3.30,16
$35,00

A5-14

4|16

Withdrawn

ON BEING HUMAN

On Being Human

Why Mind Matters

JEROME KAGAN

Yale

UNIVERSITY PRESS

NEW HAVEN AND LONDON

Published with assistance from the foundation established in memory of Calvin
Chapin of the Class of 1788, Yale College.

Yale University Press books may be purchased in quantity for educational, business, or
promotional use. For information, please e-mail sales.press@yale.edu (U.S. office) or
sales@yaleup.co.uk (U.K. office).

Set in Electra type by IDS Infotech Ltd., Chandigarh, India.
Printed in the United States of America.

ISBN 978-0-300-21736-0 (cloth : alk. paper)

Library of Congress Control Number: 2015947641
A catalogue record for this book is available from the British Library.

This paper meets the requirements of ANSI/NISO Z39.48–1992
(Permanence of Paper).

10 9 8 7 6 5 4 3 2 1

CONTENTS

CONTENTS

Michel de Montaigne was only thirty-eight years old when he retired to his chateau and began to write the essays that are still being read more than four hundred years later. When he died twenty-one years after initiating this task, in 1582, he had filled three volumes with essays whose themes ranged from liars to cannibalism. When I reread some of these narratives on a cold Saturday in March 2013, the thought of composing such a collection relevant to this century evoked a feeling I associate with action. Although considerably older and lacking a chateau, I vowed to adopt my model's strategy of avoiding pretense and choosing words with minimal ambiguity. I also decided to free myself, for the first time in fifty-two years of writing scholarly books, of the burden of providing a footnote for the source of every conclusion. Instead, a list of suggested readings is appended at the end of the text.

These essays are best read in the evening, preferably over a glass of wine, as the reflections of a retired academic psychologist who has morphed into a well-fed stowaway admiring the talented crew solving problems he could not have imagined in the summer of 1954 when he left New Haven with his pregnant wife to take his first faculty position at Ohio State University.

Only after typing more revisions than I care to remember did a semblance of structure emerge. "What does it mean to know something?" which is a complement to Montaigne's preoccupying question "What do I know?" is a seminal theme. This question assumes a special relevance when humans are the knowers because Homo sapiens is the only species that adds words, mathematical concepts, inferences of things that do not exist, and logical deductions to the products of sensation. The initial two essays argue that human knowledge combines representations of the physical features of events, which I call schemata and others call images, with words to form an extraordinarily large number of networks whose patterns of connections change with the setting, much like the collections of contacts among members of a large family from dawn to bedtime.

A person whose knowledge of Alzheimer's disease consisted only of the words *old, memory,* and *brain* has to be distinguished from the expert whose understanding contains schemata for the varied memory difficulties and density of amyloid plaques in the brains of patients. The social scientists whose only evidence consists of the words people use when they reply to questionnaires or interviews cannot be sure of the depth or the meaning of the knowledge their informants claim to possess.

Too many social scientists treat what people say about their feelings, beliefs, or past lives as faithful replicas of their actual experiences. The fact that most adults are willing to answer a pollster who asks, "How has your life been lately?" does not guarantee that the reply "Very good" has the same meaning when given by a happily married, white lawyer in Montreal, an African American health aide who is a single mother earning $25,000 a year working in a nursing home in Atlanta, and an illiterate peasant from rural Bolivia.

The titles of many papers in psychological journals have ambiguous meanings because they contain abstract words that fail to evoke the same networks in all readers. The terms *regulate, stress,* and *maltreatment,* which appear often in the titles of psychological articles, are ambiguous because readers activate different networks to these words. By contrast, the terms *default network, dorsal stream,* and *dopamine,* which appear in the titles of articles in neuroscience journals, evoke a similar understanding because they are linked to consensual networks. The first two essays elaborate these ideas and the conclusions they imply.

The social scientist's habit of using single abstract words to name processes independent of their context continues to obstruct progress. Each kind of setting selects one particular perception, emotion, thought, or behavior from a collection of candidates that could occur to a question, event, or instruction. A windowless room in a university, the narrow tube of a magnetic scanner, the living room of a home, an Internet cafe, and an airport waiting area generate dissimilar answers from college students asked by a friend or a stranger to report their major worries.

The settings that characterize a person's social class, culture, and historical era have extraordinary power to shape personality traits, abilities, values, and the interpretations of events. The greater prevalence of physical and mental illness among the poor in every society affirms this claim. The details of the procedure a scientist chooses to generate evidence are part of the setting. A single measure reveals only some properties of the phenomenon of interest. A woman's description of how she felt when she confronted a group of adolescents in a dark alley and her pattern of brain activity measured in a laboratory when she was asked to recall this event provide different evidence about her state of fear in the alley that night.

Because most behaviors and verbal descriptions can be the result of more than one set of conditions, scientists must collect patterns of measures in order to distinguish among the causal sequences that generate the same outcome. Social scientists are fond of trying to prove that a single condition whose potency depends on being part of a pattern can make a significant contribution to an outcome. The consequences of being bullied as a youth are apt to depend on whether the victim belongs to a minority or a majority group, grew up in a poor or affluent home, is excessively timid or bold, a nerd or a low-achieving student, deferential or bossy, and whether the evidence came from a questionnaire, observations of behavior, or measures of the brain.

The contexts created by historical events, woven into many of the essays, have altered the ease of social mobility, the balance between the individual and the community as the primary beneficiary of action, and sources of unhappiness. Essays 3 and 4 elaborate the influence of contexts, especially settings that characterize social class categories, on human actions, emotions, and beliefs.

The prominence of explanations of human psychological properties that emphasize genes and brains, while excluding thoughts, is another theme. Natural scientists have become reluctant to award thoughts an autonomous influence on human actions because, unlike genes and brain circuits, they are immaterial, cannot be visualized, and are absent in the mice and rats that are frequent targets of study. If thoughts had a partial autonomy from the brain activity from which they emerged, investigators would be forced to question the practice of relying on animal models to illuminate human desires and worries. They could not, for example, equate a rat's reaction to being confined in a narrow tube with the response of a single mother of three children who just lost her job. Nor could they assume that the state of a mouse who avoids entering a brightly lit alley resembles the state of an adolescent whose anxiety over a coming examination has led to insomnia. As a result, pharmacological companies could not cite the "benevolent" effects of a drug on mice who avoid lit alleys as evidence for its effectiveness in reducing anxiety in humans.

The natural scientist's conviction that material entities are the fundamental origins of all natural events makes it easy to treat thoughts as epiphenomena which, one day, will be predicted and explained by patterns of activity in neurons, circuits, and molecules. This premise denies the possibility, acknowledged by physicists, chemists, and biologists, that emergent processes can possess properties that cannot be predicted from the events that were their foundation. The properties of a fog are not present in the molecules of hydrogen and oxygen; the properties of insulin are denied to the amino acids that are its foundation. It is perfectly reasonable, therefore, to argue that a person's interpretation of a racing heart has properties that cannot be found in the brain profile that provoked the increase in heart rate.

Currently popular explanations of human altruism are burdened with a materialistic perspective. Rather than acknowledge that the thought "I am a good person" is often the only satisfaction accompanying an act of kindness toward a stranger, biologists and like-minded social scientists insist that an altruist must gain something tangible in return for giving a stranger money, food, or blood. A materialistic explanation of charitable behaviors enjoys a broad reception among natural scientists because they can point to brain circuits that respond to the receipt of material rewards, like food or sex, but cannot find a circuit that accompanies the private affirmation of oneself as a good person.

Natural scientists celebrate machines such as the electron microscope, space telescope, and linear accelerator because they make hypothetical things perceptible and, therefore, real. The magazine *Science* announced that the breakthrough event of 2014 was the landing of the space probe Philae on the comet 67P after a journey of 6.4 billion kilometers. The thoughts of the scientists and engineers who made this feat possible, which machines cannot reveal, were not mentioned.

Essays 5 and 6, on genes and brains, summarize the many fascinating facts scientists have learned about these material entities. Although this knowledge complicates an earlier and much simpler view, some scientists continue to award genes and brain states a deterministic power that ignores the cascade of events that precedes every observable outcome. The vast majority of traits require the joining of particular life histories and current experiences with genes and brain patterns.

As a result, the vocabulary that describes brain activity cannot replace the words that describe actions, thoughts, and feelings. Because neuroscientists have not yet invented a vocabulary that describes the brain profile recorded when a person looks away from a picture of a snake with open jaws, is nostalgic over a past event, or plans the day's activities, they decided to borrow psychologists' words and apply them to brain patterns—hoping that the meanings had not changed. Unfortunately, brains cannot be fearful or nostalgic and can neither plan, decode, nor compute. Future investigators will have to invent a vocabulary that is appropriate for what is happening in neurons and circuits when a person engages in a psychological process.

The person is at the center of the final six essays, which discuss the role of the family, the degree to which early traits are preserved over time, the functions of education, the significance of expectations, the interpretations of bodily feelings, and the meanings of morality. The neuroscientists' dismissal of thoughts as having causal power turned psychologists away from studying the vicarious emotions that accompany a person's identification with a family, class, ethnic group, religion, or nation. An explanation of an adolescent's depression a week after he learned that his grandfather was a callous killer must include the youth's interpretation of his genetic relationship to a grandfather he never met. The conflicts between Shia and

Sunni Muslims or between the residents in Eastern Ukraine and Kiev are fueled by emotional identifications with religion or nationality.

Almost all the research on the relation between a child's family experiences and his or her future traits emphasizes observable events, such as parental neglect, sexual abuse, harsh punishments, or lack of physical affection, and not the child's interpretation of those experiences. These interpretations depend on expectations. Children in colonial America expected to be punished harshly for disobedience. Hence, their interpretation of being spanked, locked in a closet, or deprived of pleasures for many days was more benign than the one contemporary children would impose on the same experiences.

Many psychologists defend their failure to evaluate identifications and interpretations by arguing that they are too difficult to measure. Natural scientists are less likely to use difficulty as an excuse for not studying an important process. When physicists decided they had to determine whether the Higgs boson did or did not exist, they persuaded governments to give them $9 billion to build the Hadron Collider.

I made morality the theme of the final essay because a concern with good and bad is one of the defining properties of Homo sapiens. Only humans insist on sorting things, people, and experiences into bins marked bad, good, or neither. Although children and adults hunger for a set of moral demands that must be honored under all circumstances, this prize continues to elude humanity because circumstances matter. Montaigne understood this truth.

Essay 12 distinguishes between moral behaviors, defined by conformity to a community's moral code, and a person who is loyal to his or her private conscience. Edward Snowden's defense of his actions illustrates the difference between these two meanings of moral. Humans want to believe there are some moral demands that are unquestioningly right and deserve to be honored. The historical events of the past century have frustrated that need. As a result, many seek to understand a malaise that affects many members of industrialized, democratic societies. What is its cause? What is its cure? Misdiagnosing the malaise as due to loneliness, unbridled capitalism, too much stress, or rebellious immigrants prevents recognition of a more critical basis for the mood of uneasiness.

Some facts from my history may help readers evaluate my conclusions and speculations. I was born in 1929 to an agnostic Jewish family in a small New Jersey town of close to thirty thousand residents about twenty miles south of New York City. Only recently have some of the scars created by the economic Depression of the 1930s begun to heal. I have always identified with the underdog—I rooted for the Dodgers when they were in Brooklyn—feel empathy for victims coping with conditions they cannot control, and am peeved when those in positions of authority become arrogant. An automatic skepticism toward all statements issued by such authorities is probably one of my defining traits.

The ingenuous belief that a deeper understanding of the family experiences of young children would automatically yield wise recommendations that, if adopted by parents, would create utopian societies free of crime, hatred, and misery was the reason I chose developmental psychology rather than biochemistry when, in 1950, a career decision had to be made. The bursting of that illusion combined with the events of the past century have generated an unwanted pessimism about the future state of our species. I wish I were as optimistic today as I was forty years ago. The natural scientist's declaration that the origin of the universe and the emergence of life-forms were accidents and life will disappear in about 4 billion years when a giant red sun will evaporate the earth's water call for more humility and less narcissism.

Biology's four seminal unsolved mysteries center on the conditions that led to the varied anatomies and physiologies of animals, the processes that explain why offspring resemble their biological parents, the detailed functions of cells, and the reasons for the current distribution of species across the world's regions.

Psychology's primary puzzles resemble the biologist's quartet. What patterns of conditions are responsible for the changes in an individual over a lifetime, which psychological properties are likely to be preserved and which altered or lost, how does any psychological outcome emerge from brain activity, and what factors explain the variation in adaptation to a society?

Montaigne titled his collection *Essais*, which means attempts. Readers who now know my biases should be better able to judge whether my attempts to illuminate some extraordinarily complex ideas contain a measure of truth. I used two criteria in selecting the dozen themes. I wanted each essay to be interesting but also comprehensible to readers who do not possess detailed technical knowledge but wish to have an appreciation of the complexity of the phenomena. The processes that allow perceptions of events are of great interest to scientists, but most readers do not have the background to appreciate a comprehensive discussion of this domain. But the meaning of words, the influence of social class, the relation between brain and mind, and the role of the family recruit a broad curiosity and can be discussed without an overly technical jargon.

The elegant victories of the physical and biological sciences have attracted the support of philanthropies and federal agencies that used to be friendlier to the social sciences. The media, too, are more interested in the genetic contributions to a behavior than the experiential conditions that give rise to it. I hope these essays persuade both constituencies that the events of the mind, although requiring a brain, possess a degree of independence that requires a vocabulary that is inappropriate for genes and brains. The brain's response to a hand placed in boiling water has an equivalent autonomy from the physics of the heated water molecules contacting the surface of the skin. An understanding of the feelings and thoughts evoked by listening to Beethoven's Ninth Symphony in a quiet room on a winter night, seeing the torture of a prisoner on a television screen, or walking in an autumn forest when the foliage is at peak color requires evidence that a brain cannot provide and sentences that are inappropriate for neurons and circuits.

I hope these essays will persuade those who question the power of the mind that thoughts and feelings are not wispy, ghostlike phenomena that one day will be explained away by measures of brains. I share the view of the physicist Lewis Victor de Broglie, who wrote, "Two seemingly incompatible conceptions can each represent an aspect of the truth. . . . They may serve in turn to represent the facts without ever entering into direct conflict."

I thank Robert Kagan and Charles Nelson for comments on one or more essays and Robin DuBlanc for perfectly superb editing and the ability to detect incoherence.

Schemata and Words

Humans are the only species that operates in two realities. The one we share with animals consists of representations of the salient features of objects, movements, places, smells, sounds, tastes, and feelings. Taste is salient for cookies; flying for birds. These representations, which I call schemata, are the foundations of the images that humans generate when they try to re-create an event in the mind. My schema for the face of a person I just met retains the spatial arrangement of the eyes, nose, and mouth and color and length of the hair, but usually omits the shape of the ears and length of the eyebrows. I possess schemata for the sound of an airplane, the texture of sandpaper, the odor of mothballs, my actions in the morning, and the feelings that accompany cold fingers, hunger, and the first glass of wine after a day of work.

Schemata are created effortlessly. Most adults can generate a separate schema for each of two hundred pictures they examined for only a few seconds. Eleven-year-olds living in isolated villages in Guatemala preserved for at least two days schemata of pictures of objects they had never seen—including a toaster, a telescope, and golf clubs. These observations imply that the brain can create and preserve schemata for a very large number of events.

Objects and events that are encountered frequently become prototypic schemata that contain the features that usually accompany each phenomenon. A six-month-old has acquired a prototypic schema of her mother's face that allows her to distinguish the mother from another woman. My prototypic schema for one of the pine trees on my lawn consists of the distinctive shape, height, and location that differentiate it from a nearby spruce. The features of a prototypic schema can change with experience. An adult's schema for a parent's face contains features that were missing from his schema as an infant.

When an object or action typically occurs in a particular setting—say, brushing one's teeth in the bathroom, buckling up in an airplane, or cooking dinner in the kitchen—the features of the setting are part of the prototype. My prototypic schema of the treadmill I use in a nearby athletic club contains features of the room in which the treadmill is located. When the setting is an element of a schema, adults might not notice a small change in some of the objects in that setting: for example, most adults would not detect a slightly different faucet on the kitchen sink.

Schemata allow rapid recognition of a familiar event, detection of an unfamiliar one, and facilitate the understanding of abstract ideas. Niels Bohr drew a picture of a spherical drop of water being transformed into the shape of a peanut to help him understand how a stream of bombarding neutrons could fission a uranium atom. Werner Heisenberg frustrated his colleagues by replacing Bohr's schema of an electron as a planet orbiting the sun with a mathematical operation that was difficult to represent as a schema.

Words: The Other Reality

The second reality, unique to humans, consists of words, only some of which describe the reality that schemata represent. The first humanoid species possessed schemata for the distance between two trees, the interval between sunrise and sunset, and the array of fingers on a hand. Modern humans invented special words to describe the distances between objects, the durations between events, and the number of objects in an array.

Human languages contain three broad categories. One set of words is used to evaluate a person, object, event, intention, or feeling as good, pleasant, or appropriate, as opposed to bad, unpleasant, or inappropriate. The second category consists of names for observable objects, events, or their physical features. Most of these words are linked to a schema. Amanda Holland found that four-year-olds learning English found it easier to remember new words that named a whole object than new words that named the color or texture of an object. This principle may hold for children learning any language. That is, children appear to be biased by their biology to assume that when an adult utters a new word while looking at an object, the word probably refers to the whole entity. Young children are apt to remember that the word *avocado* names an object with a particular shape, size, and color, but are likely to forget that a pineapple is "prickly" and a tulip is "turquoise" when they hear these terms for the first time because prickly and turquoise are features.

The third category contains names for abstract ideas, such as knowledge, truth, resiliency, justice, number, and time, that do not possess a particular set of physical features. A team at the Max Planck Institute in Nijmegen noted that the word *time* activates different schemata and, therefore, has dissimilar meanings for Mandarin and English speakers. The former conceive of time as approaching a passive person. English speakers rely on a schema in which an active person moves through a passive time.

Number words name a property of objects or events that is not contained in their individual features. A person looking at two decks of playing cards would be equally correct if she said there were 104 cards, two decks, or one pile. Time and number, like sacred and holy, are not inherent properties of natural events but words humans invented because they are useful. Chimpanzees walking to a grove, picking and eating bananas, and returning to the nesting area are natural events that occur sequentially. We find it useful to say that six chimps spent eighty minutes away from their nesting site. In the debate between scientists who believe that numbers are the language of nature and those who insist that numbers are mental inventions that happen to describe some phenomena, I side with the latter.

Natural scientists are suspicious of the social sciences because many of the latter's concepts—perception, memory, regulation, stress, emotion, and well-being—are not linked to a single set of features that can be imagined or, better yet, photographed. Only 1 percent of the words in the abstracts of papers published in the July 2014 issue of *Psychological Science*, a leading journal in psychology, had a link to a consensual schema. One of the abstracts contained the terms *negative emotion, aversion sensitivity, stress,* and *discomfort.* None evokes the same schema in all readers. Negative emotion could refer to fear, worry, anger, jealousy, or sadness; aversion sensitivity could mean the avoidance of parties, flying, or dirt; and stress could refer to an illness, poverty, loss of a job, social rejection, death of a loved one, or a tornado that destroyed one's home.

By contrast, 5 percent of the words in the abstracts taken from the July 2014 issue of *Neuron,* a leading journal in neuroscience, contained words such as *glia, Schwann cell,* and *interneuron,* which would evoke a similar schema in all readers. The French biologist Jean Rostand captured the ambiguous meanings of abstract words in a pithy quote: "Theories come and theories go, the frog remains." Rostand meant that a word can change its meaning over time by referring to a different phenomenon. The phenomenon, however, remains the same. The meanings of the terms *species* and *gene* in 2015 are not the meanings biologists understood in 1930.

A Brief History

The first spoken language appeared long after the first humanlike species created schemata for objects, actions, and feelings. The first written language did not appear until about eight thousand years ago, more than ninety thousand years after Homo sapiens evolved. Words, therefore, appear to be an "add-on" to talents that are millions of years old.

Humans had to first inherit an anatomy of the tongue and larynx that allowed them to articulate vowels and consonants and a brain that sent projections to the larynx. These anatomical facts explain why human infants babble but monkey infants do not. Humans also had to be able to infer that some sounds coming from a human mouth were intended to represent events. These properties had to occur before humans could invent a language that informed others of facts they needed or wanted to know, obligations they had to obey, and dangers they ought to avoid. This spoken communication united the members of a community into a more coherent collective, just as honeybees rely on their abilities to produce and detect select odors to unite the members of the hive into a coherent collective.

The Specialness of Words

An infant watching *The Wizard of Oz* for the twentieth time, seeing Dorothy release the straw man from the pole on which he hangs, anticipates that the object is about to move. A five-year-old expects to see a "scarecrow dancing." Dancing scarecrows belong to the symbolic reality of language, which carves schemata into semantic forms that often convey little or no information about the physical features of the events. The name for my schema of the space where I work—my study—wipes away the physical details of the room because the main purpose of language is to communicate information as efficiently as possible. My wife only wants to know where I am, was, or will be, and does not care about the prototypic schema residing in my brain.

The words that name the legal status and diverse roles of the person named Jerome Kagan have not changed over the past sixty years, even though his actions, beliefs, emotions, genes, brain, gut, muscles, and immune system have been altered in nontrivial ways. Words freeze-frame changing events into forms that invite the belief that nothing has changed. The fact that the Mesopotamians had words for the English terms *life, liberty, happiness, right, wrong, fair,* and *unjust* does not mean that the phenomena to which these words refer have not changed.

Words distort experience by digitizing events into bins containing different kinds of things. Most speakers, as well as the media, refer to African Americans as one group and fail to distinguish between African Americans whose families have been in the United States for generations and recent black immigrants from the Caribbean or Africa. Mary Waters of Harvard University points out that many members of these two groups live in different regions and have dissimilar educational and job histories. Hence, it would be useful to give them distinctive names. Jonathan Schooler of the University of California reported that individuals who used only words to register faces or objects, compared with those who also created schemata, were impaired when they had to recognize these events later because the words failed to name critical features. If I represent the new Tesla in a neighbor's driveway as a car, without also creating a schema for its exact shape, I may have difficulty later distinguishing it from a new model of a Lexus or Cadillac.

Consider a person who is asked one month after seeing a gang of boys tease a small child but not physically harm him whether any gang member had hit the child during the incident. If the observer had registered the scene as "aggression," he is likely to say yes because of the strong association between the words *aggression* and *hitting*. This error is less likely if the person had registered the event as a schema, with or without a semantic label. Adults who do not regularly activate schemata when planning a future action often fail to consider similar occasions in the past when a less than pleasant experience occurred. For example, a person who decides to travel the day before Thanksgiving because it is convenient and fails to retrieve schemata representing the three times she did this and was frustrated by the traffic is at risk for another unhappy experience.

The different microanatomies of the left and right hemispheres of the brain may contribute to an asymmetry in the different kinds of associations to words compared with schemata. The neuronal collections that make the most important contributions to language are in the left hemisphere and favor analysis of the features of events. The neurons of the right hemisphere are prepared to process the whole patterns that are more characteristic of schemata. The language sites in the left hemisphere are prepared to detect a single feature shared by objects with different shapes. For example, rattlesnakes and black widow spiders share the property of being dangerous. Hence, reading the word *rattlesnake* is apt to evoke a schema for a black widow spider. By contrast, a picture of a rattlesnake is unlikely to evoke a schema of or the word for spider.

Most philosophers ignore the schemata that contribute to the meanings of words. The verb *know*, for example, is often conceptualized as a yes or no dichotomy rather than a continuum of certainty. Too many philosophers and social scientists treat word meanings as natural kinds, as if the properties of the terms *good, moral,* and *truth* were as discoverable as the properties of the soft green stuff growing at the base of trees. This premise explains why some psychologists thought it was perfectly appropriate to ask the staff at different zoos to rate animals belonging to diverse species on personality traits that were invented to apply only to humans. The staff members were willing to rate lions and leopards on curiosity and self-confidence, as if these words had a meaning as fixed as eats meat, sleeps during the daylight hours, and has a tail.

Adults who have mastered a second language later in life are unlikely to activate schemata for the feelings linked to emotional words. As a result, they find it easier to swear or to say "I love you" in their second language than in their first because these words are stripped of feeling. Renaming events in order to remove a feeling linked to a stigmatizing property works. Unskilled laborers are now called entry-level workers, prostitutes are sex workers, and torture is enhanced interrogation. Perhaps "exaggerated sexual dominance" will replace rape and "chronic indifference" will become the name for parental neglect.

Words are poor at describing events that are changing, such as a bird in flight, a rush of feelings, a train of thoughts, and the movements of a person opening a bottle of wine. Words have the power, however, to dilute a feeling of uncertainty over the appropriate action to implement. A message labeled "spam" resolves unsureness over whether it should be opened and read. Transgendered adults feel uncomfortable when asked to state their gender on official documents. The Australian High Court resolved their uncertainty by ruling that they could write "nonspecific" in the box asking for gender.

The writer José Ortega y Gasset worried about the human proclivity to assume that if a word is used, it probably is the name of an observable event. "Create a concept," he wrote, "and reality leaves the room." Alfred North Whitehead phrased this truth differently: "Language . . . foists on us exact concepts as though they represented . . . experience."

The Variation in the Parsing of Experience

The world's six thousand or so languages sort many events into different semantic categories. English invented different words for mice and rats. The Thai language has one word for both species, even though Thai speakers perceive the size difference between the two animals. The ancient Greeks distinguished between physical pain and mental distress; the Romans invented only one word—*dolor*—for both experiences.

Very few English verbs describe variations of common actions. The English verb *eat*, for example, is used when a person is eating nuts, an apple, or a popsicle. An Australian language, by contrast, invented three different verbs to capture the different actions of the mouth and teeth with these foods. Barbara Malt of Leigh University asked speakers of English, Dutch, Spanish, or Japanese to describe a woman displaying thirty-six different movements. Although all the speakers had words that distinguished between fast and slow movements, some languages did not have different words for skipping in place versus skipping forward.

Speakers of Fijian use different words to describe an object that belongs to a person compared with a person's body part. English speakers ignore this difference when they say "Mary's cup" and "Mary's arm." The English term *in* ignores both the kind of object and the type of container. Speakers of Tzeltal, a Mayan Indian language, have six different ways to capture the combinations of certain objects and containers that are possible in: "The water is in the bucket," "The water is in the cup," "The water is in the ground," "The spider is in the bucket," "The spider is in the cup," and "The spider is in the ground."

Psychologists, as a language community, use some words in ways that are foreign to the general public and to natural scientists. For example, psychologists are fond of the adjectives *positive* and *negative* to describe feelings and emotions. Most adults, by contrast, say they are happy, not positive, when they receive a gift and sad, not negative, upon hearing about the death of a friend. Chemists might lose their grant if they used the words *positive* or *negative* to describe a molecule that caused a collection of neurons to either fire or grow silent.

Reward is another popular psychological term that is supposed to apply to an extremely broad range of events that animals seek to experience. Some eminent psychologists write about rewards as "value systems in the brain." This phrase implies that a similar brain profile accompanies a male mouse preparing to mount a female, a monkey in a laboratory expecting three drops of grape juice for moving his eyes to a certain location, a child in school anticipating praise from a teacher for an examination performance, two lovers anticipating their first sexual intimacy, a scientist in her study anticipating a particular result as she pores over a collection of numbers, and a speeding driver pulled over by a state trooper anticipating only a warning and not a ticket. It is unlikely that the brains in these life-forms respond to these diverse events in the same way.

Communities are unlikely to invent words for infrequent events that convey little information. There is no need, for example, to invent a word to describe a person skipping in place. On the other hand, one regularly sees a person or animal move slowly or quickly and the words *walk, shuffle, jog,* and *run* convey important information about the kind of movement and, by inference, the psychological state of the agent. People invent and use words for a purpose—they want to communicate a fact or idea that both speaker and listener care about.

Networks

The collection of schemata and words associated with an event form a network. The strengths of the associations among the members of the network vary with the number and salience of the features shared by those members. The shared feature could refer to shape (balls, apples, and pebbles are round), size (pennies, peas, and a doll's shoes are small), function (soap, water, washcloth, and sink are used to clean things), usual location (gulls, sand, and waves are found near the sea), kind of movement (slow, smooth, graceful), sound when spoken (peach, preach, teach), a contrasting relation (up versus down or bad versus good), a condition with salient consequences (a hurricane or earthquake), or a semantic category (animals, natural, manufactured, common).

The network for peach contains schemata and words for physical properties (sweet, smooth, and round), usual function (edible), locations (on trees, in grocery stores, in kitchens), category (food), and words with a similar sound (preach, beach, each, teach, reach, and leach). The network for woman, at least among Americans, has strong links to the network for mother which, in turn, evokes associations to the networks for child, food, cook, kitchen, sink, soap, clean, good, and attractive, which bring us back to woman to close the circle.

French adults familiar with Eugene Delacroix's painting *Liberty Leading the People*, whose central figure is a bare-breasted woman holding a musket in her left hand and the tricolor flag of the French revolution in her right, probably possess links between the network for woman, on the one hand, and the networks for liberty, sacred, France, and rebellion on the other. Americans, Germans, and Japanese are unlikely to possess this network of associations. Medieval Europeans had strong associations among the networks for woman, green, cold, and jealous because they regarded green as a cold color and women as both coldhearted and prone to jealousy.

Contemporary Europeans possess an association between the color yellow and a triangle and an equally strong association between red and a circle. One interpretation rests on the fact that yellow objects and triangular shapes are less common in nature than objects that have a red hue and a circular shape. Hence, the terms *uncommon* and *common* provide the link that explains why yellow goes with triangle and red with circle. The image of two wheels, each with many spokes, provides a visual metaphor for the associations between two networks: an association is represented by a spoke from one wheel touching a spoke on the other.

The discovery of the structure of deoxyribonucleic acid—DNA—in 1953 had to occur before geneticists could have made so many major advances over the past fifty years. I suggest that the future discovery of the range of network structures linked to frequently used concepts, such as woman, father, good, earth, and food, will be followed by an equally significant set of advances. This task requires measuring the strengths of the associations among the schemata and words that are part of each network. Too few psychologists are working on this problem because the appropriate methods have not been developed.

Most adults are able to detect at least one feature that is shared by any pair of words in their language because elementary contrasting word pairs, such as good-bad, active-passive, strong-weak, and male-female, provide a link that unites pairs of seemingly disparate words. For example, aspirin and vacations are good; blizzards and athletes are active; babies and raindrops are weak; and the sea and queen bees are female. Magic rituals are based on these kinds of links. A woman in ancient Egypt who wanted to attract a man's ardor melted a wax figurine of the man on the assumption that wax and a man's feelings were both capable of being softened.

Because educated, high-status parents in eighteenth-century Europe usually gave their children a middle initial, most adults possessed an association between higher status and a middle initial. Contemporary Irish college students hold the same belief. American parents during the country's first century rarely gave their children middle names. Neither George Washington, John Adams, nor Thomas Jefferson had middle names. This practice changed after the Civil War, and today almost 99 percent of American infants are given a middle name.

Most contemporary adults follow the ancient Greeks and Chinese in associating odd numbers with maleness and even numbers with femaleness. Although there is no consensual explanation of this fact, two interpretations are possible if we assume that the numbers 1 and 2 are prototypes of the concepts odd and even. One explanation relies on the fact that a person who is number 1 in a hierarchy dominates the one ranked 2—and, traditionally, men dominated women. There is only one God and he is usually pictured as male. A second, more speculative, account rests on the fact that things that cause pain often consist of a single article (a knife, pin, or needle), whereas many objects that bring pleasure consist of a pair of features (two lips that kiss, two breasts that nurse, a pair of arms that embrace). Men are more likely than women to harm others; women more likely to embrace them.

Because most of the teachers in America's elementary schools are women, children acquire an association between schoolwork and femaleness. One implication of this unconscious association, which psychologists affirmed with German children, is that young boys who are unsure of their male identity might be threatened by a conscientious approach to school assignments. As a result, they are less diligent.

Punctate or Smooth?

The brain is remarkably sensitive to the differences between punctate and gradual events. Sounds that are punctate have a short duration, higher pitch (frequency), and fast rise time (the peak intensity is reached quickly). Screams, alarms, and the nonsense word *kiki* are punctate. By contrast, gradual sounds last longer, have a lower pitch, and display a slower rise time. Lullabies, murmurs, and the nonsense word *bouba* are gradual. The shapes of objects can be punctate or gradual depending on the rate of change in their contours. Angular shapes are punctate; curved ones are gradual. Children and adults alike select objects with a punctate shape— say, a picket fence—as matching words with a punctate sound such as *kiki*, and select objects with a gradual contour—such as a ball—as a match for a word like *bouba*, which has a gradual sound. Experiences humans judge as pleasant, such as a lullaby, caress, a flower's scent, and the texture of silk, are marked by gradualness. Experiences judged as unpleasant, such as sour tastes, acrid smells, and the prick of a needle, have a punctate quality.

When the pitch of the first syllable is lower than the second in three-syllable meaningless words, as in *babopu, bibapo,* and *bopipa,* adults judge these sounds, which ascend in pitch, as pleasant and match them with pictures of puppies, babies, and heaven. However, when the first syllable is higher than the second, as in *tatoku, didago,* and *dodiga,* adults match these sounds, which descend in pitch, with pictures of snarling wolves, snakes, and sad faces. It may not be a coincidence that the first syllable in the most popular two-syllable names for American boys—Jacob, William, Ethan, and Michael—is higher than the second syllable. By contrast, the first syllable in two of the four most popular girls' names—Sophia and Olivia— has a lower pitch than the second and the sound ascends in pitch. The names of three popular cars—Chevrolet, Lexis, and Mazda—have the sound pattern of popular boys' names, whereas the names of the popular flowers azalea, begonia, camellia, and carnation match the sound pattern in girls' names.

The Setting

The setting affects the networks that are likely to be activated by an event or a sentence. If I remember T. S. Eliot's line "I will show you fear in a handful of dust" while reading Eliot's biography, I am likely to activate networks representing the First World War, Barbara Tuchman, Serbia, the film *Tom & Viv*, and my father, who served in that war. Remembering the same line while reading a biography of John Maynard Keynes, who knew Eliot, will activate networks that include reparations, Germany, Adolf Hitler, World War II, and the Marshall Plan. And if I remember the line after listening to a lecture on the conditioning of fear in rats, a different collection of networks would be activated.

I do not possess one network for "woman." Rather, I possess a number of related networks that have different probabilities of being activated when I see an attractive woman on the street, read about women presidents, think about women caring for young children, see the play *Macbeth*, or hear a radio program discussing competitiveness among professional women. The networks that are prepared to be activated by an event resemble a smorgasbord that diners sample—all items are potentially available. A person's perception of the pattern of reflected light on the crest of ocean waves provides a second analogy, for the perception is contingent on where the viewer stands.

Are Words Locatable in the Brain?

Some scholars are attracted to the idea that each word has a single home in a person's brain. It is more reasonable to assume that most words in a person's vocabulary belong to a large number of different networks located in different places. The sentence in which they appear and the setting determine the network that will be activated or, in some cases, assembled at the moment a provocative event occurs. The word *train* evokes distinct networks in sentences describing travel compared with sentences about a woman's bridal gown. Consider the seemingly simple word *female*. Some women who were born with a female genome, ovaries, and uterus cannot conceive. Others with a female genome are born with a penis and replace it with female genitals. A few individuals with a female genome ask a surgeon to remove their female genitals and prescribe male hormones so that they can look like a male. A person who knows these facts does not possess a single network for this word.

Adults often create a new network, or alter an old one, when they must answer a question they had never considered. For example, most adults would answer a psychologist who asked, "How confused have you been over the past ten years? Please rate your feeling on a ten-point scale," even though they had never considered this question until that moment. And the mental events that preceded their answer could have generated a network for the word *confused* that did not exist before the question was posed.

Alan Rosenthal, a commentator on European culture, reminds us that the names of nations form networks that change with history. The network for contemporary (but not medieval) France has strong associations with culture, art, romance, wine, and women. The network for Germany, by contrast, has stronger associations with the masculine concepts of cars, machines, Prussian generals, and war. Freud's trio of id, ego, and superego has been transformed into the current concepts of impulsivity, executive processes, and emotional regulation.

Early humans possessed a network for the idea of time that is not the contemporary understanding. The languages of premodern societies untouched by science talked about the intervals between specific events that had either occurred—"We planted corn two full moons ago"—or might occur in the future—"We will plant corn when the leaves reappear on the trees." The Egyptians invented a water clock, relying on the same principle as the hourglass, to measure the interval during which a person could take water from a public well. The network for the word *time* that includes a schema for the spatial patterns formed by the hands of a clock did not emerge until the thirteenth century when the mechanical clock was invented.

The words *month* and *year* as units of time correspond to natural intervals (the lunar and sun cycles), but *second, minute, hour,* and *week* are arbitrary. The term *week* originated in a decision by Sargon I, the king of Akkad in 2350 BCE, to name an interval of seven days as a basic unit of time because the Sumerians, whom Akkad had conquered, worshipped seven gods symbolized by the planets that were visible in the night sky. Had the Sumerians worshipped eight gods, a week might have had eight days. The citizens who took over after the French Revolution created a ten-day week and a 140-minute hour.

The idea that the numeral 4 can name a collection that consists of a goat's hoof, a clay bowl, an arrowhead, and a white stone resting next to each other in a hole in a cave does not come easily to the human mind because the four objects look different and belong to different semantic categories. That is why set theory was invented relatively late in human history. The words *time* and *number,* like *evil* and *sacredness,* are abstract concepts that have belonged to different networks throughout history. The poet e. e. cummings captured the distinction between abstract words and schemata when he wrote: "Life's not a paragraph / And death I think is no parenthesis."

Semantic Versus Schematic Prototypes

A word that possesses many features of the network held by most speakers in a community is called the semantic prototype. The word *robin* is the semantic prototype for "bird" among Americans living in the mid-Atlantic states because robins are common and combine the features possessed by most birds: small size, the ability to fly and sing, and winter migration. For Norwegian residents living close to the sea, the word *gull* is the semantic prototype.

The prototypic schema of a bird, however, can differ from the semantic prototype. My prototypic schema for bird is not a robin but an average of the salient features of robins, wrens, gulls, sparrows, and crows. Jerry Fodor and Zenon Pylyshyn in *Minds without Meaning* emphasize the distinction between a prototypic schema and a semantic prototype. They note that the word *triangularity* applies to every possible bounded figure composed of three connected lines and, therefore, differs from the usual schematic prototype for a triangle, which has sides of equal length.

The members of each scientific discipline possess a semantic prototype for an ideal member of their discipline and, perhaps, a schematic prototype of that person's face. The name Albert Einstein accompanied by a schema of his distinctive face is probably common among physicists. Francis Crick and James Watson looking at their model of the DNA molecule may work for biologists. The members of a discipline whose research resembles that of the prototype enjoy more respect and win more prizes than those who deviate from the ideal.

The Special Properties of Words

The primary purpose of words is to communicate information. The function of thought is to understand experience. Communicating these understandings is secondary, especially when they are insights about the self that one does not wish to share or thoughts filled with schemata that lack an appropriate vocabulary. I do not have words that are able to convey the train of thoughts and feelings that occurs when I am standing on a deserted, unlit beach staring at the Milky Way in a cloudless sky filled with the light of a full moon.

Many words, but especially nouns that name objects, are part of a hierarchy of terms. Every puppy belongs to the category *dog*, all dogs belong to the category *mammal*, mammals are animals, and animals belong to the category *living things*. The members of a language community select one element of the hierarchy as the basic term, which is usually *dog* in most languages.

Social scientists and the public often differ in the basic-level terms they use to describe a psychological trait. The latter prefers words that are lower in the hierarchy. Most Americans would say, "Mary was afraid of her father's harsh criticisms when she was a child." Psychologists, who prefer words higher in the hierarchy, make *stress* the basic-level term: "Mary experienced stress as a child." This sentence ignores the cause and quality of the stress and the feeling that accompanied it. Since words that are used less frequently are susceptible to more than one meaning, English speakers agree more on the meaning of *afraid* than the meaning of *stress*.

Although young children can discriminate between dogs, cats, cows, on the one hand, and boxes, telephones, and furniture, that fact does not mean they understand the meanings of the words *mammals* or *artifacts*. The brains of infants display different profiles of activity in response to patterns of moving lights produced by filming adults (with small lights attached to their limbs and trunk) adopting a happy or a fearful posture.

The psychologists who did this study concluded that the infants were distinguishing between happiness and fear. It is more likely that the infants' brains were responding to the physical differences in the light patterns generated by adults spreading their two arms, as in joy, versus bringing their arms close to the body, as in fear. The four-year-old who asks his mother, "Why is the sky blue?" is not a budding epistemologist. Developmental psychologists are tempted to attribute abstract competencies to infants based on behaviors or brain patterns that, in many instances, are simply responses to variations in physical features.

The brains of infants, like the brains of all vertebrates with intact vision, detect changes in the orientation, density, and movement of the contours of an event by activating circuits that cause the infant to orient to these changes. Psychologists who attribute an understanding of number to infants because their looking behavior indicates they can detect the difference between arrays of two and four circles, or attribute to toddlers an appreciation of geometry because they perceive the different orientations of contours in drawings of rooms are using the vocabulary of the mathematician for observations that have a simpler, less abstract, explanation. Three-year-olds who say, "Wha's that, Mama?" do not have an understanding of the linguist's concept of the interrogative.

The Attractiveness of Abstract Words

The social scientist's habit of inventing abstract concepts, such as extraversion, theory of mind, utility, and resilience, to describe different collections of events contrasts with the biologist's preference for particularity. Psychologists would profit by adopting the biologist's understanding of nature's attention to detail. A gene is expressed in a specific cell in a particular tissue, a neuron responds to a restricted range of events, a limb begins to form in an embryo at a particular time. The processes in life-forms are restricted to particular contexts and times. Psychology is a life science and its investigators would profit from heeding this principle.

Instead of assuming that social anxiety is a property an individual carries into all settings, it will prove useful to code variation in the frequency of talking, smiling, and small hand and leg movements in adolescents sitting with four strangers during a thirty-minute exchange of views on politics, compared with the behaviors the same youths display at home with their family. Psychologists should descend from the high rung on the semantic ladder they now occupy to a lower rung from which they observe particular events in specific contexts.

Both Richard McNally of Harvard University and Angelique Cramer of the University of Amsterdam urge social scientists to study the actual relations among a variety of behaviors, feelings, and beliefs rather than assume that these phenomena are simply examples of a hypothetical, abstract trait. For example, some victims of a trauma develop insomnia because their hyperaroused state prevents them from falling asleep. The lack of sleep is likely to produce fatigue which, in turn, can lead to an apathy that the person interprets as depression. This cascade of events is more faithful to the facts than the current belief among psychiatrists that insomnia, hyperarousal, fatigue, apathy, and depression are the products of a hypothetical state called post-traumatic stress disorder.

Successful writers, poets, and politicians regularly use words that activate schemata. Cynthia Emrich of Purdue University and her colleagues performed a fascinating analysis of the inaugural address and one major speech given by each U.S. president from Washington to Reagan. They computed the number of words in each speech that had either a strong or a weak link to a schema. The first term in the following word pairs is more firmly linked to a schema than the second: sweat versus work, heart versus commitment, path versus alternative, and rock versus dependable. The presidents whose speeches contained many words evocative of schemata— Franklin Roosevelt, Lyndon Johnson, Abraham Lincoln, and Andrew Jackson—were judged more charismatic by students and as more inspiring leaders by historians. Four verbs in Lincoln's Gettysburg Address on November 19, 1863—brought forth, conceived, endure, and perish—evoke schemata.

By contrast, the speeches of Jimmy Carter, Warren Harding, U. S. Grant, and William Howard Taft contained fewer schematically related words and these men were judged less charismatic and less effective leaders. The phrases in Barack Obama's second inaugural speech in January 2013 were schematically lean. He talked about "life's worst hazards," "fidelity to founding principles," and "common effort and common purpose." Perhaps it is not surprising that he is regarded as a pragmatic, rational, and intellectual leader but not a charismatic one. Compare Obama's abstract prose with six phrases from Franklin Roosevelt's first inaugural address in March 1933 given in the midst of the Depression: "terror which paralyzes," "convert retreat into advances," "money changers stand indicted in the court of public opinion," "withered leaves of industrial enterprise," "mad chase of profits," and the famous line "The only thing we have to fear is . . . fear itself."

Types of Meaning

It is time to consider the controversy surrounding the definition of the term *meaning*. When scholars disagree on the meaning of a word, the wisest strategy is to focus on the phenomena the term is supposed to name rather than defend one definition. Any event that reliably signals a second event has meaning. The sight of a piece of chocolate cake has meaning when it is followed by the anticipation of a sweet taste. At least four different kinds of phenomena meet this simple criterion.

The first refers to the occasions when one schema automatically evokes a second schema simply because they typically occur together at the same time or in the same location, as in the case of the sight of the chocolate cake and the sweet taste. No special tutoring or mental effort is needed to establish these associations. Antonio Damasio of the University of Southern California reminds us that repeatedly seeing a violin and hearing its distinct sounds create a connection between the two events. As a result, seeing a picture of a violin activates brain sites normally activated by the sounds of a violin, including sites in the motor cortex that represent the hand movements of a violinist.

A second kind of meaning has to be taught. We have to learn that an arrow pointing to the left in a parking garage means one should turn left, and a moving red truck emitting a loud siren means there is a fire somewhere.

Linguists invented the word *sign* to designate the meaning of the arrow and siren.

The third and fourth kinds of meaning are called semantic because the associations contain words. The association can be between a word and a schema—for example, a child learns that an object with a particular shape is called a fork—or between two words, as in the link between the terms *fork* and *knife*. The rest of this discussion is limited to semantic meaning. The two important facts are that sentences, not single words, are the usual carriers of meaning, and the meaning of a sentence depends on how the members of a language community interpret it.

The philosopher W. V. Quine used the sentence "Bachelors are unmarried males" to argue that all definitions necessarily involve particular events whose meaning depends on how members of a language community understand them. The words *unmarried* and *bachelor* have very specific meanings in societies that require a legal marital contract between two persons. One cannot understand this sentence without activating networks referring to men living without a partner and a marital contract.

Technical advances in reproductive biology are altering the schemata and, therefore, the meaning of networks containing the term *mother*. Although most of a woman's genes are located in the nuclei of her eggs, a small number, about thirty-seven, lie in structures called mitochondria located in the portion of the cell outside the nucleus. Because a woman possessing a deleterious gene in the mitochondria of one of her eggs might pass it on to her child, it would be advantageous to eliminate this gene but retain the majority of genes in the nucleus. Scientists have successfully removed the nucleus from the egg of one female monkey and placed it in a cell, taken from a second female, from which the nucleus had been removed. The egg of the recipient female contains her mitochondrial genes but the nuclear genes of the first female. This egg was then fertilized with sperm, placed back in the uterus of the first female, and allowed to develop into a newborn monkey.

The Federal Drug Administration is considering approval of this manipulation in cases where a mother has a risk gene in her mitochondria. Should this technique eventually become accepted medical practice (the British recently approved this procedure), it would be correct to state that the children born of this process have two mothers. A child would have three mothers if the fertilized egg were placed in the uterus of a third woman who carried the infant to term and then gave the newborn to the woman who supplied the nuclear genes.

The Embodiment Theorists

There is a lively controversy surrounding the processes that generate semantic meaning. A majority of social scientists argue that most meanings originate in learned associations between words and events. Presumably, I understand the meaning of "The forecast calls for rain" because I acquired associations between the words *forecast, calls,* and *rain,* on the one hand, and a set of corresponding schemata.

A smaller group, called embodiment theorists, favors a different perspective, especially for the meanings of verbs. They suggest that a person infers the meaning of an action verb automatically when a relevant motor circuit that simulates the action is activated. There is no role for schemata in this conception. When a person reads the sentence "Mary grasped the cup," the activation of the motor circuit for grasping awards meaning to the sentence. Benjamin Bergen in *Louder Than Words* summarizes the evidence supporting the idea of embodiment.

Alfonso Caramazza of Harvard University is skeptical of a strong form of embodiment. Adults born with no arms have no difficulty understanding verbs like *grab* and *throw.* Liuba Papeo of the University of Trento found that patients who have a serious loss of motor control due to ALS, or Lou Gehrig's disease, comprehend the meanings of action verbs and carry out verbal requests for motor acts. And Iris Berent of Northeastern University, with colleagues, found that adults can correctly perceive nonsense words, such as *blif, bdif,* and *lbif,* when the site in the motor cortex that controls the muscles around the mouth is temporarily silenced. These observations are inconsistent with a strong version of embodiment theory.

Embodiment theorists do not award enough power to the setting in which a sentence is spoken. Jana Basnakova and colleagues at the Max

Planck Institute in Nijmegen note that the context is especially critical when the intended meaning of a sentence is sarcastic, ironic, or intended to reduce another's worry. A parent who says to her adolescent daughter, "You're dressed to the nines" intends one meaning if she is wearing a new dress for a date and another if she is wearing dirty jeans and a torn blouse at the dinner table.

In one study, adults listened to dialogues that ended with the same sentence but were preceded by sentences that either made the final sentence informative or required the inference of an indirect meaning. For example, the final sentence "It's hard to give a good presentation," spoken by a teacher to a student, has informative meaning if the student had asked the teacher whether it was difficult to give an oral presentation to a large audience. However, if the student had given a presentation but was not certain of its quality and asked, "How was my presentation?" the teacher's reply, "It's hard to give a good presentation" was intended to allay the student's anxiety. In this context the student must infer the intended meaning. The brain sites that are activated by these indirect utterances are in the prefrontal cortex, which embodiment theorists regard as less relevant to discerning meaning.

Even if discerning the meaning of sentences with action words occasionally requires the activation of motor circuits, there are advantages to theorizing about the contribution of schemata. By assuming that a schema is activated when a person reads "The boy grabbed the cup," investigators can theorize about the action's properties, such as its smoothness, speed, and direction. Measures of the brain's motor cortex cannot, at present, detect these properties. As is often the case, the disagreement boils down to the best way to describe a phenomenon. Is my granddaughter's puppy best described as a dog, domesticated wolf, vertebrate, mammal, canine, or pet?

Sentences Are the Site of Meaning

The earlier assertion that sentences, not single words, carry meaning is easily illustrated because the sentence selects the specific networks that will be retrieved. The meaning of *cell*, for example, depends on whether it occurs in a sentence about animals or prisons. The word *fork* assumes one meaning at a restaurant and another in an automobile when the driver asks a question about direction.

An accurate understanding of most English verbs requires listeners to know the noun. The listener has to know whether rain or a ball is falling, a cloud or a mouse is moving, or a window or a mouth is opening in order to extract the correct meaning of the verbs *fall*, *move*, and *open*.

The same holds for the objects of verbs. Listeners have to know whether a person is regulating lust, attention, or nervous motor movements in order to understand the meaning a speaker intended. Some social scientists fail to appreciate that the meaning of most verbs depends on their noun partners. Economists are fond of the sentence "Humans choose actions in which the reward exceeds the cost." This sentence has different meanings when the reward is food and the cost is the physical effort needed to obtain the food, on the one hand, and when the reward is appointment as a professor in an elite university and the cost is the many years of lost pleasure from social relationships and favorite avocations.

Michael Tomasello wrote that apes "know" select causal sequences. Because the term *know* in that sentence referred to schemata, it is not synonymous with the word *know* in the sentence "The student knows that the square root of 36 is 6." One group of scientists used the verb *divorce* to describe the behaviors of male and female birds; another team called yeast cells "cooperative." The meanings of *divorce* and *cooperate* have one meaning when humans are the nouns but assume a quite different meaning when animals are the agents.

Philosophers are fond of using the verb *exists* without specifying the entity that has this property or the time when and place where an entity existed. Is the entity an idea, such as the Big Bang, or an observable event, such as a snowflake? Nor are readers told for whom the idea or object exists. Do quarks exist for infants, scientists, worms, horseshoe crabs, or some or all of these categories? The verb in the sentences "God exists," "Climate warming exists," "Quarks exist," and "The number zero exists" does not have the same meaning for the 7.2 billion humans alive today.

Some eighteenth-century Europeans, excited by the American and French revolutions, extended the traditional meaning of *freedom*, which applied to citizens wishing to be free from coercion by a government, to a person's freedom in pursuing sexual liaisons. If each citizen had a moral right to be free of unfair treatment by a monarch, it was reasonable to award the same freedom to individuals wishing to make love to any partner who felt similarly. Three individuals who believed in the truth of this extension—Mary Wollstonecraft, the poet Percy Shelley, and Wollstonecraft's daughter, Mary Godwin, who married Shelley—brought considerable unhappiness upon themselves. These accomplished writers, who should have known better, would never have adopted a similar permissiveness with the verbs *bury, kill,* or *dissect.* Lewis Carroll appreciated humans' tendency to select whatever meanings pleased them when he had Humpty Dumpty say, "When I use a word it means just what I choose it to mean."

The evolutionary biologist David Sloan Wilson, who titled his recent book *Does Altruism Exist?,* repeats the philosopher's error by failing to specify the agent and the target of an altruistic act. He assumed that the term *altruism* does not change its meaning when the altruist-recipient pair refers to worker bees and the queen in a hive, American college students caring for patients in a hospital in Sierra Leone, or commuters traveling to work by bicycle instead of car in order to reduce the level of carbon dioxide pollution in the atmosphere.

The philosopher Gottlob Frege distinguished between the sense and the referential meaning of a word. The former refers to the networks a speaker activates when communicating an idea. The latter refers to the events the speaker intended to name. The sentences "I thought about Meryl Streep" and "I thought about the star of the film *Sophie's Choice*" have the same referential meaning but slightly different sense meanings. James Joyce's 1939 novel *Finnegans Wake* was unpopular because it contained too many phrases, such as "a commodious vicus of recirculation," that failed to generate the same sense or referential meanings in readers.

It is obvious that sentences can have meaning if the events to which they refer do not exist. English speakers understand the meaning of the sentence "The serpent in the Garden of Eden tempted Eve to eat the apple from the Tree of Knowledge" because they possess similar schemata and semantic networks for serpent, apple, Garden of Eden, Eve, and Tree of Knowledge.

However, the English term *witch* and its synonym in the Quiché language of the Mayan Indians have different meanings because the words are linked to different schemata.

Few modern readers would guess that L. Frank Baum, author of *The Wizard of Oz*, was probably relying on his schemata of the large, electrically lit buildings he saw at the 1893 Chicago World's Fair when he described the city of Oz at the turn of the last century. It is hard to know exactly what the framers of the American Constitution were thinking in 1787 when they wrote about liberty, justice, and the general welfare since neither slaves nor women could vote.

Misunderstandings of a speaker's intended sense meaning are common because speakers and listeners occasionally activate different networks for the same words. Such misunderstandings are most likely when the speaker and listener activate different schemata for the same sentences. It takes time for spouses or lovers to learn what their partners intended to mean when they said they were tired, annoyed, or sad. Japanese adults possess slightly different understandings of the English words anxiety, shame, and fear. Erica Hepper of the University of Surrey, helped by many investigators, asked 1,704 adults from eighteen countries to rate the importance of thirty-five properties of the word in their language that best described the feeling of nostalgia. Not surprisingly, the significant properties nominated by adults in Cameroon, Uganda, and several East Asian nations differed from those nominated by English speakers.

The answers to the question "Which of these colors do you prefer?" given by speakers of English and those who speak the language of the Himba people of Namibia reveal the significance of the networks a listener activates in the service of interpreting a sentence. The English speakers preferred blue, partly because they interpreted the sentence to mean they should select the color that evoked pleasant associations, and blue has the fewest number of associations with unpleasant experiences. Among the Himba, however, blue was their least preferred color because they interpreted the sentence as meaning they should pick the color whose physical features were pleasing. They found the richly saturated colors of red, orange, and green most pleasing.

American and Belgian college students possess different understandings of the word *ideal* in the question "What are the features of an ideal society?" Americans favor a competitive individualism that places each person's interests over the interests of the community. Belgians, like many Europeans, favor a less competitive individualism that cares as much about community harmony as self-aggrandizement. This difference is accompanied by different networks for the concepts *anger* and *shame*. Many Americans believe they should not reveal signs of shame, whereas signs of anger are acceptable. Among Belgians, however, shame is more acceptable because it is linked to the idea of close relationships, whereas anger is undesirable. As a result, the members of these two societies interpret sentences containing the words *shame* or *anger* in slightly different ways.

The English term *freedom* occurs in sentences that describe minimal governmental constraints on private actions as well as in sentences declaring that each person can choose which of several actions to implement. The Russian words *svoboda* and *volya* are synonyms for these two meanings, both of which apply to an individual. The Russian language contains a third term, *mir*, missing from English, that refers to the freedom of a community of individuals, probably because Russia was a feudal society until late in the nineteenth century. The plantation slaves who learned of Lincoln's Emancipation Proclamation and the Jews who established the new state of Israel may have had a similar feeling, even if they had no unique word to name it.

The Particularity of Associations

Scientists have been surprised by the extreme specificity of the associations that are lost when a person suffers damage to certain brain sites following a stroke, accident, or infection. The location of the damage is often accompanied by difficulty in retrieving highly select associations. A team at Tel Aviv University described a patient who could recite the single numerals 1 to 9 and add two-digit numbers, but was unable to name two-digit numbers. That is, he could say "one," "two," "three" and add the numbers 31 and 42, but he could not say the words "thirty-one" or "forty-two" when he saw these numerals.

Patients with damage in other places lose the ability to name the color of a restricted set of objects. A team at the University of Rochester described a fifty-year-old man with damage to the temporal and occipital regions of the left hemisphere who had no trouble naming the colors of cars and tools, but had difficulty retrieving the correct color name for some fruits and vegetables. Apparently, the connections between the networks for certain fruits and vegetables and their color names were weakened by the stroke. This result is reasonable, for color is a salient feature of fruits and vegetables but not of tools or cars. Because lemons and limes have a similar shape and size, we use their distinctive colors to differentiate them. These observations imply that single words, such as *red*, stripped of the objects to which they apply, belong to a number of networks and the brain's representations of these words retain the objects with which they are linked.

Older adults often find they can retrieve an image of a friend or a celebrity but cannot remember the name. The connection between the schema of the person and his or her name was weakened temporarily. Retrieval of words is more fragile than the retrieval of schemata. Those in the state we call "tip-of-the-tongue" are unable to recall the name of the actress who played Eliza Doolittle in the film *My Fair Lady*, even though they can retrieve a schema of Audrey Hepburn's face.

College seniors are more likely to remember the building and campus location of a course they took as a freshman than the name of the professor, the textbook, or much of the verbal content of the lectures. The firmer preservation of schemata is not surprising. The human brain evolved from the brains of species who registered the physical features of events and locations without the help of a language.

Gender Associations

A speaker's network of associations to certain objects is altered if his language designates the gender of particular nouns. This is true for Italian, French, German, and Serbian. Italian words that are marked feminine usually end in the vowel "a" or "ione"; masculine nouns end in "o" or "ore." Children learning these languages acquire associations with the networks for masculine or feminine, even though the objects named have neither male nor female properties. For example, feminine nouns in German are preceded by "die," masculine nouns by "der." Thus, the German word for *bee* is preceded by the feminine *die;* the term for *penguin* is preceded by the masculine *der.* Even though German children might agree that bees, like many boys and men, cause pain when they sting whereas penguins, like many girls and women, are gentle and harmless, the German child's network for bee contains associations to feminine properties and the network for penguin is penetrated with associations to masculine features.

Serbian students were asked to learn meaningless words, which possessed a mark for gender, for musical instruments. Later they were asked to describe each instrument. The instruments given a word with a masculine mark were characterized as louder, rougher, sharper, and more penetrating than the instruments marked feminine, which were designated as gentler, quieter, and softer.

These facts invite the speculation that Germans, Italians, and French should have more obvious gender stereotypes than English speakers. The prudent German frau, overprotective Italian mother, and sexually seductive French woman are examples of female stereotypes. The German military officer, Italian gigolo, and French artist are male stereotypes. Equivalently strong female and male stereotypes seem, at least to this writer, less obvious in the English-speaking societies of Great Britain, Canada, Australia, and the United States. Although Old English had grammatical marks for gender, modern English, which emerged in the fifteenth century, deleted them. It may not be a coincidence that the relation between men and women in fifteenth-century England was among the most egalitarian in the world. English-speaking nations were the first to replace the sexist forms "Mrs." and "Miss" with "Ms."

Fifteenth-century China, by contrast, was a sexist society. Charles Ettner of Stanford University notes that at least 20 percent of Chinese words containing the linguistic sign for woman refer to undesirable properties: for example, ugly, envy, harm, and evil. No word containing the morpheme for man refers to an unpleasant feature.

The Universals

Because all humans have either been exposed to or thought about many of the same events, no matter where or when they lived, all societies were bound to invent names for them. With few exceptions, all languages have names for varied kinds of motion, sequences and repetitions of an event as well as for male, female, sun, moon, father, mother, I, you, think, want, feel, know, good, bad, big, small, before, after, say, do, and the numbers 1 and 2. These words, which are used frequently, are least likely to be dropped from a language or replaced by other terms. By contrast, words that are used less often—for example, designating an atypical personality trait or a rare plant—are more likely to be replaced during times of social change. The term *gay* replaced *homosexual*, *weed* replaced *marijuana*, and *cool* was used to name a person who was not easily perturbed during the social changes that began in the 1960s in the United States.

Contrasts

Humans invent a word when they want to differentiate between two as-pects of an experience their society regards as important. That is why the contrasts between fast and slow motion, males and females, and thought and action are universal. Other contrasts are local to a particular society during a certain era: for example, slave versus free, gay versus straight, rural versus urban, and genes versus experience. A team of psychologists at the University of Oregon examined the terms used to describe human traits in twelve languages spoken in parts of Africa, South America, Southeast Asia, Australia, and the Arctic, excluding the Romance languages that domi-nate the developed world. Most words referred to actions, traits, motives, or emotions that belong to the networks for good or bad and potent or impotent, which is also true for the Romance languages. Examples are the English terms *good, respectful, useful, beautiful, strong, young,* and *alive* versus *bad, disobedient, useless, ugly, weak, old,* and *dead.* These words inform each person what to expect when they interact with a member of the community. Individuals want to know whether the object, person, or situation will be a source of pleasure, safety, or kindness, on the one hand, or distress, danger, or rejection, on the other.

The motor schemata created by a glance of the eyes upward or downward and the objects perceived by these glances are a part of the semantic networks for terms associated with the networks for good or bad. Pleasant feelings and their emotional names are preferentially linked to the schema for an upward glance and the word *up*; unpleasant feelings and their names are linked to the schema for a downward glance and the term *down*. Happy and pride are up; sad and shame are down. The sun, moon, and stars have a close link to the networks for up and good; mud, puddles, and rocks have a closer tie to the networks for down and bad.

Antonyms

This discussion of contrasting networks invites an elaboration of antonyms. Antonyms are useful because they clarify the meaning of the members of a contrasting word pair. The word *nonfiction* imposes a limit on the meaning of *fiction*. The meaning of *true* loses some of its ambiguity with the addition of *false*. People are unsure of the meanings of the terms *art* and *personality* because these words have no obvious antonym.

The most frequent antonyms in all languages name opposed values on properties the society regards as important. All languages contain the antonyms good-bad, large-small, rich-poor, big-small, light-dark, and still-moving. The ancient Greeks believed that one-many, odd-even, right-left, still-moving, straight-curved, light-dark, square-rectangle, and good-bad were the most significant contrasts. Contemporary Swedes have a special fondness for the antonym pairs central-regional and oral-written. British journalists like the contrast public-private. The Chinese antonym pair yang-yin is applied to light, heat, strength, speed, and the relationship between two people. The Japanese emphasize the antonym pair inside-outside because they are particularly concerned with the difference between a person's private thoughts and his public behavior. Speakers of Hindi rely on antonyms that English speakers would translate as frugal-extravagant and primary-secondary.

Contemporary Americans worry about the increasing number of older adults, income inequality, and the size and intrusiveness of government. Hence, the antonyms young-old, advantaged-disadvantaged, and liberal-conservative are popular. The antonyms free-slave, north-south, and urban-rural were more popular in 1815 than they are in 2015.

Medieval Europeans were obsessed with the antonym pair pure-impure. A priest who voluntarily castrated himself to curb his carnal desire was pure; one who was castrated by others as a punishment, Peter Abelard's fate, was impure. Medieval Welsh and Irish monks relied on antonyms as the rationale for punishments. Work was the punishment for idleness and confinement to one place the punishment for the sin of wandering.

When both members of an antonym pair occur in the same sentence, the word for the more desirable property usually occurs first. Most Americans prefer to say good before bad, rich before poor, tall before short, present before absent, right before wrong, on before off, yes before no, thick before thin, light before dark, happy before sad, and right before left when both terms appear in an expression. The word *right*, when it refers to the hand or a direction, has a desirable connotation in every known language; whereas the term *left* carries a less desirable one in more than 90 percent of all languages. The word for the more desirable property is also more frequent when it appears alone. Google's Ngram Viewer plots the changing frequencies of words from 5.2 million books written in English between 1800 and 2000. Good, strong, rich, fast, just, and love were more frequent than bad, weak, poor, slow, unjust, and hate across the two centuries. Peter Dodds of the University of Vermont, with colleagues, confirmed that words with a pleasant connotation outnumber those with an unpleasant meaning in the books, newspapers, and media across ten different languages.

All languages acknowledge that no object can possess, at the same time, the contrasting properties of an antonym pair. Young children assume that an object can have only one name. A college student who was babysitting our three-year-old daughter one evening in 1957 told us the following story on our return. Our daughter asked the student what she wanted to be as an adult and the student replied that she planned to be a mother and a doctor.

Our daughter, who had seen only male physicians, was troubled by the answer and insisted, "You can't be a mother and a doctor."

Languages vary in the ease with which speakers can recognize semantic inconsistencies. Languages with many abstract terms that fail to specify the actor or the setting make it easier to detect inconsistencies. English has more abstract words than Mandarin. English speakers use the terms *aggressive, loving, conscientious,* and *fearful* in sentences that leave the incentive and the context unclear, as in "Mary is aggressive," "Bill is loving," "Max is conscientious," and "Alice is fearful." Mandarin speakers describe concrete actions by saying, "Fei takes toys away from her younger brother," "Fei brings food to her close friends when they are ill," "Fei studies hard for all her exams," and "Fei is afraid of flying."

Adults who are proficient in both Mandarin and English make finer differentiations between personality traits when they are speaking Mandarin than they do in English. Mandarin allows speakers to distinguish among yelling at a parent, hitting a stranger, and insulting a friend. English speakers, by contrast, are concerned with fixing the abstract category to which an event belongs. Hence, they treat all three actions as aggressive and ignore the important differences among the behaviors. An English speaker who describes a friend as aggressive will be reluctant to describe the same person as kind for that would imply the friend possessed inconsistent traits. Mandarin speakers do not detect an inconsistency when they say that a person teases her friends but lends them money because they do not use the abstract terms *aggressive* and *kind.*

Metaphors

Meaningful sentences containing networks that represent very different events are usually intended as metaphors, as in "Life is a journey" and "Anger is a boiling kettle." It is relatively easy to explain how children learn the names for objects and the categories to which they belong. It is far more difficult to explain how twelve-year-olds developed the ability to understand metaphors, like "A marriage is a flower garden" or "Happiness is up."

Most metaphors follow a simple principle. The salient feature of a word for a concrete object or event is only one aspect of an abstract term with several characteristics of roughly equal salience. For example, love is an abstract idea whose properties include pleasure, permanence, fragility, frustration, pursuit, intense feeling, and irrationality. The concrete term a speaker chooses for a metaphor depends on the feature of love he wishes to emphasize. A speaker can say, "Love is a crystal goblet," "Love is madness," or "Love is a treasure." Marriage, too, is an abstract term with many properties. The concrete term chosen for the metaphor awards salience to one of them, as in "Marriage is the Rock of Gibraltar" or "Marriage is a cache of honey."

The concrete terms in metaphors usually refer to things that can be visualized and represented as schemata, such as a part of the body, an illness, an animal, a food, a kind of motion, a color, or a feature of space. The abstract terms usually refer to an emotion, moral belief, thought, society, time, life, death, or human relationship. Each has more than one salient feature. Many metaphors contain some property of space because this network is linked to distinct schemata. The metaphors "Happy is up" and "Sad is down" are found in all languages. Spatial features are used to describe temporal properties, as in "Tomorrow is just around the corner," "It was a big day," or "Seize the moment in front of you." Spatial features are also exploited to describe moods (high or low), personality types (open or closed), and actions, as in "He grasped the idea" and "Mary ran with the opportunity."

On the other hand, languages vary in the meaning of some metaphors. Yellow is used in metaphors for cowardice in English, for wealth in Chinese, and for envy in Dutch. Seventeenth-century scholars used the machine as a metaphor for human nature because they wanted to communicate the deterministic functions of each of the body's organs. Twentieth-century writers replaced the machine with a gorilla to emphasize the human capacity for violence. Psychologists at the University of Kansas note that manufacturers of drugs for a mental illness reflect carefully before selecting a metaphor for their product. Ads for medicines designed to treat depression use the verbs *lift* and *lighten* because the mood of depressed patients is down and dark.

The Mismatch Between Words and Events

The writer Julia Blackburn captured the slipperiness of words. "I've often mistrusted the spoken word. You give a quick tug on a line and out they come from the dark continent of the mind, those little rasps of sound that jostle together, shoulder to shoulder, that are supposed to be able to give shape to what you really think, feel, or know. But words easily miss the point. They drift off in the wrong direction, or they insist on providing a clear shape for something that, by its nature, is lost when it's pinned down."

Scientists have an obligation to discover relations between and among behaviors, feelings, inferences, beliefs, experiences, and biology, not the relations among the words that purport to describe these phenomena. Imagine investigators who wanted to know the relation between the average temperature and the average amount of snowfall from October to May in the upper Midwest from 2000 to 2010. Their only sources of evidence, however, were the number of mittens and snow shovels purchased during these months over the ten-year interval. The relation between these measures would be a poor proxy for the relation the scientists want to know. The habit of relying only on verbal reports as bases for inferences about a person's actions, feelings, and intentions is analogous to relying only on the gestures of chimps, songs of birds, or waggle dances of honeybees as the bases for conclusions about the internal states of these animals.

The story of an adolescent boy in a small town with one church who wondered how the man who rang the church bells each day at noon knew when it was noon is appropriate to this discussion. The boy climbed the hill to the church one day and asked the bell ringer how he could be certain of the correct time. He told the boy that each morning after breakfast he went down to the town and checked his watch against the time on the clock in the watchmaker's window. The boy visited the watchmaker and asked him how he knew how to set the hands on his clock. "Oh," he answered. "I always set my clock by the ringing of the church bells at noon."

I recall an evening more than seventy years ago when the mischievous leader of the Boy Scout troop of which I was a member asked one of the boys sitting by a fire we had built to "please get the smoke sifter." The boy went to search for a nonexistent object he had never seen on the assumption that the leader would not name an object that did not exist. I suspect that some social scientists do not realize that they resemble this hapless boy, searching for instances of an abstract semantic concept that nature does not honor.

Words can enlighten, inform, and reassure, but they can also misinform and generate corrosive uncertainties that do not exist in the first reality of experience. The task is to distinguish between words and sentences that describe events that have occurred, or have a reasonable probability of occurring, on the one hand, and semantic inventions that do not cross the border separating imagination from nature's products. This claim does not deny the power of imagination to produce benevolent consequences and powerful theoretical ideas. It only asks for an acknowledgment of the profound differences between the smooth world of words and the rough world of events.

What Does It Mean to Know?

The first knowledge children acquire assumes the form of schemata which, readers will remember, are patterns that preserve the salient features of events. Three-year-olds know that a lit stove is hot, an ice cube is cold, and a flame can destroy paper because they have experienced these events directly. On some occasions, a schema is not a faithful representation of the event. A pencil immersed in half a glass of water generates a schema of the pencil bent at the point where it enters the liquid. A large and small dog moving randomly but close to each other create a schema of the large dog following the smaller one.

A schema need not contain knowledge of the origin of the event or the symbolic category to which it belongs. Newborn infants can detect the difference between a person speaking sentences and birdsong, but they do not know that the former sounds are spoken words. Some of the knowledge contained in schemata is not available to consciousness. Most Americans are not aware that they have acquired schemata representing the fact that sons are more likely than daughters to have single-syllable names and male candidates for a political office are more likely to have broad faces and prominent chins.

Many adults with no special knowledge of abstract art do better than chance would dictate in distinguishing between a painting by an artist and a similar artwork by a young child or a chimpanzee, even though most were unable to say how they decided which paintings were by an artist and which by a child or animal. Ellen Winner of Boston College and her colleagues suggest that these adults may have been relying on schemata for the patterns they had seen in the works of modern artists.

All species inherit a biology that places a limit on the features they can perceive and the schemata they can generate. Rats, bees, and bats detect events that are hidden from humans. The schemata children create when they visit the tropical bird section in a zoo are unlike the schemata the birds create upon seeing them.

Although elegant machines, such as the electron microscope and Hubble Space Telescope, provide humans with information denied to the senses, they remove the observer from the phenomenon and, on occasion, produce information that does not match what a person can perceive. Jeff Lichtman of Harvard University tells us that a single scientist working alone would need many years to take electron microscopic photographs of every milli-meter of a mouse's cortex and transfer the trillions of images to hard discs. A machine can perform this task more quickly, but it makes a few errors that human observers examining the same photos do not make.

A Quartet of Additional Sources of Knowledge

Humans add to perception four additional processes that contribute to their store of knowledge. Inference, which typically appears during the second year, allows children to assume that a parent is in pain or in a happy mood. Two-year-olds spontaneously pick up an object an adult dropped, even if the adult does not explicitly ask for help, and spontaneously open a door for a stranger whose hands are full because they infer the adult needs assistance. I recall watching a pair of three-year-old boys in a playroom that contained only one Batman costume. The boy who seized the costume first inferred that the other boy wanted this prize and taunted, "You can hate me if you want." Children infer the meaning of unfamiliar words that occur in an otherwise familiar sentence. A three-year-old infers that the unfamiliar word *fungus* refers to the distinctive white spots on a blos-som when the mother, pointing to the flower, says, "Look, the flower has a fungus."

Most inferences require some prior knowledge. I have learned that objects that move spontaneously in a body of water must be alive and that living things require a source of clean water. Hence, if I see a small object move in a small pool of dirty water I infer that the object cannot be alive. I made that inference many years ago when I saw a small object move in the heavily polluted water at the foot of a fountain in a Paris park. Moments later this inference was confirmed when I saw a boy with a remote device control the movements of a toy submarine.

Most inferences about the relations between two events—whether an object accidentally pushed off a table will shatter when it strikes the floor—acknowledge the features of the object and the setting. We expect different outcomes depending on whether a glass falling from a table lands on a concrete surface or a thickly carpeted floor. We infer a moment of guilt in an adult who accidentally breaks an expensive vase but do not make that inference if an infant commits the same act.

Bertrand Russell believed there was a small number of general rules of inference that applied across all domains. His colleague Alfred North Whitehead disagreed. He was equally certain that the validity of every inference depended on the system in which it was a part.

The deduction of logically correct conclusions and the detection of incorrect ones in sets of sentences or mathematical equations comprise a third process that is a source of knowledge. Peter Higgs's positing of the particle that bears his name years before physicists claimed in 2013 that they had found it is a classic example. I suspect that most adults who read that electrons had no mass right after the Big Bang do not know that this statement was dictated by the need to keep the set of equations, called the Standard Model, mathematically consistent. It is impossible to know whether the electron was massless during the first moments after the universe was born. It remains possible that future physicists will invent a more powerful set of equations that will assume the electron did have mass at the moment of its creation.

Jeroen Van Dongen points out that a young Einstein believed that mathematical models ought to be based on and consistent with observations. After the success of his equations of general relativity in 1915, an older

Einstein began to move closer to the view that a coherent set of mathematical equations that originated in intuition was a better guide to truth. Einstein's assumption that nothing can travel faster than the speed of light was dictated by the assumptions that gave rise to the equations. Although no scientist has discovered any particle that violates Einstein's premise, that does not guarantee that such an observation will never be made.

There are two ways to view mathematical descriptions of nature. Some physicists have an unquestioning faith in explanations implied by the mathematical equations that account for and predict a set of observations. They are not troubled when the equations assume events that are either counterintuitive or difficult to imagine. For example, some theorists believe that a tiny ball of energy expanded into the current universe in less than a fraction of a second 13.7 billion years ago because the mathematics that explains the known facts demands that idea.

I remember reading about the two physicists who, having measured the temperature of the cosmos, concluded that the energy implied by that temperature (a few degrees above absolute zero) represented the energy left over from the Big Bang. This bold statement was based on equations that assumed a steady rate of cooling over this long interval, without the insertion of new sources of energy. Finding this claim counterintuitive, I expressed my doubts to a Nobel laureate in physics. He responded as if I were a five-year-old who had asked a silly question. If the mathematics can explain the data, he implied, it is a valid account. Case closed.

Unfortunately, hedge fund and investment bank traders believed that the mathematical formula invented by Scholes and Black, which was intended to tell traders the optimal price of a derivative, guaranteed protection from serious loss. The traders did not realize that the equation did not adequately reflect the continuous changes in the prices of the equities and, more seriously, assigned too low a value to the probability of a financial loss.

Biologists, like the geneticists Isabelle Peter and Eric Davidson at the California Institute of Technology, care about the reasonableness of a mathematical description of a natural phenomenon and are skeptical of equations that violate what is known about a domain. The equations that assume continuous processes in the formation of body parts explain a great deal of the evidence, but happen to be inconsistent with the stubborn fact that each tissue contains a qualitatively distinct type of cell. There are no tooth cells in the lips, no cells from the cornea in the retina, suggesting that these equations are unlikely to be valid descriptions of this process as it occurs in nature.

The retired British philosopher Antony Flew had been a committed atheist until late in life when he examined the logical coherence of the physicist's explanation of the origin of the universe. Finding it wanting, he concluded that positing a God was no less logical than accepting the physicist's explanation. Francis Collins, a biologist and the director of the National Institutes of Health, sees no logical inconsistency between his belief in an omnipotent God and the scientific facts. When I stand on an unlit beach staring at the Milky Way on a cloudless night wondering about the origin of the energy in all those stars, I come closer to understanding how Flew and Collins arrived at their beliefs.

One set of equations, called string theory and intended to unite Einstein's general relativity with quantum mechanics, predicts a large number of universes—10 followed by 500 zeroes—each one following unique laws whose phenomena cannot be observed. If some eminent physicists believe in multiple universes obeying different laws, we should not be surprised by the adults who believe that a supernatural being created the universe.

I recently read a description of the patterns of gene expression and concentration gradients of the many molecules that must be coordinated in time and space if an embryo is to develop properly. Overwhelmed by the complexity of these cascades, I shared the author's sense of mystery surrounding these phenomena. I am willing to make the leap of faith needed to accept the argument that these cascades are the products of natural selection acting on hundreds of millions of years of chance events. I confess, however, that it is easier to imagine a chimpanzee striking a keyboard randomly accidentally typing a Shakespeare sonnet.

A majority of European and North American scientists and mathematicians possess an unshakable faith in the power of rational, logically coherent analyses, stripped of all sentiment, to reveal the optimal decision when experts are uncertain. American generals during the Cold War of the 1950s were troubled by their uncertainty over the Soviet Union's intentions to launch a nuclear attack. Their response was to hire mathematicians and social scientists committed to logical decision trees to supply them with a set of possible scenarios that would reduce their uncertainty.

A faith in the power of logical analyses that assign probabilities to future outcomes remains strong, despite the fact that this strategy failed to predict the recession of 2007, the attack on the World Trade Center on 9/11, the Arab Spring, the rise of ISIS, low fertility rates in Europe, and a host of other phenomena in which feelings and irrational beliefs trumped the logic applied to known facts.

Leaders in science are frustrated by their inability to predict which investigators under age thirty are most likely to make an important discovery and, therefore, ought to be supported. Experts continue to invent new predictors and stubbornly refuse to consider the possibility that accurate prediction is impossible because the probability of a major discovery depends on the laboratories, colleagues, and students a young scientist will encounter during the next thirty years of a career. These facts are unknowable the day young scientists begin their journey. There will be about thirty-two homicides in the United States each day in 2015. This number is such a small proportion of the population it is impossible to predict who will commit these crimes. The same unpredictability surrounds the likelihood of a mutation during a cell division in a particular organ or tissue. Some phenomena simply cannot be predicted with any known procedure. Einstein's reluctance to acknowledge this fact led him to criticize quantum mechanics as an incomplete theory.

The world is lucky that the leaders of nations with stockpiles of nuclear weapons made three errors of reasoning that decision theorists had claimed lead to undesirable outcomes. They made the mistake of defending the status quo, justifying past decisions, and awarding power to the evidence that affirmed the prior decision not to drop nuclear bombs on a potential enemy. By contrast, the bankers and investors who were too clever to fall prey to these mistakes brought on the recession of 2007. It is unlikely that any decision rule transcends the details of a situation. There are only rules for particular problems at a particular historical moment.

Most scientists trying to understand a social problem award special causal power to conditions that can be assigned a number. For example, some theorists argue that the number of unrealized years of productive work is the criterion to use when deciding the value of a life that was compromised by accident or disease. The person's level of distress is an unattractive criterion because it is difficult to assign a number to an emotional state. The two psychiatrists at Virginia Commonwealth University who assigned a number to represent a person's level of resilience under stress ignored the exact nature of the stress as well as the reaction to the stress by individuals from different social classes or cultures. Physicists and mathematicians award some numbers a reality as fundamental as the one reserved for plates, pencils, and pebbles. Planck's constant, pi, and the ratio $1/137$, or $.007299$, are three examples.

A fourth class of knowledge originates in the intuition, usually accompanied by a feeling, that certain actions, intentions, and values are more ethical, fairer, or closer to an ideal. The beliefs that parents should love their children, that altering the forms that occur in nature is dangerous, that all life is sacred, that freedom from government surveillance is a right, and that governments should help the poor do not originate in either perception, inference, or logical deduction. Many contemporary Americans have the intuition that explanations of mental illness that make the brain the major cause are more likely to be correct, that a person's happiness ought to have priority when personal or governmental decisions are made, that all humans are entitled to equal dignity, that all value systems are to be respected as long as they do not harm others, and that laissez-faire capitalism is the best way to organize an economy.

The Statements by Authorities

Faith in one's intuitions rests, in part, on statements by respected authorities. This fifth source of knowledge is usually contained in sentences that can refer to events neither experienced directly, inferred, nor deduced. My beliefs that single cells without a nucleus were the first living things on earth and the ability to perceive red and green evolved later than the ability to detect blue are two examples. The treatises on nature written by scholars from ancient Greece and China during the six hundred years from 400 BCE to 200 CE provide an example of how bright minds can invent very different, but equally coherent, views of the same phenomena.

The Greeks decided that a small number of invisible, but stable, elements were the foundation of the phenomena we perceive. The Chinese, by contrast, assumed that the balance between the forces of yang and yin explained the same events. The Greeks wanted to know the discrete elements that composed a snowflake. The Chinese wanted to understand the processes that allowed a snowflake to form. The Greek view promised certainty; the Chinese perspective accepted the uncertainty inherent in the continually changing balance between different energies. Contemporary physicists combine both ideas. They side with the Greeks by positing basic particles, such as quarks. They agree with the Chinese by positing forces, called bosons, that particles require in order to actualize their properties. The Higgs field is a boson.

The Source of the Evidence

The meaning—and therefore the validity–of statements by authorities is seriously dependent on the evidence that is the basis for the statements. This seemingly radical idea became necessary during the 1920s when the novel observations and concepts of quantum mechanics challenged the existing understanding of words such as *cause, particle,* and *certainty.* These events motivated the physicist Percy Bridgman to write an influential book in 1927, *The Logic of Modern Physics,* arguing that all scientific concepts had to be defined by the procedures that generated the evidence for the concept. The opening chapter of Susan Fahrbach's 2013 textbook on developmental neuroscience is devoted to descriptions of the methods neuroscientists use to arrive at their conclusions because these investigators understand that the validity of every conclusion depends on how the observations were generated.

It is difficult to persuade social scientists who rely only on answers to questionnaires that there is often a minimal relation between what people say they believe, feel, or do and what they actually believe, feel, or do. A 2011 poll of adults from twenty-four countries revealed a surprising result. A larger proportion of adults from countries, such as Indonesia, India, and Mexico, that have a relatively small GDP and many residents living in poverty, told an interviewer they felt very happy, compared with the proportions in South Korea, Germany, France, and the United States, which have a much larger GDP. It is likely that the adults from these different societies were using dissimilar definitions of the phrase "feeling very happy."

Qi Wang of Cornell University in *The Autobiographical Self in Time and Culture* notes that bilingual Chinese Americans asked to describe their personality traits chose different properties when they answered in English compared with Mandarin, partly because the latter language has more terms referring to social relationships. But these individuals do not have two personalities.

Daniel Schacter describes three common sources of error when adults report memories of the past. Many recall events that only resemble the ones that actually occurred, imagine events that never happened, or incorporate a later event into the memory of an earlier experience. Carl Weems of the University of New Orleans found that adolescents who initially reported many traumatic memories of Hurricane Katrina in 2005 often failed to report these memories four years later if their experience with Hurricane Gustav, which occurred in 2008, was benign.

An unknown number of adults are convinced that one of their parents was either cruel or kind when they were young children. The selection of either belief depends partly on the narrative the adults constructed to explain their current personality and circumstances. I once interviewed a large number of twenty- to twenty-five-year-olds about their childhoods. In this instance, however, I had access to reports of observers who made semi-annual visits to the homes of these respondents when they were young children. Some of the young adults who were satisfied with their lives told me they had kind parents, although the reports revealed that they had grown up with an unusually harsh, punitive parent. I suspect they decided that their parent must have been kind because if that were not true they ought to be less happy. Several adults who said they were unhappy but actually had affectionate parents reported that one or both parents were unloving. The English words *know* and *believe* capture the distinction between knowledge that originates in personal experience and beliefs that are based on the statements of others. I know I have two hands; I believe I have trillions of bacteria in my gut.

Close to 75 percent of Americans, most of whom knew little or nothing about economics and the finances of large communication companies, offered a confident opinion when a pollster asked them if a proposed merger of Comcast and Time Warner would affect their rates or access to better programming. That fact explains why George Beam, a critic of telephone- or Web-based surveys, warned, "If you want to find out what's really going on, don't ask."

Beam's skepticism is supported by the adults who say they detect deep metaphorical meaning in the drawings of four-year-olds if they believe that the drawings are works of abstract art painted by famous artists. This observation reminded me of a short silent film I saw many years ago. The film depicted a man standing on a scaffold pouring paints randomly on a large canvas a few feet below. The man descended, walked over the canvas for a few minutes to spread the paint, cut the canvas into twelve smaller pieces, and placed them on a beach. Minutes later a small plane landed, a man in a suit emerged, greeted the artist, examined each of the twelve canvases carefully, selected one, gave a check to the artist, and departed. When the plane was gone the artist kicked the remaining eleven canvases into the sea.

The age of the earth provides a persuasive example of the principle that the validity of all statements depends on the nature of the evidence. Contemporary physicists tell us that the earth is 4.5 billion years old. Lord Kelvin, arguably the most respected scientist of the nineteenth century, arrived at a far younger age for the earth because his estimate of the rate at which the earth's interior had cooled since its origin was incorrect. Scientists who rely on evidence from fossils write that the domestic dog evolved from the wolf about twelve thousand years ago. Geneticists who use genes as evidence claim that the dog emerged about thirty thousand years ago. The difference between these estimates is not trivial.

Linda Bartoshuk of the University of Florida provides a persuasive example of how a slight change in the nature of the evidence can affect the conclusion. The human tongue contains different kinds of taste buds that are sensitive to the varied sensory qualities of foods. It is reasonable to assume that those who possess more taste buds for sweetness should experience a food, say Coca-Cola, as sweeter than those with fewer taste buds for sweetness. This intuition is disconfirmed if the psychologist asks adults to rate the sweetness of a sip of Coca-Cola on a scale from 1, meaning "not sweet," to 7, meaning "very sweet." A slight change in the procedure, however, reinstates the original intuition. When the person is asked to adjust the loudness of a tone to match the intensity of sweetness, those with more taste buds for sweetness select a louder tone than those with fewer taste buds. The answer to the question "Do adults with more taste buds for sweetness experience a sweeter sensation than others?" is: "It depends on the evidence."

Conclusions regarding prejudice honor the same principle. The psychologists who found that many Americans have automatic associations of aggression to the words *black* or *African* claimed that these adults were prejudiced against blacks, even if they strongly denied a bigoted attitude. Millions of white Americans who possessed these associations to *black* or a picture of an African American voted for Barack Obama—twice. Automatic associations, conscious thoughts, and actions are different sources of evidence for conclusions about prejudiced beliefs. My automatic associations to the word *German* include "Nazis," "cruelty," and "genocide," but my beliefs about and behaviors with the many Germans I know are free of bigotry. The millions of twenty-year-olds whose associations to the word *grandfather* or a picture of an old man include the words *forgetful, weak, tired,* and *sick* are unlikely to hold a prejudiced attitude toward their own aged grandfathers. These facts imply that the meaning and truth value of the sentence "Max is prejudiced against Hispanics," like the statement "People with more taste buds for sweetness experience a more intense sensation of sweetness," depend on the evidence.

This claim applies to conclusions about states of fear or anxiety in rats or mice. Many investigators assume that mice or rats who avoid brightly lit areas or the center of large spaces are anxious, even though a British scientist from the University of Sunderland argues that the evidence does not support that assumption. A moment of reflection reveals the potential error in assuming that an animal or person who avoids an object or location is anxious. I avoid spicy foods, large cities, cocktail parties, and country music because I do not like them, but I do not feel anxious when I experience these events. Rats, mice, and humans avoid places that evoke an unpleasant bodily state, but that state is not always synonymous with human anxiety, which is often created by anticipating an event—being bitten by a snake, injured in an airplane, or coming down with a malignant cancer—that has never occurred.

A similar skepticism applies to the popular assumption that increased secretion from the sweat glands on a finger or hand (called the skin conductance response) or an exaggerated eye blink reflex to a sudden loud sound (called potentiated startle) delivered while the person anticipates or is presented with an aversive event—say, a bloodied body or a loud scream—are reliable signs of anxiety. The evidence does not always support this premise. Adults who report being anxious when they anticipate an aversive event do not display a larger skin conductance response or a potentiated startle than the average person. Most adults report feeling anxious when they breathe air enriched with carbon dioxide or place a hand in very cold water for ninety seconds, but they do not show an exaggerated eye blink to a loud sound. On the other hand, adults trying to solve an anagrams problem do show a potentiated startle.

Studies of the effectiveness of various forms of therapy for a mental illness typically rely only on the patient's verbal report. Matthew Price of the University of Vermont, with colleagues, remind us that these judgments are colored by the patient's optimism regarding the efficacy of the therapy. Most patients are reluctant to say that the therapy they chose was a waste of time. Price found that veterans with post-traumatic stress disorder (PTSD) who expected to be helped by a therapy reported, after six sessions, that their symptoms were less severe. However, they failed to show reduced secretion of the stress hormone cortisol, suggesting that their recovery may have been less successful than their verbal reports implied. The main point of this discussion is that biological, behavioral, and verbal report measures award different meanings to the terms *anxiety* or *fear*.

When a discipline is young and without a consensual theory, many terms have multiple meanings because they belong to different networks of words and schemata. None of the social sciences possesses a broad consensual theory; therefore, few concepts have a single meaning that all investigators accept. Under these conditions the source of the evidence determines the meaning of the term. Niels Bohr was among the first scientists to recognize that the investigator's procedure is always a participant in the conclusions drawn from every observation.

Readers should appreciate that the evidence for many facts about human personality in psychology textbooks comes from verbal reports to questionnaires. It is possible, even likely, that these textbooks would contain radically different content if the conclusions had been based on observations of youths or adults in their usual settings. This claim is supported by Sean Wojcik and colleagues, who found that politically conservative Americans say they are happier than liberals. But, surprisingly, liberals display fuller smiles in photographs and their written comments contain more words implying a happy, optimistic mood. The authors end their paper with useful advice, "Reliance on any single methodology is likely to lead to an oversimplified account of not only who is happier than whom but also what it means to be happy at all." Amen!

Each source of evidence can be likened to a lens with a fixed curvature. A viewer can polish the lens to render perceptions a little clearer, but each lens can reveal only a limited set of objects. A curtain punctuated with many tiny holes separates scientists from the phenomena they want to understand. The view from a single hole, analogous to reliance on one source of evidence, cannot satisfy this wish.

If, subjectively, I feel free of anxiety, no investigator examining my biology or behavior can deny that claim. A scientist examining my brain who concludes I am anxious is adopting a different definition of *anxiety*. It is possible, of course, that the brain measure is a better predictor, or provides a better explanation, of an outcome that theory says reflects an anxious state than my subjective report. But the two sources of evidence award different meanings to anxiety. No source of evidence is privileged over all others across all domains of inquiry.

Does the Brain Provide a Privileged Source of Evidence?

Neuroscientists would like to persuade the public and funding agencies that measures of brain activity enjoy a privileged status for conclusions about psychological states. I confess to being surprised by a paper, written by a team of scientists led by Jing Jiang, which suggested that brain measures might be useful in selecting the most effective leaders in politics or business. The basis for this bold claim was an observation in an artificial context that invites more than one interpretation. When a college student, assigned as the "leader" of two students told to be followers, spoke on an assigned topic, the brain activity of all three at a site related to language processing showed a modest level of synchronization between the leader and the two followers. There was no synchronization when one of the followers spoke.

This observation has an obvious explanation that has nothing to do with the leader's potential effectiveness. A student told to play the role of follower would be expected to pay more attention to the speech of the assigned leader than to comments by the other follower, independent of the charismatic potential of the assigned leader. That interpretation would account for the correspondence between brain activity at a site that is usually active when one person is speaking and others are listening.

Popular explanations of the occasionally impulsive decisions of youth provide another example of the attempt to replace psychological processes with brain patterns. I suspect that 90 percent of any sample of sixteen-year-old boys would, if asked, insist that they were capable of inhibiting an urge to rape a woman, stab a rival, steal a woman's purse, or set fire to a car, and these declarations would be affirmed if we observed each boy in these settings.

Nonetheless, some scientists argue (and some juries agree) that adolescents have difficulty inhibiting asocial actions because their brains are not fully mature. These scientists fail to tell their audiences that crimes of violence are far more common among poor youths from a minority group than among affluent adolescents with the same immature brains who belong to a dominant ethnic group. The majority of homicides in the United States over the past ten years were committed by black males between fifteen and twenty-five living in the South. There is no evidence to indicate that the brains of these youths were less mature than the brains of boys of the same age who grew up in advantaged families living in other regions. These facts provide a persuasive example of the danger inherent in replacing a psychological frame of reference with a biological one and arguing that the latter has a privileged validity.

Judges and juries have, on occasion, been persuaded that the integrity of a defendant's brain is relevant to decisions about punishment. They are willing, for example, to give lighter sentences to adolescents who commit a serious crime if scientists testify that an adolescent's frontal lobe, which is a critical region contributing to inhibition of impulsive behaviors, is not fully mature until the midtwenties.

A sensitive sign of an "immature frontal lobe" is incomplete pruning of the synapses in this site, which is measured by the thickness of the gray matter in this part of the cortex. A study by scientists at the University of Alberta challenged this belief. Although there was a general trend favoring a thinner cortex over the long interval from age five to thirty-two, many ten-year-olds had thinner cortices than some thirty-year-olds, and youth between ages twelve and eighteen showed similar levels of thickness in the frontal lobe. It is useful to remember that most adolescents born before 1800, although they also had incompletely pruned frontal lobes, were working to help support their family. Over the course of human history, most rapes, murders, and robberies have been committed by men between twenty and forty, most of whom probably had mature frontal lobes.

Some juries are a little more likely to give less severe sentences to adult criminals if an expert testifies that their brain scans reveal an abnormality, even if they and the scientists do not understand how that abnormality would lead to criminal behavior. Most adults with a brain abnormality do not commit crimes and most criminals have no known brain abnormality. A twenty-four-year-old woman, J.F., smothered her newborn infant moments after its birth in her boyfriend's apartment. J.F. was judged legally sane and intellectually competent, but measures of her brain revealed less than the expected amount of gray matter in a location in the frontal lobe that contributes to control of impulsive actions.

Most adults with this same brain feature do not murder anyone and most law-abiding adults over age seventy have lost equivalent amounts of gray matter in this location. Thus, we have to ask: could J.F. have controlled her urge to kill her infant or did her biology render her incapable of suppressing her action? I do not know the answer but I do know that defense attorneys will increasingly use information about the brain to argue that their clients were not completely responsible for their crime.

The Privileged Position of Science

The knowledge that originates in a scientist's declarations enjoys a privileged position in modern societies, even though everyone understands that all facts are subject to revision. The discovery of an infectious protein that could cause a brain disease is an example. This idea evoked strong resistance among scientists because it was inconsistent with the fundamental principle that only a form that contained DNA or RNA could be infectious. But Stanley Prusiner, with the help of specialists, persisted against harsh critiques and eventually persuaded a majority of biologists and the Nobel Prize Committee that genes, diet, or an environmental event could transform the shape of a normal brain protein into one with an abnormal shape. The deformed protein, called a prion, could convert normal proteins into an increasing number of abnormal ones, which eventually coalesced into toxic plaques that caused the symptoms of mad cow disease in cattle or Creutzfeldt-Jakob disease in humans.

I noted that natural scientists are suspicious of statements by social scientists about mental phenomena because it is difficult to imagine how a thought or feeling is represented in the brain. Sitting alone by the sea one summer afternoon, I was surprised to find myself wondering why the water did not rise. I knew that the gravitational force between the water and the earth's core explains why the sea does not ascend. I even remember Newton's equation for this force. But because I do not have a schema for "gravitational force," I have the uneasy sense that I do not fully understand why the sea remains in place. I have a firmer understanding of the physicist's explanation of why water boils because I have a schema for water molecules bouncing against each other in a heated pot. A schema of a large object bending the space around it, as a large, heavy ball would distort the surface of a trampoline, aids understanding of Einstein's explanation of why the earth orbits the sun in his theory of general relativity.

A person who is unable to retrieve schemata to support a belief is especially vulnerable to an authority's declarations. Students who were told by an authority that biological measures of their body indicated they had slept very well during the prior night performed better on cognitive tests than those who were told their sleep had been poor. The students' memory of how well they slept had no effect on their performance. This observation points to the ease with which an authority can persuade a person to accept a fact that is not true.

Most Americans during the second third of the last century had not seen a child who displayed seriously disturbed language and social behavior. As a result, they were ready to believe the experts who wrote that a cold, aloof mother could produce these abnormal behaviors. Even the belief that seventeenth-century Italian violins made by Stradivari produce sounds superior to anything a new violin can create is subject to challenge. The ten renowned solo violinists who, blindfolded, played a violin made by Stradivari and a new violin preferred the sound of the latter instrument.

Social scientists often ask adults to play a game with strangers in a laboratory setting that is unlike the subjects' life circumstances. John Nash, the central figure in the film A Beautiful Mind and a Nobel laureate in economics, invented a logically elegant model that predicted the optimal strategy a player should adopt in a multiplayer game. However, Nash's model made four unrealistic assumptions: all players are able to evaluate their motives correctly, possess equivalent bargaining skill, know the preferences of all the other players, and cannot communicate with each other. No successful portfolio manager, quarterback, poker player, or political candidate would meet the Nash criteria.

Explanations that support what the investigators, and often the public, want to believe are prevalent in psychology and psychiatry. The popularity of Freud's writings between 1910 and 1960, especially in the United States and England, illustrates the seductive power of conclusions that supported the public's belief in the power of early family experience. We do not fully understand why a majority of psychiatrists and psychologists as well as a fair proportion of educated Americans believed Sigmund Freud's explanations of the causes of neurotic symptoms, for these ideas have not been supported by the evidence.

Freud's hypotheses were attractive to many middle-class Americans in the beginning of the last century because they believed that early experiences were important and because they were coping with moderate guilt, shame, or anxiety over sexual urges. Asti Hustvedt notes that Freud's experiences while visiting Jean-Martin Charcot in Paris helped him arrive at the notion that repression of sexual ideas and feelings created the symptoms of hysteria. Many of Charcot's hysterical patients at the Pitié-Salpêtrière hospital spoke about sex openly and frequently because they had been seduced or raped many times when they were young women.

In addition, the automobile, radio, empowerment of women, the First World War, films, and a faster pace of life had created a mood of uncertainty whose cause was difficult to specify. Hence, a large proportion of Americans and Europeans were receptive to an expert who offered an explanation of their tension. The millions for whom Freud's account had the ring of truth were willing to believe that repression of their sexual urges brought on by improper childhood socialization was the reason for their feelings. Carl Jung recognized that Freud had misinterpreted a temporary attitude toward sexuality in middle-class European society at the end of the nineteenth century as a deep truth about human nature.

An attraction to proving the truth of a favorite idea is a product of the history of the young discipline of psychology. Many of the first psychologists were nineteenth-century scholars trained in physiology who wanted to understand human perception. Younger scholars who were attracted to the philosophical issues surrounding mind and morality soon joined this new discipline. Freud's popularity temporarily turned the balance of power between these two groups to favor the philosophical types.

Even experts in a mature discipline are susceptible to believing a colleague's statement if it affirms a popular idea. The media announced in the spring of 2014 that scientists at the South Pole using a highly specialized telescope aimed at a small patch of sky had discovered traces of gravitational waves created only a fraction of a second after the Big Bang as the universe expanded. Although many physicists accepted this fact as true, a few skeptics, who later examined the same evidence, suggested that the observations were better explained as the consequence of the scattering of interstellar dust by the magnetic fields in our galaxy. This is now the consensual understanding.

During the years 1880 to 1920, an unknown number of middle-aged men spent the current equivalent of $10 to buy a cloth belt they placed around the waist that created mild electric stimulation of the skin. The belt consisted of wooden cylinders wound with zinc and copper wires that had been soaked in vinegar. These men believed the advertisements promising that electrical stimulation of the body, especially the genitals, supplied the energy needed to cure the impotence they believed was brought on by excessive masturbation during adolescence.

Mental Illness

The public is unaware of the evidence that led some psychiatrists to announce an epidemic of autism, a word invented about seventy years ago to describe the condition of children who displayed serious abnormalities in language and social behavior. The prevalence of autism in the United States, which was about one in one thousand only seventy years ago, rose to one in sixty-six in 2014. It would be a cause for worry if the number of autistic patients had increased by a factor greater than ten in less than a century. However, parents can relax; there is no epidemic of autism. The reason for the increased prevalence is that clinicians altered the criteria they had been using to arrive at a diagnosis. Most of the children currently diagnosed as belonging to the autistic spectrum had been categorized earlier as brain damaged. Damage to the brain can result from a very large number of causes, including varied genetic mutations, maternal infections during pregnancy, immune reactions, or problems during delivery. Doctors and scientists are now pooling these many causes of different forms of brain damage into one catchall category called the autistic spectrum. If physicians pooled everyone who complained of feeling tired into one category called the fatigue spectrum, the media would inform us that there is an epidemic of fatigue.

The American Psychiatric Association published its fifth manual of mental illnesses in 2013. Belief in the validity of the categories described in the manual depends on one's faith in the wisdom of the individuals who composed it. Unlike most physical diseases, very few mental illnesses are defined by their origin. Rather, each illness is based on the opinions of professionals who have treated, or in some cases studied, individuals who report less common behaviors or moods. Unfortunately, less than half of the illness categories in the latest manual are supported by robust scientific facts. The majority of the categories are based on professional opinions that are not always consensual. As a result, there has been a flurry of books criticizing the validity of the current long list of illnesses.

For example, although the manual states that chronic gambling is a mental illness, it excludes the men and women working for investment firms who rise each day before dawn to buy and sell millions of dollars of equities. These men and women are gambling and many find this activity as exciting and addictive as those who play poker online or visit gambling arcades. If gambling performed as part of one's job is not a sign of illness but gambling for pleasure is, psychiatrists should classify women who choose to be highly paid prostitutes to support their family as healthy, but diagnose women who enjoy changing sex partners frequently as mentally ill. Surely there is something illogical in this reasoning.

Allen Frances, a distinguished psychiatrist who is disturbed by the addition of many normal states to the list of illnesses, writes in *Saving Normal* that the current psychiatric manual has the "harmful unintended consequence of triggering and helping to maintain a runaway diagnostic inflation that threatens normal and results in massive overtreatment with psychiatric medication." Frances's suggestion is supported by the fact that one of every two Americans who received a diagnosis of anxiety, depression, or substance abuse disorder returned to their usual, less distressed state within three years without the help of any treatment. This fact implies that a bout of worry, sadness, or heavy drinking brought on by loss of a job, a failed relationship, or chronic illness is a common human reaction and not always a sign of abnormal genes, a damaged brain, or a traumatic childhood.

A pediatrician who had studied a small number of infants in the 1920s discovered that it took about four hours for the infant's stomach to empty following a feeding. That slim source of evidence was disseminated to thousands of American pediatricians who, in turn, told millions of new mothers to wait four hours between feeding their infant. My mother, who received that advice but didn't ask the doctor for the evidence behind this prescription, told me it required considerable willpower for her to ignore my screams of hunger.

The Increased Number of Scientists

The extraordinary increase over the past century in the number of scientists was accompanied by the creation of many narrow specialties. The scientists working in each domain claimed the right to decide which conclusions were true and which false. The members of a specialty—say, particle physics, molecular genetics, or neuroscience—are willing to be persuaded by other members of their group but usually ignore claims made by scientists from another specialty. The era of the generalist has passed. As a result, changing the beliefs of a majority in a specialty requires persuasive arguments by colleagues within the discipline. This indifference to the views of others slows reform. When there were fewer scientists and fewer facts, a scholar in one domain with a good idea or novel observation was able to influence those in a different discipline. Ivan Pavlov was a physiologist, Gregor Mendel and Johannes Kepler were members of the clergy, Karl Popper and W. V. Quine were philosophers. All four had a major influence on the natural and social sciences.

Not surprisingly, the swelling in the number of scientists was followed by an extraordinary increase in the number of published papers. Essays addressing this problem in the October 4, 2013, issue of *Science* magazine noted that a book containing all the scientific papers published in 1880 would be about one hundred pages long. More than sixteen longer volumes would be required in 2015 because a page of prose is added to the scientific literature every fifteen minutes. Close to 3 million papers were published in American journals in 2012.

There are at least three reasons why the expansion of the technical literature has eroded the quality of an unknown number of papers. First, it is difficult to conduct thorough reviews of every paper submitted to every journal. Second, many young investigators, eager for promotion and knowing that the critical requirement for advancement is publication of many papers in a few years, are tempted to lower their standards. A final reason is the recent emergence of many "for-profit" publishers who charge authors between $500 and $2,000 for publishing an article in one of their journals. Because these companies want to make money, they accept reports of flawed studies without a thorough review. Some experts estimate that at least one-half of the findings in these "for-profit" journals could not be repeated—and therefore the conclusions should not be believed.

One biologist discovered how permissive the reviews can be when he sent a fictitious paper about a possible cure for cancer that contained obvious errors to 304 different journals that conduct inadequate evaluations of manuscripts. More than half of the editors accepted the deeply flawed paper. This sad fact means that scientists, journalists who report on science, and the public should remain skeptical of conclusions published in journals known to implement inadequate reviews unless they have been verified by another scientist.

No Silver Bullets

Social scientists are attracted to finding single causes of complex outcomes. One of the robust truths in science is that the more complex the phenomenon the larger the number of conditions needed to produce it. Geneticists acknowledge that most physical and psychological traits require a pattern of many genes combined with critical experiences. Nonetheless, many psychologists continue to search for single conditions, such as day care attendance, security of attachment, abuse, neglect, lack of friends, being a victim of bullying, divorce, or maternal depression, that increase the

probability of an unwanted psychological trait or biological state, independent of the child's gender, social class, ethnicity, talents, and culture.

Norbert Wiener's childhood years contained at least six conditions that
psychologists regard as risk factors that are supposed to interfere with future
adaptation. He was clumsy, nearsighted, socially inept, friendless, full of
self-doubt, and lived with a demanding father who infantilized him. But
these single features were elements in a larger pattern that included exceptional talent in mathematics, mentoring by leading European mathematicians and philosophers, a Harvard professor father who had many friends
able to help his son's career, and coming of age in the 1920s when the proliferation of telephones and electricity was accompanied by problems that
Wiener's mathematical discoveries could resolve. As a result, he became an
esteemed professor at MIT, was happily married, and enjoyed a productive
life despite his six childhood burdens.

There is a robust relation between a childhood spent in poverty and the
development of a chronic inflammatory state caused by high levels of
proteins, called cytokines, that increase the risk of a serious metabolic
disease such as diabetes, heart attack, or stroke. A majority of scientists agree
that the stress of growing up poor is a major cause of the adult's compromised physiology. But we do not know which patterns of conditions associated with poverty, which include an inadequate diet, many infectious
illnesses, lack of proper medical care, quality of schools attended, asocial
values of the peer group, lack of physical exercise, stressful prenatal events,
and the socialization practices of parents, create the inflammatory state.

Almost every psychological outcome and a majority of biological ones
are the result of more than one causal cascade. Therefore, improved understanding and prediction require discovery of each of the causal cascades that
end up with the same outcome. Sadly, few social scientists are trying to find
the variety of cascades. Oncologists, by contrast, are trying to find the
different genetic abnormalities that produce the same form of cancer.

The popular assumption that the experience of being bullied leads to
unwanted outcomes, independent of any other conditions, ignores the fact
that bullies typically select victims who deviate from the peer group in some
way. They might have a small stature, an unattractive face, be excessively timid

or arrogant, belong to a minority religious or ethnic group, live in a poor family, or perform poorly in school. Any one of these properties could contribute to a later psychological problem, without the experience of being bullied.

Danish scientists studying youths from thirty-five nations discovered that those who were most often bullied came from poorer families but were attending schools in which most of their classmates came from affluent homes. Hence, the feelings generated by their perception of relative disadvantage could have been an important determinant of their later personality. A popular child from the majority ethnic group who has good grades is rarely bullied, and if he were a victim I suspect that the outcome would be more benign. A large number of Jewish adults born to middle-class, supportive families early in the twentieth century in Europe or the United States frequently experienced harsh anti-Semitic bullying but failed to develop the maladaptive features that are presumed to be an inevitable accompaniment of being bullied.

It is unlikely that a single condition can make a significant contribution to the disproportionately high prevalence of homicides, incarceration, unemployment, academic failure, and foster care among contemporary African American men. This state of affairs requires a combination of conditions that includes economic disadvantage, a perception of white prejudice, migration from communities containing extended family members to urban centers, the availability of drugs, less adequate schools, lack of college-level skills, the loss of manufacturing jobs, and an anger that often finds expression in a refusal to adopt the values of the majority society. It is unlikely that any one of these factors alone could generate the profile described above.

Parental maltreatment has become one popular explanation of criminal activity among youth. A parent who is poor, divorced, uneducated, and rearing several children is more likely to punish harshly or abuse a child when frustrated. Youths who grow up in these homes are at the highest risk for robbing homes, joining a gang, or engaging in other antisocial acts. But other conditions associated with poverty, especially a less adequate diet, more infections, attendance at less effective schools, and lower levels of academic achievement, could make critical contributions to later antisocial behaviors even if the child had not been maltreated. Cathy Widom and

Christina Massey of the John Jay College of Criminal Justice affirm this claim. Adults who had experienced many of the above risk conditions as children but were not physically abused were just as likely to have been arrested for a crime as those who had been maltreated.

Historical changes in a society are rarely due to one condition. The economy and skill level of Chinese citizens lagged far behind those in Russia and India in 1980. By 2014 the GDP and skill level of Chinese youth exceeded those in Russia and India because China took advantage of a distinctive combination of societal features after Mao Zedong was no longer in power. These include respect for authority outside the family, a strong desire for enhanced status, the absence of a caste system, pride in being the oldest continuous civilization, an emphasis on education as the vehicle for social mobility, a concern with the harmony of the community, and the fact that American and European corporations were outsourcing work to China because of its cheaper labor costs. This collection of factors, rather than any single condition, explains the dramatic changes in Chinese society over the past thirty-five years.

Investigators wanting to prove that one condition in a larger pattern can lead to a particular outcome appreciate that the condition is often corre-lated with social class, ethnicity, gender, or all three. They have been told that a statistical technique can remove the contribution of the correlated properties, leaving only the influence of the single condition of interest. Consider the popular idea that children who attend a day care center during their first two years are at risk for having a lower IQ as ten-year-olds. Because children's IQ scores are always correlated with their social class, investiga-tors use the statistical procedure to remove this contribution. They first compute the magnitude of the relation between social class and IQ scores, and then compute the relation between day care attendance and IQ after the contribution of social class has been removed. If the resulting correla-tion is significant, the psychologist concludes that day care attendance alone can affect later intelligence.

There are two potential errors in this conclusion. Children from econom-ically disadvantaged families are not only more likely than affluent ones to attend poorer-quality day care centers, but they also obtain lower IQs, even if they never attended a day care center. These facts leave open the possibility that a pattern that combined growing up in a disadvantaged family and attending a poor-quality day care center for the entire day leads to lower IQ scores at age ten. Attendance at a day care center, independent of its quality, the number of hours spent there, and the family's social class, is unlikely to have a substantial influence on IQ scores.

One problem with this statistical technique is that it assumes a linear relation between each of the causal conditions and an outcome. When there is a linear relation between two measures, a given increase in one measure is always accompanied by a proportional increase in the other. The relation between an individual's weight and height during the first eighteen years is linear; that is, for every gain of five pounds there is a proportionate increase in height. But after a person's height stops increasing the linear relation to weight disappears. Because the relation between the predictor and outcome measures in psychological outcomes is rarely linear, the statistical technique is questionable. The following example is instructive.

Scientists wanting to prove that children's IQ scores at age six predict the number of years of formal education they will attain as adults know that a family's annual income is related to both the predictor and the outcome and, therefore, researchers use the statistical technique to remove the influence of family income. However, the relation between family income and years of education attained by offspring is not linear. Among American families living in urban areas, a rise in annual income of $10,000, say, from $20,000 to $30,000, has a smaller effect on the predictor and outcome than an equivalent gain in income for families who had been earning $100,000. This is because the poorer families are less able than the wealthier ones to use the extra $10,000 to move to a neighborhood with better schools and to provide the child with other opportunities that improve IQ scores. As a result, the statistical manipulation designed to evaluate the contribution of childhood IQ to years of education with family income removed makes the incorrect prediction that children from poorer families with an income gain of $10,000 will attain more education as adults than they actually do.

It is easy to arrive at incorrect conclusions when scientists use statistics to remove the contributions of conditions that are essential to the outcome.

Rainfall, warm temperatures, and sunshine are required for the growth of plants. No biologist would remove the contribution of rainfall and temperature to discover the influence of hours of sunshine because no plant grows in a very cold place with little rainfall.

A pair of social scientists interested in the relation between life satisfaction and place of residence used the problematic statistical technique to remove the contributions of income, age, gender, ethnicity, years of education, and employment in a sample of 1.3 million Americans. Because the six conditions that were removed make important contributions to life satisfaction, their analysis revealed that the happiest Americans lived in Louisiana and the least happy adults lived in New York State. This counterintuitive result rubs against the fact that more Americans prefer to live in New York rather than Louisiana as well as the results of a Gallup poll that found residents of Louisiana were among the least happy Americans.

Most psychological outcomes are the product of patterns in which all the conditions are necessary. The experience of being bullied or attending a day care center contributes to a later trait only when each is part of a pattern that includes, at a minimum, the child's gender, social class, ethnicity, and cultural setting. Social scientists should refrain from writing, "The experience of being bullied makes a 10 percent contribution to the development of depression." Rather, they should first discover the pattern of conditions that predicts a bout of depression. The implementation of this strategy might lead investigators to conclude, "Twenty-five percent of girls from poor, minority families who were chronic victims of bullying during early adolescence developed a recurrent depression during the adult years. By contrast, only 5 percent of girls from poor, minority families who were not bullied, and 1 percent of girls from wealthy families belonging to the majority ethnic group who were bullied, developed recurrent depression." This statement contains far more useful information than the first.

It is also relevant that over 90 percent of the correlations between a social condition or biological property and a psychological outcome are less than 0.40, and most are smaller. A pair of Canadian psychologists affirmed my sixty years of analyzing data by demonstrating that significant correlations less than 0.40 are usually due to the participants whose scores were in the top or the bottom 10 to 15 percent of the distribution. For example, two psychologists at Stanford University reported that the more often mothers spoke to their young children directly, the larger the child's vocabulary. However, this relation applied only to those children who experienced either the most or the least amount of child-directed speech. Only 10 percent of the children had both very high vocabulary scores at two years of age and experienced very frequent maternal speech, and another 10 percent had the opposite profile. There was no relation between these two measurements for the remaining 80 percent of the group.

Silver bullet outcomes are as rare as silver bullet causes because most verbal reports or behaviors can be the product of different causal cascades. Yet most studies in the social sciences rely on only one measure to affirm a prediction. Developmental psychologists, for example, use the total time infants look at particular events as the sole basis for bold conclusions about the understanding of causality or awareness of another's goals. These conclusions require the assumption that a violation of expectation is the only determinant of differences in time looking at each of two events. But infant looking times are affected by the physical features of the events, the infant's ability to remember the sequence of events presented, and the fact that events that are serious deviations from the infant's expectation recruit less looking than events that are only moderate deviations.

Maddalena Boccia and colleagues at the University of Rome provide a lovely example of the need to examine patterns of outcomes. A brain site called the parahippocampal place area is always activated when a person is looking at or imagining a scene containing one or more objects, animals, or people. Boccia asked Italian college students to imagine the locations of various cities on a map of Italy, the locations of various buildings on their campus, and the locations of the clock hands at various times. The three kinds of scenes evoked equal activation of the critical brain site. Only a pattern of activation involving nine separate brain sites captured the brain's differential response to the three types of scenes.

Physicians always request several kinds of information before deciding on a diagnosis. Economists gather measures on employment, gross domestic product, money supply, inflation rate, and balance of imports and exports before arriving at conclusions. And climatologists measure changes in ice sheets, sea temperatures, and carbon dioxide levels in the air before making statements about future ocean levels. It is odd, therefore, that many social scientists assume that one measure can provide sufficient evidence for an important conclusion.

Solve a Puzzle

Most biologists choose puzzling phenomena they do not understand as targets for prolonged study. Peter and Rosemary Grant went to the Galápagos more than forty years ago hoping to illuminate three puzzles: what conditions cause a new species of finch to form, does competition for food affect the evolution of finch species, and why do some species possess greater variation in a trait, such as size of the beak, than others? Their forty-year effort taught them that unpredictable climatic events, such as a drought or a period of heavy rainfall, helped to resolve all three puzzles.

The young Jacques Monod in 1941 was curious about the factors influencing the growth of a colony of bacteria when he noticed something he did not understand. He knew that when the food supply contained only one kind of sugar, the growth rate of the colony of bacteria was linear. When he fed the bacteria two different sugars, there was a brief lull in the growth rate before the expected linear increase. Monod's pursuit of the reason for the puzzling lull in growth rate led to a discovery that won him a Nobel Prize.

A fair proportion of psychologists are more interested in proving the validity of a favorite idea rather than probing a puzzling observation. Individuals vary in the frequency of bouts of depression. A biologist is likely to focus on this variation and try to discover all the responsible conditions. Psychologists more often select one particular cause—say, loneliness—and try to prove that this condition can bring on a depression. This strategy ignores the possibility that those who are depressed possess a biology and life history that predate both the loneliness and the depression. An overweight, unattractive woman with no close friends who grew up in poverty, dropped out of high school, and cannot get a good job is susceptible to a metabolic illness, which can precipitate a bout of depression. Although she might tell a psychologist that she feels lonely, this feeling may not be the major cause of her melancholic mood.

A majority of the papers in the February 2015 issue of *Psychological Science*, a high-prestige journal in psychology, were attempts to prove that a particular condition, for example, insufficient hugging, increased the risk for asthma, heart attack, or a cold. Biologists would have taken the differential susceptibility to each of these illnesses as a puzzle and explored the many conditions that contribute to these susceptibilities before deciding that the absence of hugging can bring on a cold.

Most social scientists agree that the reasons for the profound differences in cognitive talents between children raised in poor homes compared with affluent ones represent a puzzle crying for solution. I am not aware of any psychologists who are filming the experiences of infants and young children, in and out of the home, over several years in order to illuminate this puzzle. The psychologists who want to prove the utility of an idea they find attractive should take Karl Popper's recommendation more seriously and spend more time trying to prove the falsity of a favorite idea.

The public is willing to accept many declarations by scientists, even if some contradict strongly held convictions. For example, some neuroscientists have announced that free will is an illusion because every thought, feeling, and action is determined by a person's genes and the brain's store of past experiences. That statement strikes most nonscientists as counterintuitive nonsense, yet some are willing to accept it as true.

The biologist's explanation of human altruism does not match the public's belief that adults who visit a sick friend in the hospital or send money to a disaster relief fund do so because they believe these actions are the morally right thing to do. Evolutionary biologists insist that humans act altruistically because they possess some of the same genes that lead social insects, such as bees and ants, to act in ways that benefit genetic relatives. These genes presumably bias humans to be more altruistic toward family members, with whom they share many genes, than toward strangers. This explanation rubs up against the fact that adults make sacrifices for adopted children, bring food to a sick adult who moved into a neighborhood, and donate blood to a stranger they will never meet.

The recent discovery that many of the genes responsible for "altruism" in social insects are novel DNA sequences implies that whatever genes contribute to human altruism, they are unlikely to be the same genes that mediate altruism in worker bees. The advocates of a genetic basis for altruism fail to recognize that, unlike animals, humans often award more importance to shared beliefs than to shared genes when deciding on a charitable act toward another. A black Muslim living in Dakar shares fewer genes with a white Muslim in London than with a black, Christian neighbor in Dakar. But I suspect that the Dakar Muslim is more likely to be altruistic toward the London Muslim because they share the same religious beliefs.

Facts Are Insufficient

What are we to do? Decisions must be made by individuals and governments when there is a lack of certainty about all the facts. What should governments do about the warming of the oceans; the inequalities in income and health; threats of hacking the computers of banks, corporations, and defense agencies; and chemical pollution of food, water, and air? Consider, as an example, the possible health dangers posed by chronic exposure to plastics. There are very few places in the world that are not penetrated with plastic cups, dishes, containers, and wrapping. A chemical called bisphenol A, used in the manufacture of plastic materials, is present in the urine of more than 90 percent of Americans. This molecule affects the brain's receptors for estrogen and can feminize the brains of male embryos. Infant mice born to mothers given variable doses of bisphenol A over many days of the pregnancy displayed a number of abnormal behaviors. Moreover, the genes in the cells that become the ova of female mice were altered in abnormal ways after exposure to small amounts of bisphenol A.

These facts raise an obvious question: is bisphenol A in plastics sufficiently dangerous to humans that Congress should ban all plastic objects that contain this molecule? So far scientists and the FDA are not certain enough to make that suggestion, even though there are several examples of chemicals that proved to be toxic that were not banned in time—thalidomide is one. Most of the time public sentiment must be added to the facts in order to provoke legal action. The public became sufficiently exercised over passive smoking that municipal authorities banned smoking inside buildings, even though the evidence pointing to the dangers of passive smoking was less persuasive than the facts pointing to the perils of bisphenol A. Evidence alone is usually insufficient; the public's attitudes are critical. Facts, reason, intuition, and community sentiment join in determining the beliefs that a majority will accept as a persuasive reason for action.

Settings Matter

E vents that recruit attention, whether a smile on the face of a friend or the knob of a door, occur in a setting. Scientists who probe the separate features of a phenomenon often forget that the features can vary with the setting. Most individuals understand this truth. A woman imposes different interpretations on the smile of a clerk in a store and the smile of the same person encountered at a party. Each setting—an airport, department store, party at the home of a friend, or dinner with one's family—automatically evokes a small collection of expected events and preparation for a limited range of responses.

Not surprisingly, the brain contains a circuit dedicated to registering the setting of every event. Even when individuals are told to attend only to the shape of an object, their brains automatically register features in the background. Laboratories, homes, schools, playgrounds, villages, and cities are settings that vary in their physical features, familiarity, number and types of people, and expected behaviors. Therefore, a person's response to an event, say, a long period of silence or a loud siren, often depends on the setting in which it appears. Anger at a peer is more likely to lead to an act of aggression in an urban ghetto than a suburban neighborhood; an adolescent has a higher probability of being physically attacked in St. Petersburg than in Minneapolis; and a fatal automobile accident is three times more likely in Montana than in Massachusetts.

When the art critic Arthur Danto first saw Andy Warhol's 1964 simulation of a Brillo box in a gallery, he realized for the first time that the decision to classify some objects as works of art depended on the setting in which they appeared. A Brillo box, metal tree, pile of tires, or porcelain urinal are art when they are on display in a museum gallery. The same objects lose their artistic property in a hardware store.

I noted in the prior essay that the procedures scientists use to gather observations of behavior or biology are always part of the setting. One investigator's failure to confirm another's evidence, common in all the sciences, is often due to the use of a slightly different procedure. Neuroscientists measure brain activity in rooms that are unfamiliar to subjects who remain perfectly still and quiet. The relation between a brain pattern and a psychological state in this unusual setting might not be repeated if one could measure brain activity when the same person was at home, at work, or on a vacation.

One team assumed that the brain activity recorded in men whose penises were being stimulated by their spouse or lover as they lay perfectly still on their back in the narrow tube of a noisy scanner would resemble the pattern generated if they had been recipients of the same stimulation in their bedroom at home. Timothy Pleskac and colleagues at Michigan State University remind these investigators that the responses people display in a laboratory do not always correspond to those seen when they are in their usual contexts. Biologists have learned that observations of cells in a dish outside the body (in vitro) do not always match observations made when the cells are studied in a living animal or person (in vivo).

The meaning of a behavior often varies with the cultural setting in which it occurs. New Guinea preadolescents who perform fellatio on older adolescents because they believe this behavior provides them with the seed they will need to father a child are neither gay nor suffering from gender identity disorder.

A sixteenth-century French bandit who stabs a stranger to steal his money, a seventeenth-century Ottoman sultan who murders his brothers and the pregnant concubines in the harem when he ascends to power, a member of Napoleon's army who shoots a Russian soldier in battle, and a twenty-first-century Iraqi Sunni suicide bomber who kills twenty Shia to honor his religious beliefs have all committed violent acts. But because the killer in each of these settings has different reasons for his murderous behavior, it is not obvious that these acts should be assigned to the same category.

It may not be surprising that the physical attractiveness, voice quality, and interactive style of a researcher conducting a study with human participants can influence their behavior or physiology. But it is surprising that the sex of the human examiner can affect the behavior of mice. A McGill University team discovered that mice in a state of pain displayed fewer signs of distress (typically, licking the paw and grimacing) when a man was sitting about a foot away than when a woman was resting in the same place. The animal's detection of olfactory signals in the man's sweat raised the pain threshold.

A rat mother usually licks her male pups more than her female offspring when the litter contains both sexes because detecting the difference between the smells of male and female pups is required for the differences in licking. The maternal preference for licking males vanished when scientists from Baylor University manipulated the litters so that the nest contained only males or only females. In these settings the mother was unable to make a discrimination between the smells of the sexes.

Stanley Milgram performed a series of studies in the 1960s designed to show that ordinary Americans would obey an authority figure who ordered them to administer extremely painful electric shocks to a stranger whenever he made an error in a learning task. The stranger, however, was a hired confederate who was not really receiving any shocks. Milgram regarded this setting as simulating the behaviors of staff at Nazi concentration camps.

Although a majority of the subjects administered what they believed were painful shocks to a confederate, who emitted screams of pain, features in the setting were relevant. Subjects administered the strongest shocks when the confederate was sitting in a separate room (though they could hear his cries of pain) and the experimenter, the authority figure, was in the room with them. They were least likely to administer strong shocks when the confederate was sitting next to them and the experimenter was giving instructions from a different room.

More important, most subjects believed their participation in the experiment was a contribution to scientific knowledge and therefore assumed that the experimenter, who was representing Yale University, would not allow them to harm the confederate. That is why they were willing to do what they were told. The guards in Nazi concentration camps who were ordered to gas, shoot, or cremate innocent victims did not hold these beliefs. Thus, Milgram's results do not explain why German guards and officers behaved as they did.

The language used to present a problem can affect a participant's moral judgments. In one study, adults were asked to read about a moral dilemma either in their native language, which in most cases was English, or in a second language learned later in life, and then decide on the right action to take. The dilemma described a person standing on a footbridge overlooking a railroad track who sees an oncoming train that will definitely kill five people standing on the track unless the onlooker sacrifices the life of a single man by pushing him onto the track to stop the train.

Subjects were more likely to select the utilitarian alternative, pushing the man onto the track, when the dilemma was posed in their second rather than their native language. One explanation holds that the automatic associations to guilt or uneasiness over harming others, which are acquired while children are learning their initial language, were missing from the language learned later in life. There is a similar absence of feeling when adults swear or express love in their second language.

Everyday actions are often classified as ethical violations if they occur outside their usual setting. The display of urination, defecation, or sexual behavior in an atypical place—say, in a public park with strangers present—is a serious deviation that most adults classify as disgusting. I suspect that if Bill Clinton had chosen to have oral sex with Monica Lewinsky in a hotel room rather than in the Oval Office the public outrage would have been muted. Had Dominique Strauss-Kahn, who asked a chambermaid for oral sex in his New York hotel room, made the same request of the same woman in a posh brothel, few journalists would have treated this event as worth reporting.

Settings and Suicide

The probability of suicide is affected by the setting. A team at Osaka University, aware that blue light activates select brain sites, persuaded a Japanese railway company to install lamps emitting blue light at some stations. The number of suicides, across a thirteen-year interval, was lower at these stations than at those without the blue lamps. However, railway stations are a special setting. Suicides are typically highest in the spring, when the hours of sunlight, which contain blue frequencies, are increasing. Benjamin Vyssoki and colleagues at the University of Vienna found a small but significant relation between the number of suicides in Austria across a forty-year interval and the probability that the sun was shining on the day the person committed suicide. The explanation rests on the mismatch between the apathy felt by the depressed person and the mood appropriate on a sunny day, which reminds the depressed person of his inability to enjoy life.

The suicide rate among younger Chinese women living with their family in a rural area is higher than the rate among those in the same demographic group who have migrated to a city. The urban setting freed such women from guilt-inducing parental pressures, an unhappy marriage with a dominating husband, a hypercritical mother-in-law, or the misery of poverty in an isolated region. City residence also made it more difficult to commit suicide because of reduced access to the toxic pesticides rural women use to end their lives.

Some regions within the United States contain settings that affect the probability of a suicide attempt. Readers should know that at least half of the suicides by Americans are committed by white males older than forty-five. Suicide rates in the rural western states of Wyoming, Alaska, and Montana, which have low population densities, long winters, and a large proportion of men who own firearms, are twice as high as rates in New York, New Jersey, and Massachusetts, which are urban, have denser populations, milder winters, and a smaller proportion of men with firearms.

Historical Changes in Settings

Michelle Obama was born in 1964 to parents who encouraged a high level of achievement in a daughter who possessed the potential to develop many talents. But these twin advantages required settings where her talents could be enhanced and exploited. Ms. Obama's childhood coincided with the passage of civil rights legislation and a more racially tolerant ambience in America.

These conditions allowed her to attend an integrated high school for gifted students in Chicago during the early 1980s, a time when elite colleges were trying to recruit more minority candidates. I suspect that without these historical changes in the settings Ms. Obama experienced, the probability of her being admitted to Princeton University and later to Harvard Law School, meeting Barack Obama, and becoming the first African American first lady would have been far lower.

The depressing job prospects for today's young biologists affirm the power of a historical era. There were about five hundred thousand scientists at the end of the Second World War; there were more than 7 million in 2014. A college graduate in 1950 who pursued graduate training in biology was almost guaranteed a satisfying career. A graduate in 2014 with the same skills and motivation who made the same career choice is far less certain of the future because there are many more PhDs in biology than universities and pharmaceutical corporations can hire.

The Internet and television make it easier for adolescents who have no friends and are doing poorly in school to withdraw to their bedroom for long periods of time. The Japanese call this syndrome *hikikomori*. A century earlier, friendless youths with poor grades would be less likely to choose this behavior because they would have nothing to do if they retired to their bedrooms. Perhaps many of these youths in 1900 would have developed a constructive hobby or perfected a special talent.

David Colander, an economist, and Roland Kupers, a physicist, urge social scientists to acknowledge that new inventions, institutions, and laws affect likely life paths by altering the contexts that people encounter. Fifteenth-century western Europe was unique because the state, large landowners, urban merchants, artisans, and the church were competing for the power to decide on the rules its members should follow. In no other region of the world were five separate groups competing for special privileges. That competition may have been a catalyst for the intellectual advances of Europeans during the succeeding centuries.

The rise in the number of small entrepreneurs and increased social mobility in eighteenth-century Britain was accompanied by an enhanced ethos of individualism and a trio of ideas that defined the Enlightenment:

reason based on scientific facts replaced faith, equality replaced inequality, and an individual's freedom trumped a responsibility to the larger community. The events of the succeeding 250 years generated material advances, large corporations, value diversity, geographic mobility, stronger central governments, technologies, supermarkets open 24/7, and a reduced need to form close relationships with nonfamily members.

Too many explanations of the rise in adolescent gangs, murders, and drug use ignore the changed circumstances that contribute to these behaviors, especially limited work responsibilities, easy access to drugs and guns, violent films and video games, a permissive posture toward some antisocial behaviors, and the absence of a safe place to withdraw. These conditions were missing in earlier eras when most youths were working to help support their family. I noted in the prior essay that many scientists claim that the adolescent's immature brain helps to explain youths' antisocial actions. I suspect that contemporary settings make a more important contribution to the incidence of robbery, rape, and murder among sixteen- to twenty-one-year-olds than the structure of their brains.

A new research practice that was impossible before the Internet allows social scientists to recruit subjects they never meet personally. Psychologists are paying Amazon a small fee in order to ask adults among the company's five hundred thousand employees questions over the Internet. These investigators seem unconcerned by the fact that they know neither the psychological characteristics of these people nor the setting in which they are performing. Gabriele Paolacci at Erasmus University and Jesse Chandler of the University of Michigan point out that a majority of these hired hands are in their thirties; Caucasian, Asian American, or Indian; have a college degree; hold politically liberal views; and are less religious but more anxious than the average person. The evidence this atypical group of adults provides might not resemble the observations provided by a more representative sample of adults.

Younger social scientists are most likely to exploit this arrangement because they must have a long list of publications in order to be promoted, and renting subjects makes research easier. Those with the funds can go further: pay another for-profit company to analyze the evidence and hire a third firm to write the paper. All the psychologist has to do is think up a hypothesis that can be evaluated by having strangers sit in front of a laptop providing answers to questions that, in many cases, are of minimal theoretical significance. The rest is handled by hired minds who have no interest in the hypothesis or the conclusions.

A biologist is establishing a commercial arrangement in which a natural scientist at one university who does not have the money to purchase the expensive equipment needed for a study can contact an investigator at another university who does and, for a fee, the latter's assistants will run the experiment. I suspect that Darwin, Pasteur, the Curies, Planck, McClintock, Hubble, Levi-Montalcini, and Monod would weep if they were aware of this new way to do science. An experienced investigator who cares about the question being asked often makes a major unexpected discovery by noticing a subtle anomaly while conducting an experiment. The plan to rent assistants to run complex machines in a distant laboratory is part of a dangerous trend to replace sophisticated minds deeply invested in a problem with disinterested employees. Suppose Darwin had hired three students to make the *Beagle* voyage, write down what they observed, and bring their notes to him when they returned.

Some inventions have created contexts with health implications. Electric lights alter the body's circadian rhythm by allowing individuals to remain awake deep into the night. This disruption in the natural rhythm of day and night is a risk factor for depression and obesity. The pleasures enjoyed by the many generations born before the explosion in electronic artifacts required some delay and were not always under the individual's control. Contemporary youths and adults possess gadgets that provide pleasure on demand. This immediacy might be creating an increased impatience among those who are accustomed to receiving a jolt of pleasure whenever and wherever they wish. I hope that the current generation does not prefer an iPhone picture of a sunset at peak color to sitting by a lakeshore for a half hour to watch the same scene form and gradually dissipate.

Judicial decisions do not escape the reach of historical changes in the setting in which decisions are made. Richard Posner, a judge on a U.S. Court of Appeals, worries that the increase in caseloads during the past twenty-five years forces overworked federal judges to ask their law clerks, who tend to rely on literal analyses of legal prose, to write the opinions they would have composed themselves forty years earlier. Decisions about firearms provide an example. The Second Amendment states that the right to own a firearm should not be infringed because a state needs a militia to defend its security. The Supreme Court in 1876 concluded that this language was not intended to imply that every citizen has a right to own a weapon. This decision was written at a time when it was impossible to order a variety of weapons over the Internet, violent crime rates were lower, and there were no gangs fighting turf wars over drugs. The law clerks assigned a case on firearms are more likely than the older judges to base their decision on a literal interpretation of the words in the Second Amendment and ignore the social context that existed when those words were written.

Erik Erikson's writings on the concept of identity in the 1950s had the ring of truth to many first-generation youths born in America to European immigrants as they brooded on the psychological categories to which they belonged. Were they primarily Americans or were they Poles, Jews, Irish, Italians, Germans, or Swedes? Large numbers of men from blue-collar families returning from military service at the end of the Second World War had to decide whether to return to their father's trade or train for a profession with the help of the GI bill, which paid their college tuition. Further, many women who had been working in defense plants were faced with a choice of remaining in the workforce or returning to the traditional female role. Erikson's personal preoccupation with his identity in his influential book *Childhood and Society* struck a familiar chord with these readers. If Erikson had written this book in 1900 or 2015 rather than 1950, it might not have attracted the same degree of interest.

Historical events have contributed to the current preoccupation with the dangers of anxiety. For most of human history, adults understood they had to cope with loss, failure, harm, and illness. Freud's writings and the events of the last century transformed the idea of anxiety from an inevitable emotion that was conquerable into a dangerous state that must be avoided. This new belief is one reason why there are many more studies of the brain's contribution to fear in mice and rats than its contribution to sexual behavior, even though humans between thirteen and sixty are more often sexually aroused than afraid of being harmed.

Too many Americans believe that anxiety in a child is especially toxic because they assume children have great difficulty coping with this feeling. Hence, parents and teachers feel obligated to protect children from this danger. It is refreshing to read Olga Ulturgasheva's observations of the Eveny people of northeast Siberia, who herd reindeer in forests near the Arctic Circle. Eveny adults, who accept the inevitability of anxiety, teach their children *khinem*, which means a resilient response to all hardship.

The American psychologists and psychiatrists who flew to Sri Lanka after the 2004 tsunami to be of help anticipated large numbers of people suffering from post-traumatic stress disorder. Instead, they found a composed mood among the majority, who honored the Buddhist imperative to bear catastrophe with grace and dignity because "to suffer is to survive." A similar philosophy was more common in America prior to 1940 when there were far fewer experts warning the public about the undesirable consequences of worry.

Asian and European Biases

Asians have traditionally resisted separating an object from its setting. Chinese scholars writing two thousand years ago insisted that the context affected the balance between the forces of yang and yin. A young man's yang is dominant when he is with a woman; his yin force prevails when he is listening to a lecture by an older expert. The Chinese definition of a person always includes his or her relationships in specific settings. Western novelists often write about a person's identity as a woman, a black, or a musician. No Chinese novelist would invent a hero or heroine who asked, "Who am I?" because each person's relationships provide the answer.

The Japanese invented the words *tatemae* and *honne* to capture the different styles of interaction a person is supposed to adopt in public compared to private settings. A wife adopts the formal style of tatemae when she is with her husband at a party but the candid honesty of honne when they are alone at home.

Because Asians are sensitive to the different meanings that settings impose on actions, they understand that a person need not behave the same way in every context. A woman is a mother at home, a lawyer at work, a guest at a party, and a wife when with her husband. The opinions, emotions, and behaviors displayed in one setting are often inappropriate in another. The Chinese language, as we saw in an earlier essay, supports this understanding by making it difficult to talk or write about abstract traits, such as an "affectionate" person. Whereas Americans say, "Alice is affectionate," the Chinese say, "Fei hugs her friends at parties."

More than 90 percent of written Chinese words are combinations of two or more meaningful characters, and the meaning of one character often depends on the character with which it is combined. The Chinese characters for a verb usually specify who is doing the action and its outcome. English speakers use the same verb *broke* in sentences such as "The dog broke the vase," "The teapot broke," "The heat spell broke," and "The woman broke the engagement." Chinese speakers would use different characters for this verb in each of these sentences.

This cultural variation is also revealed in an important difference between Western and Chinese law. An American who steals $300 has committed the same crime, and is subject to the same punishment, whether the victim was a stranger or a cousin. Chinese law regards stealing from a member of the family as a different, and more serious, crime than stealing the same amount from a stranger.

Cities and Nations as Distinctive Settings

The sociologist Sudhir Venkatesh in *Floating City* described a feature that distinguishes Chicago from New York. Chicago has a number of stable neighborhoods composed of families from the same ethnic and class group. This condition leads to a psychological boundary that limits the geographic mobility between neighborhoods with different class/ethnic compositions. New York neighborhoods, by contrast, are more heterogeneous in ethnicity and class, and therefore the boundaries between neighborhoods are more permeable. This fact affects the attitudes of the disadvantaged residents in each city.

A pedestrian's willingness to help a stranger varies across the world's cities. Scientists observed the frequency of three actions a pedestrian might show toward a stranger on a city street: returning a pen to someone who had dropped it, helping someone with a lame leg retrieve personal items he or she had dropped, and assisting a blind person across a street. The pedestrians in Rio de Janeiro, Brazil, and San José, Costa Rica, were the most helpful; the adults in Kuala Lumpur, Malaysia, and New York City the least. Among Americans, pedestrians in New York, Los Angeles, and Philadelphia were minimally helpful; those in Rochester (New York), Houston, and Nashville the most helpful. These facts do not mean that New Yorkers do not help friends, colleagues, and relatives. It means only that when the setting involves a stranger walking on a busy street who appears to need help, New York onlookers are unlikely to behave altruistically. The same New Yorker who ignores an unfamiliar person on her home ground might help a stranger she encountered while vacationing in Rio de Janeiro, and a citizen of Rio visiting New York might not help a blind man cross a street. Context trumps character when a stranger needs help.

Some large cities display, at least temporarily, an ambience of tolerance toward minority groups combined with an admiration for intellectual accomplishments, motivating talented people who are victims of prejudice in their homelands to migrate to these cities. Budapest, which possessed these properties in the years between 1867 and the onset of the First World War, was the adult home of the physicist Leo Szilard, the mathematician John von Neumann, the biologist Albert Szent-Györgyi, and the writer Arthur Koestler.

The birthplaces of the Nobel laureates in physics, chemistry, and physiology-medicine support the claim that the values and institutions of certain nations create an ambience that favors a scientific career. The six nations with the highest number of Nobel laureates in one of the natural sciences (excluding the United States, which has the most) are Germany (82), the United Kingdom (82), France (36), Switzerland (20), the Netherlands (16), and Sweden (15). The latter three countries do not have larger populations than Spain (2), Italy (12), Norway (3), or India (4). A similar asymmetry applies to the birthplaces of American presidents elected before 1900. Almost half of these men were born in either Virginia or Ohio.

The Swiss psychiatrist Carl Jung, who was originally attracted to Sigmund Freud's ideas, eventually broke with the older man because of disagreements that had a partial origin in the different contexts in which they lived and worked. Jung was a member of elite Zurich society, whereas Freud felt he was a victim of the harsh anti-Semitism that pervaded Austria. Their distinctive experiences led Jung to view societies as benevolent structures that had constructive influences on development. Freud concluded that societies contributed to neurotic symptoms. Because Freud's ideas were friendlier to the egalitarian premise held by American social scientists, his ideas were promoted and Jung's were not.

It is also relevant that Jung spent a great deal of time in the rural villages that dotted the mountains outside Zurich. With the exception of vacations, Freud spent most of his days in Vienna. Jung once told a journalist that Freud attributed too much power to sexuality because city folk had little opportunity to witness the naturalness of sexuality among the domestic animals in rural settings. Jung also suggested that the recent availability of inexpensive condoms allowed adults to entertain ideas about sexual affairs without a fear of pregnancy. Freud's clients, Jung argued, were experiencing excessive anxiety or guilt over their sexual impulses because of historical events that lifted a prior suppression of sexuality but left other reasons for feeling anxious. Freud rejected this argument because it replaced his belief in the universal threat of sexual urges with an account that awarded power to historical contexts.

The different settings in which the two men worked are relevant. Jung spent considerable time in a hospital with many schizophrenic patients whose thoughts and emotional displays seemed less related to sexual conflict than to an abnormality in brain function. Freud's patients were primarily middle-class adults who grew up in families that socialized the suppression of ideas and actions that violated the ethics of a conservative Austrian society. In that setting, it seemed reasonable to Freud that childhood socialization of sexual impulses had formative power.

Why Interventions Fail

The context in which an intervention intended to help children with academic or emotional problems is implemented helps to explain why most are not as successful as their advocates hope. The majority of interventions take place in a laboratory, Head Start center, or school rather than in the home or on a playground, where maladaptive habits are typically displayed. A child learns to suppress a bad habit and acquire a new one in a certain setting. There is no guarantee that an adaptive habit acquired in one setting will be displayed in a different one.

This suggestion is supported by the results of an intervention with black and white kindergarten children described by both parents and teachers as frequently disobedient who grew up in a poor neighborhood in Durham, Nashville, rural Pennsylvania, or Seattle. All 362 six-year-olds in one group were tutored in reading while their parents participated in group discussions about parental practices. A second control group of 356 children and their parents enjoyed neither advantage.

This intervention continued for more than ten years at a cost of about $58,000 per family and a total cost of more than $40 million. Nineteen years later, when all the participants were twenty-five years old, the investigators interviewed them and a close friend of each and also examined police records for arrests. The effects of the intervention were more modest than Karen Bierman of Pennsylvania State University and her colleagues expected. The children who had received the ten-year intervention became adults who were not much different from those in the control group. Both groups had equivalent rates of incarceration, failure to graduate high school, and unemployment. The only happy result was that slightly fewer adults from the intervention group confessed to abusing a drug or alcohol or committing an asocial behavior (59 versus 69 percent). This intervention effort had little effect on criminality, educational attainment, or employment because the life settings these youths encountered day after day remained unchanged. The flawed premise in this and similar interventions is the belief that improvements in reading skill and academic motivation can trump a child's daily experiences in family, school, neighborhood, and playground.

Modern Settings

Most advanced, industrialized democracies are characterized by the following pattern of twelve facts or assumptions that have created historically unique settings.

1. The interests of the younger members of a society dominate those of older citizens.
2. The proportion of the population older than sixty-five is larger and the proportion younger than ten smaller than ever before.
3. The many useful technologies bias the public to look for technological solutions to pressing problems rather than attempt to alter minds.
4. All persons are entitled to equal dignity, justice, and freedom despite differences in values, skills, motivation, and contribution to the society.
5. The world population exceeds 7 billion and is growing, with two-thirds concentrated in regions east and south of Istanbul.
6. Natural scientists declare that the universe and the presence of life are accidents with no special purpose or divine meaning.
7. A growing awareness of the dangers of climate change and pollution of earth, air, and water.
8. An antielite attitude that resists status hierarchies and the awarding of privileges to persons who have special traits or hold positions of responsibility.
9. A rational approach to problems that relies on facts rather than sentiment as the optimal strategy when individuals or governments make decisions.
10. A large and growing level of economic inequality among and within the world's societies.
11. High levels of ethnic and religious diversity within many nations.
12. The assumption that each person ought to place his or her self-interest above the interests of others or the community.

The current lack of agreement on a set of values that the vast majority honor in their behavior contrasts sharply with the high level of conformity during the 1950s when social scientists and writers were bemoaning the loss of an inner-directed individuality. The American social scientists William H. Whyte, C. Wright Mills, and David Riesman as well as the novelist Sloan Wilson described the pervasive worry over being different from others, partly the product of a rise in the number of large bureaucratic organizations following the end of the Second World War. By the 1990s, a more contrarian trend emerged in which being different became the more desirable property, even though large bureaucracies had not vanished.

The features of modernity have accelerated the rate of change in the structure of many societies. It took about 3,000 years, about one hundred generations, for the first modern humans to establish large, well-functioning cities in the regions that are now Iraq, Turkey, and Egypt. It took only 300 years, ten generations, for the first European settlers of North America to build comparable urban centers. The establishment of Silicon Valley in northern California required only 150 years, or five generations.

National surveys reveal that a majority of Americans say they are dissatisfied with their society because of excessive selfishness, large inequalities, destruction of natural resources, a feeling of anonymity, and the perception that everyone is trying to "find their beach." One of every three employees working for a large corporation, such as FedEx or a large hotel chain, is paid by an outside contractor rather than the corporation. This arrangement does not generate a loyalty to the entity whose success depends on the workers conscientiousness.

No film intended for a mass audience made before 1960 would end the way the second season of the Netflix series *House of Cards* did in 2014. In the final scenes the antihero Francis Underwood becomes president of the United States thanks to his orchestration of a pattern of lies, deceits, betrayals, and murders. Americans recognize the mood of cynicism that permeates their society and wish for a community in which trust replaces betrayals by friends, salespersons, government officials, and business leaders.

History's muse has altered the problems requiring the most urgent attention as well as the villains who are blamed. Seventy years ago, when criminals, alcoholics, and delinquent youths were among America's significant social problems, experts told the public that childhood experiences in the family were the causal conditions that had to be altered.

The current chapter in the human narrative replaces the individual's woes with the issues of climate change, the need for new forms of energy, pandemics, hackers breaking into corporation computers, and the accumulation of nuclear and nonbiodegradable garbage. These potential calamities affect populations, not individuals—and equally important, their solutions require materialistic manipulations rather than altering family practices and establishing new beliefs. The problems that affect single individuals have lost their alpha position, but they have not disappeared.

Burke Versus Paine

The waves of historical events that carried humans to the current moment have favored Edmund Burke's pragmatism over Thomas Paine's idealism. Yuval Levin in *The Great Debate* reminds us of Burke's insight that societies and generations must adjust their principles to deal with new circumstances. Chinese leaders understand Burke's advice. Paine, by contrast, believed that nature intended each individual to be free and equal to every other person. This means that all governments have a continuing obligation to maximize these ideals under all circumstances.

The weight of historical evidence favors Burke. Many decisions by the liberal minority in the Supreme Court session for 2013–14 relied on Burke's arguments. So did Pierre Mendès France, premier of France in 1954–55, who told a journalist asking about the qualities that made a great leader: "He must not be too sentimental." Mendès France meant that leaders must not be restrained by an unquestioning commitment to an abstract principle that must be honored under all circumstances.

The changes in Swedish society over the past twenty-five years also affirm Burke. Sweden during the 1990s was admired for its social conditions: low levels of inequality, health and education were guaranteed by the government, a new parent was entitled to a long leave from work, violent crime was rare. Sweden's citizens were among the happiest in the world. Then circumstances changed. An influx of immigrants and conservative governments bent on reducing taxes led to a serious increase in inequality, higher crime rates, youth rejecting traditional values, and a growing dissatisfaction among the majority. As a result, new leaders were forced to raise taxes to reinstate the welfare benefits that the public had grown to expect.

The establishment of public schools during the nineteenth century provides a persuasive illustration of the power of new circumstances. Now children were required to sit still for six to eight hours a day. The children for whom this setting posed an excessive burden became restless and distractible. A century later they were labeled ADHD. These traits were less apparent and posed a minimal problem when such children were assigned chores that did not require sitting for long periods sustaining attention to letters and numbers.

If many southern states had not passed laws in 2013 punishing local school systems that had many pupils who did not meet certain levels of achievement, the significant rise in diagnoses of ADHD would have been avoided. The school officials in these states understood they would lose funds if the average scores of their pupils did not improve, and they knew that poor, minority children had the lowest scores. Hence, they classified these children as having ADHD. This move had two advantages. It meant that extra funds would be available for tutoring and, in addition, a school's average score would rise in districts that allowed teachers to exclude ADHD children from the average. Local circumstances, not genes, diet, or television, generated the increased number of cases of ADHD.

The Economist's Blind Spot

Economists are fond of abstract principles they apply to all economies at all times, even though, in practice, these precepts apply only to some nations some of the time. Economists ignore the influence of a sequence of historical circumstances because they want to be treated as scientists whose predictions, like those of the physicists they admire, are based on mathematical equations. Unfortunately, these equations make assumptions about human choice that do not correspond to the evidence. This blind spot is an important reason why their predictions are often wrong. When they are right, it is usually because the equations took into account the new social conditions history created.

The critics of Thomas Piketty's widely praised book *Capital in the 21st Century* note that his analysis of the rising inequality in the United States ignored each nation's politics. American voters are less willing than German citizens to elect representatives who favor taxing the rich at a higher rate.

Paul Volcker is fond of a joke that satirizes economists' attraction to recommendations based on abstract theory while ignoring the special characteristics of a society. A squirrel who wanted to add fish to his diet consulted a wise owl who, he hoped, might help him satisfy this desire. The owl thought a while before telling the squirrel that the solution was to scamper up a tree and imagine being a kingfisher. The squirrel climbed a tree and tried to implement the owl's advice. After several failures, the squirrel complained to the owl that his advice was of no help. The owl, irritated by the criticism, replied, "You came to me with a problem; I gave you what I believed was a useful policy recommendation. The rest is operational detail."

The evidence from diverse domains invites the conclusion that very few rules, principles, or conclusions transcend all settings. Particles decay more slowly when they are moving; the meaning of a word depends on the sentence in which it appears; the protein products of a gene depend on the gene's location in the body; replies to a stranger asking about one's worries depend on the context; the probability of a suicide at a railway station, at least in Japan, depends on the presence of blue light on the platform. It is time for all investigators to acknowledge that nature's rules apply to certain events in particular settings.

Hunters and Bird-watchers

The contexts in which contemporary science is conducted favor those who discover principles that transcend settings. In my earlier book *Psychology's Ghosts*, I wrote that most scientists can be classified as either hunters or bird-watchers. Hunters want to solve a problem with an unambiguous answer that transcends settings, can be assigned numbers, and resists challenge. Hunters are reluctant to acknowledge that a discovery with one species of bacteria or one strain of mice might be restricted to that species.

Ben Barres, an eminent neuroscientist at Stanford University, confessed that had he studied under a professor interested in kidneys rather than the brain, he would have pursued problems involving kidneys and been just as happy. Francis Crick and James Watson might have studied the structure of hemoglobin rather than DNA if that had been the puzzle with the highest priority in the 1950s.

Many biologists study less complex organisms because it is easier to find a crisp answer that seems related to a puzzling phenomenon. Sydney Brenner was not especially curious about the tiny worm C. elegans, only one millimeter long. He chose it as a model organism because it was easy to grow in the laboratory and had a short life cycle and a small number of cells. These advantages meant that scientists would be likely to discover a significant fact that might apply to many species.

Hunters want evidence that "strikes you between the eyes." David Hubel, a neuroscientist who, with Torsten Wiesel, discovered neurons in the visual cortex that respond to contours in particular orientations, once said, "If your experiment needs statistics, you ought to have done a better experiment." Daniel Bessner notes that during the Cold War the mathematicians at the RAND Corporation working on America's strategy against the Soviet Union derided the work of the social scientists who insisted on the importance of the prejudices, values, and feelings of the leaders of both nations. The mathematicians ignored these psychological factors because they could not assign them numbers.

Bird-watchers are a different breed: they care deeply about the phenomenon they selected to study and accept the constraints of settings. Biologists who are bird-watchers are curious about a particular species—for example, the life history of tigers in India, the evolution of finches on one of the Galápagos Islands, or the behaviors of chimpanzees in a forest. Bird-watchers do not expect crisp, unambiguous answers. They derive pleasure from learning more about their favorite target, accept the lack of complete control over circumstances, prefer natural to unnatural settings, and are willing to study phenomena that resist being summarized with a mathematical equation. Nikolaas Tinbergen, who received a Nobel Prize for his naturalistic study of birds, is an exception to the rule that bird-watchers win very few prizes. So are Peter and Rosemary Grant, who won several prestigious prizes for their forty-year study of finch species on Daphne Island in the Galápagos chain.

I began my career as a bird-watcher who wanted to understand more about the development of children. Late in life I came to appreciate the hunter's insight that only some questions are amenable to a preliminary solution at a particular time because of the limitations imposed by the available procedures. Human love is a set of important phenomena. Unfortunately, psychologists do not possess procedures sensitive enough to measure this emotion. Hunters, therefore, ignore it; bird-watchers insist on trying.

The discovery of a coherent answer to an intriguing question provides hunters with the special satisfaction that bubbles up from the hope that perhaps they have found a new truth about nature that will last longer than their lifetime. Bird-watchers are satisfied simply to pursue an answer to a puzzling feature in an aspect of nature that is a target of their affection. Science needs both kinds of investigators, Tinbergen and the Grants as well as Crick and Watson.

Status Gradients

Humans are addicted to sorting people and their properties into bins labeled bad, good, better, and best, and comparing themselves with select others in order to decide the bins to which they belong. Children award special significance to variation in strength, language fluency, motor skills, and fearlessness. Adolescents add physical attractiveness, popularity, their family's status, and in industrialized societies their academic standing. Adults add their own and their family's wealth, education, vocation, and accomplishments.

The comparisons between the self and those who share some of the self's features have the most emotional impact. Children choose their nearest sibling and peers of the same sex and age. Adults rely on comparisons with those of a similar age, social class, and occupation. A janitor at a hotel compares his salary with that of the hotel clerk; a junior lawyer compares her status with that held by a senior partner in the firm; a scientist selects investigators from the same domain who are at a similar stage in their career.

A preference for close comparisons is a protection against the failure that is likely when one reaches too high. A small proportion of youths decide to invest the effort necessary to gain resources or positions they judge to be attainable given their talents and motivation. The young Sonia Sotomayor dreamed of being a judge like the ones she saw on *Perry Mason*, not a member of the Supreme Court. The continuing comparisons create self-conceptions that generate either a confidence in one's ability to cope

with challenges and dominate others or a corrosive doubt and an anticipation of being intimidated. Michael Kraus and Wendy Mendes asked pairs of
men who were strangers to each other, one wearing a T-shirt and jeans and
the other a buttoned-down shirt, jacket, and expensive trousers, to negotiate
a deal. The men wearing the less expensive costume were most likely to
submit to the demands of their better-dressed partners.

The unquestioning confidence possessed by a small number of adults
who enjoyed a childhood of privilege can, on occasion, cloud good judgment. Egas Moniz, a Portuguese neurologist who grew up in an aristocratic
family, invented a surgical technique to sever the connections between the
frontal lobes and the rest of the brain with the hope of curing seriously ill
mental patients. Moniz was so certain of the effectiveness of this operation
he announced prematurely that he had discovered a cure for these diseases.
Neurologists performed this operation on thousands of patients in subsequent years before it was discovered that the surgery not only failed to cure
these patients, it impaired their already compromised cognitive functions. If
John Wilkes Booth had not belonged to a family of distinguished actors,
there is the slim possibility that he might not have persuaded himself that he
had a right to murder Abraham Lincoln.

The delicate balance between confidence and doubt often hinges on the
social setting. Consider a forty-year-old professor of English literature with a
PhD from an elite university who lives in a small town twenty miles from her
faculty office. She exudes confidence at local parties with friends because
she is the best educated person in the room and her position as a professor is
respected. She feels equally potent when attending professional conferences
on English literature with faculty from other universities because her department is among the best in the country. But she feels less comfortable serving
on a faculty committee that contains many natural scientists because she
knows that the natural sciences enjoy greater respect within the university
and most scientists she knows treat her with condescension.

Adults who have a choice of where to live usually prefer regions and
cities where the people they meet most of the time share their interests,
values, and class position because these conditions allow them to feel more
relaxed. Americans who like NASCAR races and country music do not

choose to live in Boston, and those who enjoy lectures on art and chamber music concerts do not willingly move to Nashville. Many families who settled the land west of the Appalachians before the Civil War wanted to escape from a city or town where knowledge of European books, styles of dress, and food preparation were signs of sophistication.

Because some who belong to a minority group that is exposed to harsh prejudice perceive themselves as outsiders during their childhood years, they feel freer to question the beliefs of the majority. It may not be a coincidence that a disproportionate number of Nobel laureates in the natural sciences were Jews who grew up in anti-Semitic societies.

Occasionally a subordinate group distinguishes itself from one it views as more advantaged by adopting attributes that are very different from those the privileged celebrate. Many middle-class adults in the antebellum South were intimidated by the northern states, which had more colleges, wealthier banks, respected writers, and honored a private conscience rather than conformity to majority values. The South's reaction was to celebrate religious piety, courage, skill with guns, exploration of nature, and adherence to the community's moral standards.

The principle hiding in these facts is that many who believe they occupy a subordinate position, and live in societies that permit a measure of freedom, enjoy challenging the views and practices of the majority. Their status as outsiders frees them from excessive worry over pursuing an unpopular idea or failing to conform to the dominant values. Outsiders enjoy uncovering the majority's clay feet through intellectual inquiry or acts of rebellion. Although born into a peasant family, Mao Zedong attended a school that served mainly wealthy youth who ridiculed his language and crude habits. These experiences created an anger at the privileged classes that he satisfied after assuming power in 1949. It is not a coincidence that the men and women who initially supported Freud's unpopular ideas during the early years of the last century were Jews from anti-Semitic European nations. A few African American scholars have suggested that the high rates of academic failure and criminal activity among disadvantaged black males are intended to inform white, middle-class Americans that they do not feel bound by their values.

Social Class

A person's social class position in a community always exerts a significant influence on his or her confidence, values, and actions. The social scientists' conception of class has two related, but not synonymous, definitions. The most popular, because it is objective, is based on variation in the properties that a majority in the society regard as good, desirable, and worthy of attainment. A combination of education, vocation, and income composes the index of social class in most contemporary societies.

Each person's subjective judgment of the degree to which he or she possesses these desirable features represents a second definition. Nancy Adler invented a simple technique to measure subjective class. An examiner shows an adult a ladder with many rungs. The top rung represents Americans who are rich, well educated, and have respected jobs; the bottom rung represents those who are poor, have little formal education, and work at low-prestige jobs. The subjects put an X on the rung that matches the status position they think they occupy. Although the objective and subjective measures are modestly related, they are not similar enough to be interchangeable because many who occupy a low rank on the objective index say they occupy a slightly higher status.

The ancient Chinese relied on the properties of the male head of the family to arrange citizens into relatively fixed social classes, with literate landowners at the top and peasants who worked with their hands at the bottom. The Aryans who invaded the region that is now India and Pakistan around 1500 BCE imposed a rigid caste system on the population that was inherited and dictated occupational and marital choices. Light-skinned Brahmins were at the top and darker-skinned Untouchables at the bottom of this gradient.

The nineteenth-century British reserved highest status for aristocratic families that held large estates over many generations; nineteenth-century Germans awarded a privileged rank to military officers. Adults who have acquired the technical skills needed to operate computer networks, analyze genomes, locate and produce new sources of energy, measure brain activity, and diagnose the causes of pandemics have replaced landowners, nobles, philosophers, and generals in the twenty-first century.

Although acquired skills that aid the economy have become a critical requirement for a job with a high income and more privileged status, each person's level of talent is relative, not absolute, because it is based on his or her performance relative to others in that society, or across several societies. If a mysterious virus reduced the verbal fluency, mathematical knowledge, computing skills, and reasoning abilities of every human by 10 percent nothing would change. The same youths would be admitted to the same colleges and accumulate the same amount of wealth because each person's rank on the properties that contribute to adaptation is all that matters.

An annual income under $3,000 defined poverty in the United States in 1966. The income that defines poverty in 2015 has increased by a factor of ten. But the larger absolute income of the poor has not changed the fact that the proportions of adolescent pregnancies, type 2 diabetics, and victims and perpetrators of violent crimes are highest among those living in poverty in 2015, as was true in 1966.

Class and Adaptation

Although most individuals living in democratic societies are more acutely conscious of their gender, age, and ethnic group than their social class, the latter affects their behaviors, view of society, likely marital partner, health, patterns of social interaction, interests, purchases, favorite television programs, ethical values, moods, personality traits, and fertility. College-educated adults with an adequate income have fewer children than those without a high school diploma. Americans who grew up in working-class homes prefer to buy items that are similar to those bought by their friends. Upper-middle-class adults tend to purchase goods that render them distinctive. Advertising agencies, aware of this fact, design ads for cars in magazines read by those who did not graduate college that emphasize the satisfaction of possessing the same car bought by others. The ads addressed to wealthier college graduates emphasize the sense of being different from the majority.

The social class of the family during the child's first ten to fifteen years predicts the amount of education, scores on tests of reading and mathematics, occupation, income, physical and mental health, longevity, sleep quality, criminal behavior, and a feeling of well-being in the adult. The joint income of the parents of youths who entered college in the fall of 2013 was an excellent predictor of the youth's score on the Scholastic Aptitude Test. The scores of the seventeen-year-olds from the poorest families were 388 points lower than the scores of those who grew up in the wealthiest families.

A team led by Ronald Kessler at Harvard Medical School asked more than five thousand American soldiers, who were not in combat at the time, to report any psychological symptoms they had experienced during the past thirty days. The largest number reporting anxiety, depression, and/or substance abuse had the least amount of formal education, held the lowest enlisted ranks, and three out of four had these symptoms before they enlisted in the army.

American experts on children's mental illnesses invented a new diagnosis called "sluggish cognitive tempo," defined by low motivation, slow movements, drowsiness, daydreaming, and boredom. The vast majority with these symptoms live in economically stressed families, often with a disabled parent who cannot work. Many are sleep deprived, have inadequate diets, are rarely encouraged to persevere in school, and spend hours watching television. We should not be surprised that they possess a "sluggish cognitive tempo."

Nineteenth-century experts used the pejorative label "degenerate" to describe a related profile in children from poor families. Contemporary experts prefer the less damning label "sluggish cognitive tempo." A more accurate diagnosis is "poverty syndrome." When children living near a waste dump containing cancer-causing chemicals develop leukemia experts acknowledge the causal role of the toxic environment and do not place the origin of the symptom in the patient.

A Nigerian Muslim woman's class position predicts her attitude toward female genital cutting. Less advantaged women are most likely to hold a favorable attitude toward this ritual surgery. An American woman's social class even predicts the time of year she is most likely to give birth. College-educated women usually plan their pregnancy so that their infant will be born during the warm spring or summer months. Poor women with only a high school diploma are less likely to reflect on the possibility that the winter flu season might compromise their health or the health of their newborn infant. Many conceive in the spring, come down with a bad cold or the flu in late fall or winter, and give birth in late January or February to an infant whose birth weight is below the norm.

A team from the University of Oklahoma found that women who grew up in a disadvantaged family and had two or more children were at a higher risk for maltreating their next infant if that child was difficult to care for because of prematurity or a serious birth defect. British and American mothers whose education is limited to a high school diploma or less describe their infants as more difficult to manage than do college-educated mothers, even when objective evidence reveals that the children from the two kinds of families are behaviorally similar. As a result, the former treat their infants more harshly when they cry.

Peter Hotez of Baylor College of Medicine notes that the poor are susceptible to a number of parasitic and related infections that can have debilitating consequences. For example, the eggs of a parasitic worm shed by dogs and cats are ubiquitous in disadvantaged urban and rural environments. Contact with these eggs can infect a child with larvae that migrate to the brain. An estimated 2.8 million African Americans suffer from this infection. The relation between class and illness burden is not a recent phenomenon. Christi Sumich reminds us that the poor were more likely than the affluent to come down with the bubonic plague that swept through seventeenth-century England.

The different rearing practices of parents from divergent social classes have consequences that can be observed before a child's second birthday. College-educated parents talk more and use more varied speech forms with their young children who, in turn, develop larger vocabularies and have higher IQ scores. Kenneth Kendler with colleagues in Sweden compared the adult IQ scores of pairs of brothers. One brother in each pair was reared by his biological parents; the other by adoptive parents who had more education than the biological parents. Not surprisingly, the latter males had higher IQ scores. All the female larvae of a particular generation in a beehive are genetically identical. The adult worker bees feed one diet to all but one of these larvae and a different diet, called royal jelly, to the single larva that will become the future queen. Royal jelly is analogous to the distinctive experiences enjoyed by children born to families with many years of education and high incomes.

The child's social class can, under some conditions, influence select genes. The ends of each chromosome are capped with unique DNA sequences, called telomeres, which gradually become shorter as individuals age. Telomeres are especially short among disadvantaged adults who have been exposed to the chronic stress of poverty. Investigators from the University of Michigan found that nine-year-old African American children from disadvantaged homes had shorter telomeres than those growing up with advantaged families. African gray parrots and seabirds also show a relation between stress and shortened telomeres.

The failure to recognize that advantaged and disadvantaged adults can have the same symptoms or personality traits for different reasons poses a problem. When a childhood trait predicts a later outcome, scientists often conclude that the early property was the main cause of the adult feature. A group of Finnish scientists claimed that a newborn's attentiveness to visual events predicted the child's visual skills five years later. The researchers did not consider the possibility that this result might reflect the fact that the attentive infants who developed better visual skills were born to advantaged families, and therefore their distinctive experiences from infancy forward explain the relation. In many cases, the variation in the daily experiences that accompany membership in a social class, which include diet, illness, family practices, access to medical care, schools attended, pollution of air and water, and amount of physical activity, is the cause of both the early and the later traits. A marble placed in a groove moves in a straight line because the groove allows no other direction, not because the marble possesses an inherent bias to move in a straight line.

Some adults who grew up poor vow to become wealthy, famous, or powerful; others choose to be angry rebels; most remain frozen in the grip of helplessness. The contrast between viewing the world as a place filled with opportunities or one fraught with unpredictable threats separates the privileged from the disadvantaged. The advantaged see themselves as capable agents striving to gratify their personal desires with minimal constraints. Disadvantaged youths see life's tasks as avoiding attack, maintaining interdependent relations with friends and relatives, and remaining vigilant against exploitation and degradation. An affluent white lawyer who was continually suspicious of her employer and the shopkeepers she patronized would be diagnosed as having a paranoid personality. Social scientists from Washington University in St. Louis argue that this diagnosis is inappropriate for poor black adults who hold the same beliefs because they have a more realistic basis for their suspicions.

The Gini Coefficient

When social scientists discovered that the magnitude of income inequality in a country or region predicted some outcomes that a family's average income did not, economists invented an index of income inequality called the Gini coefficient. A Gini coefficient of o means that everyone in the society has the same income; a coefficient of 1.0 means that one family earns all the income. The Gini coefficient can also be used to index inequality in total wealth. The coefficients in most contemporary societies range from 0.3 to 0.6. Canada, Japan, and the Scandinavian countries have low coefficients (less than 0.3); South Africa, Brazil, Nigeria, and China have the highest (from 0.4 to 0.6). The Gini coefficient for the United States in 2013 was a moderately high 0.45, compared with 0.38 in 1950, which implies that 10 percent of Americans in 2013 owned more than two-thirds of the country's wealth.

The Gini coefficient for the United States was much lower two hundred years earlier when most families owned a house and livestock and a college education was a less important requirement for accumulating wealth. The currently high level of inequality is accompanied by an imbalance in the degree of influence on legislation. Two social scientists report in *Perspectives on Politics* that between 1981 and 2002 close to one-half of the laws Congress passed were favored by a small proportion of very wealthy Americans. By contrast, only 18 percent of the proposals a majority of the public favored, but the wealthy opposed, became law.

The magnitude of income inequality in Europe and North America has cycled over time. The high level in France in the 1780s was reduced by the French Revolution. Industrialization, however, reversed this trend. The level of inequality in England in the 1830s, which was probably higher than the current values for China, Brazil, and the United States, motivated Karl Marx to write his influential *Das Kapital*. China had a very low Gini coefficient in 1978. The economic reforms instituted after Mao's death led, in less than forty years, to significant differences in income between the poor peasants in rural areas and the entrepreneurs in the cities. China's Gini coefficient of 0.55 in 2014 exceeds that of the United States.

Gini coefficients in industrialized nations peaked during the 1920s, followed by gradual decreases in inequality due to the effects of the Second World War, increased numbers of college graduates after the war, imposition of higher income taxes on the wealthy, and social insurance for the less advantaged. This downward trend ended in the 1980s, when inequality began to rise. It appears that a society's attempt to keep its level of inequality within reasonable bounds resembles the cyclical attempts of an overweight person to keep his or her weight within a certain range.

Although most populations enjoy better health and more material comforts than their ancestors did in 1800, those who live in nations with a high Gini coefficient usually have a greater disease burden; shorter life span; higher incidence of depression, schizophrenia, suicides, and homicides; greater distrust of strangers; and more frequent child maltreatment. The Gini coefficient in each of thirteen isolated Bolivian villages in the Amazon basin was correlated with the incidence of fear, anger, and sadness.

The twelve states with the highest Gini coefficients in 2013 (California, Louisiana, and New York are in this group) had higher homicide rates than the twelve states with the lowest coefficients (Wyoming, Utah, and Iowa are in this group). Because the former three states have a larger proportion of nonwhite adults, some might say that a combination of income inequality and minority status makes an important contribution to homicide rates. The substantial relation between the Gini coefficient and homicide rate within each of thirty-nine nations, however, points to the greater contribution of inequality. Most Latin American countries had both high Gini coefficients and high murder rates. Nations within the European Union had the lowest Gini and homicide values, even though there is more ethnic diversity in Europe than in Latin America.

The magnitude of inequality has to pass a tipping point before civil unrest is triggered. Most people are willing to tolerate some inequality in privilege, but resentment rises when the level of inequality violates their understanding of fairness. This point was reached in Paris in 1789 when Robespierre, envious of those with elite status and supported by like-minded citizens, established a despotic regime that murdered thousands in the wake of the French Revolution. Contemporary France confronts the anger of its Arab immigrants from North Africa who have higher rates of unemployment than the indigenous French.

A tipping point was passed in the United States during the 1880s when blue-collar workers became more conscious of what they perceived as unjust exploitation. As a result, the interval from 1880 to 1920 witnessed many violent strikes. During the Depression of the 1930s Americans who believed that a laissez-faire capitalism was the reason for their unhappiness were tempted to join or support the Communist Party. Today jihadi movements, such as ISIS, serve that function for an unknown number of marginalized Muslims residing in European nations. Men and women who cannot find a job that matches their skills become angry, and groups like ISIS provide an outlet for their anger.

Even though the United States has a relatively high Gini coefficient, Americans have been spared serious civic rebellions for close to a hundred years because a majority born after 1920 assumed that most privileged persons earned their wealth fairly. A Pew poll conducted in 2011 found that close to 90 percent of Americans believe that the wealthy either earned their money through hard work or had the good luck of being born into a rich family. Americans are more likely than Europeans to endorse the idea that hard work usually brings a justly earned life of ease and privilege. This premise finds support in the fact that about half of America's thirty- to thirty-five-year-olds have a higher income than their family earned when they were children.

The belief that most poor Americans are lazy and fail to exploit their opportunities was more prevalent in 2011 than it had been in 1983, even though this premise fits the facts better in 1983 than in 2011. But the accuracy of this opinion is irrelevant. A perception of fairness combined with the traditional American belief that anyone who exerts sufficient effort can become rich are all that matters. Alexander Hamilton, Andrew Jackson, Abraham

Lincoln, U. S. Grant, Andrew Carnegie, Sonia Sotomayor, and Oprah Winfrey are often cited as proof of this premise. The decrease in the proportion of poor youths who enjoyed a major gain in income and status over the past thirty years, compared with the first half the twentieth century, challenges the assumption that hard work and a college education usually pay off.

The New Halo on Victims

Franklin Roosevelt's 1944 inaugural address represented the first time an American president declared that every American was entitled to a job, a home, an education, and adequate medical care. Twenty years later Lyndon Johnson announced the "War on Poverty," Congress passed civil rights legislation, and Americans became far more sympathetic toward the victims of poverty, marginalization, prejudice, or a mental illness. This change is revealed in the sharp increase between 1960 and 1970 in the frequency of the words *victim, empathy,* and *disadvantaged* in books written in English. The increasing number of Europeans siding with the Palestinian cause and criticizing the Israeli government signifies a growing sympathy for victims of coercion. Brazilian legislators, under pressure from parents of children diagnosed as high-functioning autistics, passed a law in 2012 that classified autism as a legal disability. This change in label meant that the society was obligated to make it easier for these individuals to function in many roles.

This sentiment is spreading to animals. The European Union issued a directive to scientists who perform experiments with animals requiring them to evaluate the pain the animal might be experiencing and to obtain prior authorization before performing experiments that were capable of inducing pain in a dog, cat, or monkey. Vocal citizens persuaded the American Congress to pass rules for the treatment of animals in research supported by federal funds. These rules cover diet, cage temperature, ways to dispose of an animal, and a requirement to put interesting objects in the cages—toys—to enrich the animal's experience.

An essay in the *New York Times* of July 27, 2013, noted that those who grow up in poverty are vulnerable to serious illnesses that could have been avoided if their families had been more affluent. Compare this sympathetic perspective toward the poor with the harsh attitude of Europeans three hundred years earlier, when many commentators declared that the economic health of a society depended upon large numbers of impoverished workers willing to work for low wages.

The kinder attitude toward the poor represents a return of the Catholic Church's benevolent evaluation of the meek. Luther and the Protestants who followed withheld the gift of virtue to the poor unless they were conscientious. Listen to the Boston minister Cotton Mather telling members of his congregation in the early 1700s that their first obligation was not to pray but to acquire a skilled trade. "If the Lord Jesus Christ might find thee in thy storehouse, in thy shop, in thy ship, or in thy field, or where thy business lies, who knows what blessings He might bestow upon thee?"

Most Americans hold one of two explanations of the persistence of poverty over two or more generations. Those favoring a social Darwinian view of society claim that the poor are to blame because they did not learn an appropriate skill, made impulsive decisions, and refused to give up bad habits. This view is most common among older, wealthier, white adults who would have agreed with Montaigne's view: "No one suffers long save by his own fault." I suspect that some members of this group use Barack Obama's election in 2008 and 2012 as evidence that the high levels of poverty among black families cannot be a product of racism because more than 40 million whites voted for Obama. Moreover, a small proportion of children born to poor families do rise in status and income: one of ten ends up in the top fifth of the income distribution. This fact allows some white middle-class adults to argue that the maladaptive decisions and actions of the unsuccessful poor must be the reasons for their failure.

The African American philosopher Tommie Shelby offers a slightly different interpretation of the continued underachievement of a large number of African Americans born into poor families. He suggests that many blacks, and especially males, refuse to adopt the work habits of the white majority because to do so would be equivalent to confessing that they had failed to honor a moral standard that they and their society value. As a result, they would become vulnerable to a further loss of ethnic pride. It is more satisfying, Shelby argues, to maintain a defiant posture toward the ethical code the majority culture celebrates. A related dynamic operates when a school-age child who values good grades but dislikes his parents refuses to study because of a desire to frustrate them.

A larger group of Americans, typically less than fifty years old and holding a second explanation of the persistence of poverty, believes that the poor face serious structural obstacles in American society. Inadequate schools and the absence of good jobs in disadvantaged neighborhoods have become the politically correct explanation offered by Americans born after 1970. This sympathetic attitude toward the poor and minority groups is being extended to any person who suffers because of factors beyond his or her control. The celebratory reviews of Andrew Solomon's book *Far from the Tree*, which describes the suffering of the deaf, autistics, and gays, support this claim. The plight of victims is the major theme in more than 70 percent of the novels the *New York Times* staff nominated as the best books of 2014. The media cooperate through dramatic portrayals of the cruel treatment of American Indians, slaves in the antebellum South, Jews in Nazi Germany, and the children of indigenous families in Australia.

The hero in the 2003 film *The Station Agent* is a self-sufficient dwarf who evokes genuine affection from a lonely food vendor and an equally lonely woman. The several women in the 2012 film *The Sessions* who care for a man paralyzed from the neck down because of polio, including his sex therapist, fall in love with him because his optimism renders him heroic and attractive. Neither the dwarf nor the polio victim is to blame for his suffering. The suffering of victims of war, poverty, illness, or a personal flaw was a central theme in 50 percent of the films awarded a best picture of the year Oscar from 2001 to 2012, compared with 10 percent of the films from 1927 to 2000. Many films that won Academy Awards before 1970 celebrated elites: for example, *The Life of Emile Zola, Lawrence of Arabia,* and *A Man for All Seasons.* The winners after 1980—*Rain Man, Driving Miss Daisy, Dances with Wolves,* and *Forrest Gump*—awarded heroic status to an autistic adult, an African American chauffeur, American Indians, and an ingenuous American who profits from circumstances over which he has no control. I do not believe that the script for *Forrest Gump* would have appealed to Hollywood executives or American moviegoers before 1970.

The different themes in the books written by writers awarded Nobel Prizes in literature before and after the civil rights movement render this argument persuasive. Neither Thomas Mann, T. S. Eliot, Bertrand Russell, nor Winston Churchill wrote about the anguish of the dispossessed. Eliot's 1949 essay "Notes towards the Definition of Culture" celebrated elites as essential to an advanced culture. By contrast, the works of Toni Morrison, J. M. Coetzee, and Herta Müller, who won their prizes after 1990, were concerned with the psyches of the marginalized. None of these authors would or could have written an essay with Eliot's message.

Americans typically favor the underdog in professional sports. When the New York Yankees were winning the World Series regularly, most fans who did not live in or near New York disliked the Yankees and cheered for the other team, no matter what it was. Most football fans who live outside New England dislike the New England Patriots because they have won too many divisional titles.

Americans admire those who have attained great wealth or fame despite the absence of social or economic advantage. In honoring these individuals Americans celebrate the ordinary American. The recent increase in the number of celebrities from film, television, sports, or music who grew up in modest circumstances and were awarded honorary degrees supports this claim. Oprah Winfrey gave the 2013 commencement address at Harvard; Yale gave honorary degrees to Paul McCartney in 2008 and to Willie Mays in 2004. The selection of commencement speakers from those who rose from humble circumstances was less common before 1960. Admissions officers at elite colleges who read the essays hopeful applicants compose recently noticed an increase in confessions of mental illness, poverty, or abuse. Apparently, some American seventeen-year-olds believe they will be judged more attractive if they have suffered. This is a historically unique premise among American youth.

National polls reveal a growing concern with the disadvantaged. A 2013 Pew poll revealed that 48 percent of Americans, compared with 25 percent in 1993, believed the government should do more to help the poor, even though the election results of November 2014 were inconsistent with the poll results. An empathy for the less advantaged is an essential element in the egalitarian ethic that began to grow in eighteenth-century Europe and now permeates most democratic societies. This ethic rests on the premise that every individual is entitled to the same degree of dignity, justice, and access to resources required for a feeling of well-being, independent of their talents, traits, values, gender, ethnicity, religion, class, family pedigree, or accomplishments. Because this is a new idea in human history it requires an explanation.

I suspect that one element contributing to this new premise was a shift in the primary beneficiary of decisions and laws: from the welfare of the family or community to each individual's happiness, as the Declaration of Independence affirmed. Because a subordinate status generates unhappiness, it follows that serious income inequality violates the imperative demanding universal happiness.

The attempts to create a society in which every individual has the resources required for happiness has had some unintended costs. The recent suggestion that the growing inequality in educational attainment between children of college-educated parents and others is a serious violation of a moral standard is one. This position fails to acknowledge that college-educated parents are more likely to socialize the value of academic achievement in their children. It seems a bit unfair to blame conscientious parents for the current inequalities in occupational status and fail to assign some responsibility to the families who failed to inculcate adaptive study and work habits in their children.

A Resurgent Antielitism

An excessive anger toward those in elite positions is a second cost. The open expression of this emotion forces some doctors, lawyers, judges, politicians, clergy, scientists, professors, bankers, and corporation executives to realize that they do not enjoy the unquestioned halo of respect they hoped to command when they chose their careers. Harris polls conducted in 1966 and 2011 asking Americans to report their confidence in the men and women who fill positions in our leading institutions tell the story. During this forty-five-year interval, confidence in every major institution dropped—from 50 to 24 percent for the Supreme Court, 42 to 6 percent for Congress, 61 to 30 percent for universities, and 29 to 11 percent for the press.

The student rebellions of the 1960s were marked by harsh attacks on scientists for creating societal ills. This view was shared by the first director of the linear accelerator at Stanford University, Wolfgang Panofsky, who told a journalist that scientists share some responsibility for creating a world in which many could be killed by nuclear bombs. Julius Stratton, the president of the Massachusetts Institute of Technology, told an audience of graduating seniors in 1964 that the advances brought about by scientific research were accompanied by the unintended costs of pollution and a disillusionment with the idea of progress.

Many writers, including James Watson in his lively description of the discovery of the structure of DNA, portray scientists as entrepreneurs who are as hungry for fame and wealth as rock stars. A comparison of the celebratory biographies of George Washington written prior to 1900 with recent narratives reflects a new eagerness to reduce the size of the shadow that elites cast. Several of the books written during the past thirty years question Washington's brilliance as a general and portray the first president as an ambitious, vain, unimaginative man who loved elegant clothes and worried constantly about his reputation.

I even sense a subtle hostility toward the small proportion of adults with elite status whose contributions are simply beautiful rather than practical. Governments and philanthropies favor scholars who work on practical problems. Some contemporary scholars who create beautiful products—for example, mathematicians—have begun to apologize for their choice of career. Sections of Michael Harris's recent book *Mathematics without Apologies* are attempts to defend the legitimacy of pure mathematics bereft of any pragmatic benefit for society. It is hard to imagine Newton, Hardy, or Dirac apologizing for their careers.

It would be an occasion for weeping if the majority in contemporary industrialized societies, who are finding it harder to find beautiful moments, resented the few who do. About twenty-five years ago, I was surprised and saddened when the former president of a small but respected university asked me to describe the practical gains that might emerge from my research on young infants. When I said that I saw no such gains but enjoyed the beauty of the findings, he asked why I continued the work.

The rise in the public's use of unproven therapies implies a growing indifference to the opinions of medical experts. Congress questioned the opinions of Nobel laureates in physics when it voted to stop work on a multibillion-dollar accelerator in Texas despite an outcry from eminent scientists.

Hollywood films criticizing elites became more common during the 1970s. The 2013 film *Elysium* portrays a selfish elite that has retreated to a fortified residence in orbit, leaving the masses to suffer on an earth that is approaching a slum. The message in the widely acclaimed 2013 film *Dallas Buyers Club* is that many doctors, as well as scientists working for the Federal Drug Administration, know less about AIDS than an electrician and part-time rodeo cowboy with no training in biology or medicine.

The Organization for European Cooperation and Development indirectly challenged the conscientiousness of university faculty and administrators by proposing to rank the world's colleges and universities based on the knowledge their students had acquired. I can imagine a time in the future when an organization decides to evaluate the spirituality of the leaders of the world's religions by measuring the frequency of worship among its members. The hidden aim in these evaluations seems to be a wish to prevent any elite group from escaping the scrutiny that might expose its clay feet.

I attended my last faculty meeting before retiring from Harvard University in the spring of 2000. The issue being debated by the Faculty of Arts and Sciences was the dean's traditional practice of sending all faculty a notice, printed on expensive paper, announcing the death of a former member. The faculty members at this meeting who were less than forty-five years old argued that professors were not the only employees entitled to this honor. The same cards should be mailed when any member of the university community—secretaries, janitors, police, librarians, and those who maintain the buildings and grounds—passed away. The Australian phrase "Lop off the tall poppies" captures this sentiment.

Pascal Bruckner recognized the new mood in *The Tyranny of Guilt* when he wrote, "We doggedly examine great figures in order to cut them down to size. Only victims receive our compassion; our Parthenon is composed only of the afflicted or defeated and we compete with each other in weeping over them."

Attacks on the integrity of those who occupy elite positions have a hidden danger. Elites in most societies enjoy a measure of moral authority that makes it easier for them to persuade others to their views. Nelson Mandela possessed this authority among Africans, Albert Einstein among scientists, Mahatma Gandhi among Hindus.

Consistent criticism of those holding positions of responsibility may tempt some to lower the standards they bring to their obligations. A survey conducted in 1995 on more than thirty-eight thousand adults from thirty nations revealed that when most members in a society lose respect for those in authority, the authorities begin to believe what others say about them and behave in ways that match the popular judgment. If adults in positions of responsibility believe that a majority in their society assume they are flawed, an unknown number will cooperate by confirming the community's assumption.

A survey conducted from 2011 to 2013 asked citizens from twenty-nine nations, "All things considered, can the doctors in your country be trusted?" The United States ranked twenty-four out of twenty-nine, just ahead of Russia, Poland, Bulgaria, Croatia, and Chile, with only 58 percent affirming the trustworthiness of America's physicians. This loss of faith contrasts with the 73 percent of Americans in 1966 who had great trust in doctors. Some of the doctors who recognize the public's attitude may spend a little less time with a new patient.

The early twentieth-century Swedish writer Pär Lagerkvist captured, in a short story, the importance of the private beliefs each person holds regarding his or her daily work. A collection of dead people were complaining of the boredom and tragic futility of their former lives as doctors, architects, engineers, or lawyers. An older man rose to tell the group he did not understand their cynicism. He wanted them to know that he had enjoyed, and taken seriously, his many years cleaning the lavatories at the Stockholm railroad station.

When those at the top of the status pyramid sense that the contract they thought they had with members of their society is broken, the pride that accompanies a perfect performance as well as loyalty to the behavioral code associated with their role become muted and the strength of commitment a little weaker. The American Medical Association is troubled by the increasing number of doctors who are abandoning a long-standing ethical prohibition against criticizing another physician to a patient. Doctors who regard themselves as highly paid laborers in the health care system, rather than members of a sacred profession, might be expected to behave this way.

The reluctance to award elites a special respect has one benevolent face. It persuades youths from nonelite families that they, too, can enhance their status. Martin Luther's rebellion against the elites in the Vatican permitted sixteenth-century Europeans to entertain the idea that no person or institution was inherently sacred and immune from scrutiny. All are vulnerable to challenge if they violate their obligations, and anyone can, through effort and character, rise in status. This bold idea helped Europe, which was a backwater region in 1400, to become a world leader in science, education, democratic governments, commerce, and military power only 250 years after Luther mounted his criticism of a pope who had abrogated his responsibilities. It is too early to tell which scenario will develop from the currently hostile posture toward elites, allowing us to entertain the hope that history will follow the second path.

Hyping Genes

The machines that allow us to talk to a friend three thousand miles away while walking to a restaurant, receive an instantaneous answer to almost any question, examine a picture of a brain, replace a risk gene with a healthy one, and watch a soccer match in London while sitting on a couch in Toledo are the dividends of an intellectual gamble whose successes could not have been anticipated. That gamble was the intuition that the things we see, hear, smell, taste, and touch were built from a small number of invisible entities the Greek philosopher Leucippus called *atomos*. More than two thousand years later, physicists asserted that a small number of invisible entities, given the fanciful names quarks, leptons, and bosons, were the building blocks of atoms which, in turn, were the foundations of everything we are able to sense. Although many events in the world humans sense appear to obey deterministic laws, those in the invisible world of quarks, leptons, and bosons do not.

Impressed with the explanatory power of atoms and the mysterious entities of the quantum world, scientists studying living things nominated genes as the foundation of an animal's anatomy, physiology, and psychological properties. Some biologists are certain that research will eventually reveal direct links between particular genes and equally particular talents, mental illnesses, and personality traits. This hope is overly optimistic.

Even the most vocal cheerleaders for genes acknowledge that a person's developmental history affects the outcomes the genes favored. When one

member of a pair of identical twins develops the hallucinations characteristic of some forms of schizophrenia, more often than not a twin brother or
sister living in the same family is free of this symptom because this sibling's
life followed a different path.

A gene known to be a risk factor for obesity in adults who are sedentary
poses little or no risk for those with the same gene who are physically active.
James Rosenquist of Massachusetts General Hospital and colleagues studied
a large group of Massachusetts adults and their offspring for more than forty
years. The adults possessing one of the risk genes for obesity who were born
after 1942, when more occupations were sedentary and Americans were
eating more foods with sugar and fat, weighed more than those with the
same gene who were born before 1942. This result implies that the conditions of daily life during a particular historical era can render a gene more
or less of a threat to health.

The Attractiveness of Material Causes

The assumption that material things are the foundations of everything in
nature, more popular in Europe and North America than in the Far East,
sustains the confident search for the genes that contribute to psychological
properties and maintains an indifference to the effects of history and current
circumstances. Werner Heisenberg's conviction that "the unity of nature
can be understood in the following way: All . . . phenomena can be reduced
to the same basic structures" gives sturdy legs to this dogmatic position. At
least five historical facts contributed to the attractiveness of Heisenberg's
claim.

Europeans have always awarded respect to the artisans who combined
material elements in exactly the right way to build clocks, lenses, looms,
waterwheels, printing presses, and steam engines. Today a new kind of
artisan makes iPhones, laptop computers, hybrid cars, drones, satellites,
space stations, and robots. It was reasonable, therefore, to expect that nature,
too, was composed of material things arranged in just the right way. The
observations produced by linear accelerators, electron microscopes, radio
telescopes, X-ray crystallography, and magnetic scanners strengthened this

premise and made it easier to believe that mental states must be lawful derivatives of material entities. A fair number of scientists would accuse anyone entertaining the notion that thoughts possess distinctive properties that cannot be predicted or explained by combinations of genes and brains as a heretic.

Wealthy Americans who donate large amounts of money to scientists usually support those who study material phenomena. Bill Gates, Paul Allen, and Larry Ellison have given many millions of dollars to investigators who study the stars, distant galaxies, genes, brains, neurons, viruses, bacteria, and molecules. Very few wealthy Americans give funds to social scientists who study human thought, emotion, or behavior, although a few rich Europeans do. I interpret this fact to mean that the former are convinced that psychological phenomena will eventually be understood as the outcomes of brain states. I was pleased but surprised by the editorial in the January 1, 2015, issue of *Nature* magazine, which publishes mainly natural science papers, calling for more support of the social sciences because, as the author wrote, "If you want science to deliver for society, you have to support a capacity to understand that society."

The celebration of material foundations for psychological phenomena is present in Galen's humors, which nineteenth-century scholars replaced with nerves varying in level of excitability. Nineteenth-century European and American experts on crime went far beyond the evidence when they told the public that abnormal genes were the primary cause of criminality. The extraordinary discoveries in genetics during the past half century potentiated the faith in material causes. Because everyone prefers to "go with a winner," it is not surprising that private philanthropies and governmental agencies are more generous in their support of research on genes than of studies designed to reveal the effects of life experience, despite the evidence pointing to the significant contributions of experience. A team at the University of North Carolina, for example, found that the family experiences of identical twins were more important than their genes in accounting for changes in brain activity during the first two years of life.

Stress and lifestyle can affect genomes. I noted in the last essay that every chromosome has a cap at each end, called a telomere, that maintains the integrity of the genes on that chromosome. Scientists at the University of California found that the caps of middle-aged women (most were white) who experienced many psychological stressors over the course of a year and in addition did not maintain a healthy lifestyle shortened the most over the year.

A reluctance to blame victims of poverty or prejudice for their unhappiness has made it politically incorrect to suggest that the parents who reared the adolescents who are failing in school, committing crimes, or having children bear some responsibility for these outcomes. Genes, therefore, are an attractive alternative because no one can be blamed for inheriting genes that lead to the restless inattentiveness that causes academic failure, a vulnerability to drug addiction, or the emotional callousness that makes criminal activity more probable. Matthew Lebowitz of Yale University notes that therapists who believe a patient's bout of depression or anxiety is due primarily to genes, rather than life experiences, are less empathic because they assume that the patient's distress was not caused by unhappy experiences. This premise leads them to prescribe pills rather than psychotherapy.

The Influence of Thought

Investigators searching for the genetic foundations of academic failure, crime, or mental illness pay insufficient attention to the person's social class, which, I noted, is a far better predictor of these adaptation difficulties across cultural settings than any known collection of genes. Danielle Dick and colleagues at Virginia Commonwealth University are critical of the claim that the combination of a risk gene and a childhood filled with stressful experiences represents a serious risk for a mental illness. Dick et al. argue that a childhood spent in poverty, which makes stressful experiences more likely, must be present in order for symptoms to develop. A stressful experience alone, be it neglect, being bullied, or attendance at a day care center, is less likely to generate symptoms in those who grow up in affluent or affectionate families. Winston Churchill was a neglected child from an elite British family. The Nobel laureate Eric Kandel was bullied by anti-Semitic peers but grew up in a nurturing, middle-class family. The young Barack Obama was abandoned by his biological father and was aware of white prejudice toward blacks but was raised by a loving, educated mother and equally affectionate middle-class grandparents.

Investigators who find that a combination of childhood adversity and a genetic feature has a modest association with aggression, depression, or substance abuse typically emphasize a gene and say little about the child's thoughts prior, during, or following the adversity. After noting that about 1 percent of American children are neglected or abused, one research team concluded that any resulting pathology was due mainly to changes in gene expression brought on by the abuse. The researchers never entertained the equally reasonable possibility that a neglected child's brooding over a parent's indifference could lead to symptoms without the help of any genes. The fact that maltreatment, abuse, and neglect are more common among poor, less educated families than among affluent, educated ones means that the patina of experiences associated with being a member of a disadvantaged class, especially parental values, quality of schools, diet, illness, and peer relations, could contribute to a maladaptive outcome.

Ben Shephard reminds us that the development of the symptoms that define post-traumatic stress disorder (PTSD) in soldiers returning home after a war depends on the veteran's thoughts about the war. Was it just, did his nation win or lose, and did the majority of the citizenry support the war? The answers to these questions explain why the prevalence of PTSD symptoms was far greater after the wars in Vietnam, Iraq, and Afghanistan than after World War II.

Poverty, job insecurity, chronic physical illness, and social exclusion are accompanied by the secretion of proteins called cytokines, which help wounds heal, fight infection, and activate brain sites responsible for the fatigue and malaise that accompany a torn muscle, broken bone, or the flu. The person's interpretation of these feelings determines whether a depressed mood will occur. Most adults interpret a feeling of fatigue or malaise as meaning they are ill, especially if they have an injury or signs of an infection. When this information is missing, some interpret the feeling as meaning they are worried over something: lack of money, isolation from their community, or a compromised social status. These interpretations are often the culprit that precipitates a depression, especially if the person believes there is little he or she can do to alter the situation. Thoughts must be added to a person's biological state to explain why only a small proportion of adults coping with chronic stress become depressed as well as why those at risk for depression who attend religious services regularly and believe in a supernatural force are protected. When a river becomes polluted, ecologists look for causes in the practices of industries located near the river and do not attribute the polluted state to inherent properties of the waterway.

Thoughts had to contribute to the sudden depression of the German adolescent Rainer Hoess after he learned that his grandfather, whom he had never met, was the commandant at Auschwitz. If contemporary adolescents did not believe they ought to have many close friends, they would not interpret a lack of friends as violating an expected norm they were supposed to meet. If twenty-first-century American youths did not believe that a shy, quiet posture at social gatherings was an inappropriate trait, the prevalence of social anxiety disorder would plummet.

Laura Moisin in *Kid Rex* described her descent into anorexia after concluding she had lost control of her life when she moved to a large city. That thought motivated a search for an action that would assure her some measure of control. She decided that restricting her eating was a way to deal with the threatening thought. The anorexia developed because she needed proof that she was "strong enough to need no food."

German adults whose surname is a symbol of noble rank (examples include Konig for king, Kaiser for emperor, and Furst for prince) are more likely to be a manager rather than an employee. Youths who thought about the enhanced status their name symbolized might be more motivated in school and workplace than those whose names symbolized ordinary vocations (Bauer for farmer, Becker for baker, or Muller for miller). My former colleague David McClelland told me of the moment of pride he felt as a child when he learned he had the same name as the biblical hero who slew Goliath.

Discoveries by a team at McGill University point to the dangers inherent in a one-sided biological perspective that pays too little attention to the influence of the context of development. Michael Meaney and colleagues discovered in the 1980s that the rat pups whose mothers licked and groomed them frequently during their first weeks were more resilient to stress as adults than the pups whose mothers licked them less often. The maternal licking altered the expression of a gene in a brain site that, in turn, created a physiology that was more resilient to stress.

Twenty years later Meaney and his student Frances Champagne found that the adaptive consequences of the maternal licking could be eliminated completely by raising the infant rats, after weaning, in a large area with other rats and many objects, rather than alone in a small, bare cage. A small, bare cage, which is an abnormal place to grow up for any animal, was the home of the rats in the original study. The fact that few scientists, including Meaney, cite this study, even though it was published in a respected journal, implies a reluctance to acknowledge the power of environments to dilute or offset the power of genes.

Kenneth Kendler, a psychiatrist at Virginia Commonwealth University who is also bothered by the imbalance in explanations of psychological outcomes, reminds investigators that a correlation between a set of genes and a mental illness does not mean that the genes were the major cause of the symptoms. Each person's interpretations of his or her history and current life circumstances make a more significant contribution than genes to drug addiction, gambling, social anxiety, anorexia, attention-deficit-hyperactivity disorder, or depression. The most effective cures for mental illness will not be developed until scientists acknowledge the contribution of the thoughts provoked by life circumstances.

Natural scientists dislike awarding power to thoughts because they are transient, change in unpredictable and occasionally illogical ways, are tinged with the concepts good and bad, cannot be studied in animals, and are difficult to visualize. Biologists prefer to study phenomena that are stable, change in predictable ways, are untouched by ethical considerations, and can be imagined. Seeing is believing, and it is hard to generate an image of a thought. If scientists acknowledged that a woman's shame over her father's repeated acts of sexual abuse in her childhood, guilt over not resisting his advances, and anger over his actions were important causes of her bout of depression, they would find it harder to rationalize measuring the biological consequences of restricting mice in a very narrow tube as a strategy to understand why abused children are at risk for depression.

I suspect that few younger scientists know that during the first half of the last century many scientists attributed the rising incidence of insomnia, fatigue, and anxiety to the social changes of industrialization, rise of bureaucracies, the Depression of the 1930s, a more strident competitiveness in the workplace, a faster pace of life, larger cities, a more permissive sexuality, and the emancipation of women. These commentators argued that a sick society, not abnormal genes, was the source of the stressors that created these symptoms.

Too many biologists regard thoughts as politically incorrect obscenities. Listen to Nessa Carey, British biologist and author of *The Epigenetics Revolution.* "If we don't accept . . . a molecular basis" for the consequences of experience, "what are we left with? . . . We prefer to probe for a measure that has a physical foundation." The rejection of mental processes as having any autonomous causal power because they are invisible and nonmaterial is a serious flaw in current theorizing. Genes can only affect brain states. They are powerless to influence the interpretations of the products of brain states. Because identical twins, who share the same genes, often impose different interpretations on the same experience, it is necessary to acknowledge the vital contribution of thought to actions and emotions.

The popular twentieth-century American journalist H. L. Mencken once wrote, "For every complex problem there is an answer that is clear, simple, and wrong." With a small number of exceptions, no collection of genes guarantees the emergence of a psychological trait. A combination of small contributions from a large number of genes combined with the rest of the person's genome and history of experiences are required to generate most psychological outcomes.

What Is a Gene?

Research during the past fifty years has complicated an earlier, far simpler understanding of a gene. Before Crick and Watson discovered the molecular structure of DNA in 1953, a gene was a hypothetical entity that contributed to a physical property of a plant or animal. This was Mendel's understanding of why some peas had a wrinkled and some a smooth surface. The current definition of a gene is a repeated sequence of four molecules (called bases), whose first letters, A, T, G, and C, stand for adenine, thymine, guanine, and cytosine, that are transcribed by another molecule, called messenger RNA, to become the amino acids that are combined to make the proteins that are the building blocks for all the body's tissues. This definition of a gene is purely functional, not unlike defining a knife as an object that cuts or ice as something that cools a liquid.

The human genome consists of 3.2 billion pairs of bases, or a total of 6.4 billion bases. A paired arrangement of the bases in which A is joined to T and G is joined to C, held together by a scaffold of sugar and phosphate molecules, is called deoxyribonucleic acid, or DNA. Early twentieth-century scientists who knew the chemical structure of nucleic acids rejected the possibility that this molecule could be the foundation of life. It was counterintuitive to assume that four molecules, composed only of carbon, oxygen, hydrogen, and nitrogen, were all nature needed to create every living creature. Erling Norrby of the Royal Swedish Academy of Sciences reminds us that most biologists were unconvinced by Crick and Watson's claim in 1953 that DNA was the basis of all life-forms. It took additional experiments to persuade them.

The twenty-three pairs of human chromosomes that house the genes vary in length and number of base pairs, from 57 million pairs on the small Y chromosome to 247 million base pairs on chromosome number 1. Surprisingly, less than 2 percent of the 3.2 billion base pairs are the foundation of the estimated twenty thousand DNA sequences that are the source of the body's proteins. These sequences are called coding genes, and a typical coding gene contains about ten thousand pairs of bases. Each coding gene is composed of a large number of DNA sequences that can be transcribed, called exons, which are interrupted by other DNA sequences, called introns, that will not become parts of a protein. The specific collection of exons, that messenger RNA selects for transcription varies across the body's tissues. Because messenger RNA transcribes different exon collections in varied tissues, and each collection means a different protein, a coding gene can be the source of more than one protein.

Although all body cells in the young embryo contain the same genes, changes in the sequence of one or more bases, called mutations, can occur in one gene in a single cell when that cell divides. The number of cell divisions over a life of seventy years is larger than the number of sand grains in an eighty-foot-high dune (approximately 10 followed by sixteen zeroes). Although the probability of a mutation during any one cell division is extremely low, estimated at one mutation for every billion base pairs transcribed, there is always the possibility of a mutation because there are 6.4 billion bases.

Geneticists at Johns Hopkins University estimate that about two-thirds of all cancers are traceable to such chance mutations during a person's lifetime. This fact does not imply that a person's lifestyle has no effect on the likelihood of a mutation. A healthy lifestyle is likely to lower the probability of a mutation. The most common cancers occur in tissues whose cells divide frequently, such as the colon and bone marrow. The least common cancers are found in tissues whose cells divide less often, such as bone and thyroid gland. The large increase in the world's population over the past thousand years has been accompanied by a parallel increase in the number of rare mutations that are found in less than 1 percent of the population.

Most studies reporting a relation between a particular gene and a psychological trait were based on examining the genes taken from cells in the mouth or blood under the assumption that the same genes were present in the rest of the body. This is not always the case. Adults who learned about their genome by sending a sample of mouth cells to a laboratory might possess a different genome if cells from their blood or nose had been analyzed. The genes within the receptors for smell that line the nasal epithelium are more variable than the genes in the receptors in the ear that detect sound.

The human genome contains many variations on most genes. The most common is replacing one base with another (called a SNP and pronounced "snip"). There are about 10 million locations in the human genome (out of 6.4 billion) where any two persons selected at random would have a different base in that location. Other variations include adding, repeating, or deleting or changing the location of one or more bases. Deletions involving more than fifty base pairs and changes in the location of a sequence of bases are least frequent. Some variations are unique to a single person. It is estimated that each infant is born with about three dozen variations that no one else possesses.

About 75 percent of all mutations occur in a sperm rather than an egg. Males during their reproductive years produce millions of sperm each day and close to a trillion over a lifetime. Therefore, the probability of a mutation in a single sperm is higher than it is for an egg. As each male ages, the probability of a mutation in a sperm increases across the approximately seven hundred cell divisions within the testes from puberty to age forty-five. Brian D'Onofrio notes that within families with more than one child, children whose fathers were older than age forty-five when they were conceived were two to three times more likely to develop a serious mental illness, including mental retardation, autism, or schizophrenia, than siblings conceived when the father was less than thirty years old. Because only about four hundred ova mature in a typical female, the probability that one of these eggs will have a mutation is much lower. The message to a woman selecting a father for her child is clear—look for a man in his twenties to early thirties.

Regulating Coding Genes

A coding gene cannot contribute to a protein if it is not expressed. I noted earlier that gene expression occurs when messenger RNA transcribes the exons of a coding gene, at a remarkable pace of four thousand bases a minute, and transports this copy to a structure outside the nucleus but within the cell that manufactures proteins with the assistance of two additional RNA molecules, called transfer RNA and ribosomal RNA. The RNA molecule contains three of the four DNA bases (A, C, and G), but replaces T with U (uracil) and has a different sugar.

I will not burden the reader with the complex cascade of processes that generates proteins. I suspect that if the current understanding of the approximately twelve steps that occur between the transcription of a coding gene and the arrival of a protein at the appropriate site in the body had been presented a century ago to a thousand eminent biologists, all would have rejected the description as counterintuitive and probably incorrect.

Those who appreciate the complexity and inefficiency of these cascades have one of two choices. They can accept, as I do, the biologist's argument that the cascade is the result of several billion years of chance events. On the other hand, they can argue that God knew humans would try to figure out how he created life, so he encrypted the processes to make the task difficult. Either position requires accepting a premise on faith alone. It is as difficult to imagine how an extraordinarily large number of chance events could have led, over 3 billion years, to the current genetic mechanisms that produce proteins as it is to envision a supernatural force generating the same system.

A number of regulatory processes affect the level of expression of coding genes as well as where and when each gene will be expressed. One kind of regulator, called a promoter, is a DNA sequence located next to the coding gene whose level of expression it controls. This control is exerted through a special protein that binds to the promoter and alters its shape in ways that make it easy or hard for messenger RNA to contact and transcribe the coding gene.

A second type of regulator, called an enhancer, determines when a coding gene will be expressed in a specific tissue. The enhancer for a gene called SRY, which is responsible for the formation of the testes in a particular site in the male embryo about seven to eight weeks after conception, is located on the Y chromosome. Once the testes are formed the enhancer has done its job. A team at the Max Planck Institute in Nijmegen suggested that the important role of the left hemisphere in language is due, partly, to the fact that the enhancers for many genes expressed in the brain are expressed more in the left than in the right hemisphere.

Although the enhancer is located many base pairs away from the coding gene it regulates, it is often spatially close because of the coiled shape of the genome, like the tail of a scorpion that bends forward to touch the head. When the enhancer binds to a protein, it bends in a way that allows it to contact the promoter region of a coding gene. The differences among species—say, mice versus gorillas—are due mainly to enhancers that determine which proteins will be synthesized in specific cells at particular times. The conductor of an orchestra furnishes an analogy, for his hand movements instruct particular musicians to play louder or softer at specific times in the composition.

A third regulator is composed of small strands of RNA. Two of the shortest strands, called micro RNA and small interfering RNA, prevent a coding gene from being transcribed into an amino acid by interfering with messenger RNA. As a result, no protein is made. The collection of these short RNA strands regulates as many as half of the coding genes in the human genome. Several years ago I asked Matthew Meselson, an eminent biologist, what new fact in genetics surprised him the most. His reply, given without hesitation, was the discovery of these short RNA strands.

A fourth regulator, which is especially susceptible to experience, assumes two forms. Because neither one alters the sequence of bases in a gene, these regulators are called epigenetic. In one frequent form a chemical mark (a methyl group) is added to or removed from C when C is followed by G. Some places in the genome contain a single C adjacent to a G. In other places there are many repetitions of C-G pairs. Close to 70 percent of the former sequences are found in promoter regions that regulate a coding gene, and most of the C bases in these regions are methylated. Although less common, a methyl group can be added to A or to T when they are not next to G. Nature resists absolute rules.

Because the addition of a methyl group to C in a regulatory region usually silences the gene, the fact that T replaces C in about two-thirds of known mutations implies that many unwanted traits are partially attributable to the activation of a gene that is normally silenced. The uncontrolled growth of cancer cells is an example.

A second epigenetic regulator consists of a chemical alteration in the four pairs of proteins that form a unit around which a string of 147 base pairs is wrapped, like a thread around a spool. Because the DNA has a negative electric charge and the protein spool has a positive charge, the two are drawn together, making it difficult for messenger RNA to transcribe the DNA sequence. The addition or deletion of various molecules to the amino acid tails that protrude from each protein spool reduces the difference in electric charge. As a result the spool expands, the DNA of the coding gene becomes exposed, and messenger RNA is able to transcribe it. These changes in the spools are more reversible than adding a methyl group to C in a DNA sequence.

Patients with a form of leukemia called chronic leukocytic leukemia whose spools are expanded live longer than patients whose spools are close together. Although patients with schizophrenia, major depression, or bipolar disorder display different symptoms, a consortium of investigators examining the genomes of sixty thousand individuals with one of these illnesses found that a small proportion of patients with one of these disorders shared the same epigenetic alteration in a histone. David Moore's book *The Developing Genome* provides an excellent summary of these phenomena.

Major stressors, such as famine, war, abuse, chronic poverty, poor diet, lack of exercise, smoking, infection, and chronic pain, can generate epigenetic changes that suppress or enhance a gene's expression. Regular exercise often induces epigenetic changes in the genes of muscle cells. A pregnant mother's diet and lifestyle can induce epigenetic changes in her fetus. Ryohei Sekido of the University of Aberdeen notes that one reason male and female brains differ is that the SRY gene on the Y chromosome can alter epigenetic marks on the cytosine bases in DNA sequences as well as the histone spools in the genes of neurons. Readers may remember that the single female larva in a beehive destined to become the queen is the only one fed a diet of royal jelly. It turns out that the proteins in the royal jelly generate chemical changes that, in turn, alter epigenetic marks in the future queen.

Although offspring are unlikely to inherit most of their parents' epigenetic marks, the mother's physiology during pregnancy can induce epigenetic changes in her unborn child. For example, a girl who was abused as a child could acquire epigenetic marks that enhance the brain's response to stress. If, years later, this woman experiences a stress when pregnant, her brain will secrete molecules that pass through the placenta to affect her fetus. As a result, her infant might be born with a vulnerability to stress, even though the vulnerability was not caused by inheriting genes or epigenetic marks from the mother.

The array of epigenetic marks varies across different tissues, such as blood, mouth, and brain. This fact delays discovery of the relations between these marks and psychological traits because investigators usually examine only one tissue. The belief that life experiences can affect features in the next generation is an old idea. The ancient Greek physician Hippocrates successfully defended a white princess accused of adultery when she gave birth to a black infant by arguing that the portrait of a Moor hanging over her bed altered her physiology in ways that led to the birth of a black baby.

Epigenetic changes induced by experience are a significant addition to—some would say they require a reformulation of—the evolutionary theory of the 1940s. The traditional view held that any alteration in the pattern of gene expression was due to chance mutations in coding genes that were independent of the animal's environment. New discoveries indicate that each person's life history from conception forward can generate changes in gene expression that induce new physiological processes. Most experts believe that only a small proportion of these changes in gene expression will be inherited.

The surprisingly large number of regulators implies that coding genes require close supervision lest their expression lead to the overproduction of proteins that can precipitate a disease. About two of every one hundred healthy American adults are born with at least one coding gene known to be a risk factor for a disease. These individuals neither display nor complain of any symptoms because the effect of the risk gene depends on the rest of the genome, the person's lifestyle, and epigenetic marks. Two members of a family can possess the same mental illness but not share the same risk genes. The same principle applies to tameness in an animal species. Scientists at the Max Planck Institute in Leipzig confirmed that different sets of genes distinguish tame dogs from wolves, tame pigs from boars, tame fox from wild fox, and tame from wild rabbits.

Imprinting

One more phenomenon intrigues geneticists. Two members of a family can possess the same gene but develop different traits depending on whether that gene came from the mother or the father. In these cases, the epigenetic marks on the gene in the sperm differed from the marks on the egg that the sperm fertilized. This phenomenon is called genetic imprinting. A possible analogy is the meaning of a sentence in a novel published in two different languages. The exact meanings of many sentences in Tolstoy's *War and Peace* depend on whether they are in Russian or English.

More genes that have a maternal origin are expressed when the brain's cortex is developing, whereas more genes from the father are expressed when the hypothalamus, which contributes to sexuality, is being formed. Although genetic imprinting is restricted to less than 1 percent of the human genome, most imprinted genes affect the growth of the embryo. Growth is enhanced if the gene that came from the mother is silenced and the gene from the father is expressed. This fact helps to explain why most male newborns are larger and heavier than most females.

Genes Are Not Equally Mutable

Animal and human genes vary in their susceptibility to a mutation. The mutations that allowed the brain cells of human embryos to divide for a longer time, resulting in a much larger brain, occurred about two hundred thousand years ago. Mutations that result in different kinds of proteins are common. Many animal species, including humans, possess a collection of genes, called the MHC complex, that is the source of the proteins that coat the surface of cells in the immune system. The same genes are responsible for the distinctive odors of a mammal's sweat and urine. Dogs, cats, monkeys, and humans are biased to select a mating partner whose body emits a different odor because it possesses a different collection of MHC genes. This strategy is adaptive because it guarantees that the offspring of this mating will have an immune system capable of responding to a broader set of infectious agents.

Genes Restrict Ranges

Coding genes and their regulators make it easy or difficult for a person to develop a particular trait, but they rarely guarantee any trait. My genome prevents me from developing the extraordinary tennis skill of Roger Federer, but I have played moderately good tennis all my life. A boy born with genes that protect him from experiencing intense fear could become an astronaut, trial lawyer, or neurosurgeon, on the one hand, or a rapist, serial killer, or chronically dishonest investment advisor, depending on his life history.

This claim is easy to demonstrate. About 6 percent of Caucasians possess a variant of a gene that is necessary for the synthesis of acetylcholine, a molecule that facilitates the ability to sustain attention over a long interval and to resist being distracted by sounds or sights. Anne Berry and her colleagues at the University of Michigan found that adults with this gene could nonetheless maintain attention on a boring task as long as there were no distracting stimuli. Most adults with this gene are functioning well in their settings and attain the same level of education as those without this variant, despite their vulnerability to being distracted. Because of the dramatic increase in the number and intrusiveness of distracting events, such as radio, television, iPhones, and the sound of a police car or ambulance, which interfere with prolonged concentration, this gene poses a greater risk to adaptation in 2015 than it did in 1715.

If we assume, for the sake of illustration, that each person has the potential to actualize ten thousand different psychological properties, the genes possessed by a particular infant may limit the actualization of one thousand of those properties and facilitate the development of another thousand, leaving eight thousand properties untouched by the child's genome. The number of psychological outcomes is far smaller than the number of genes and life circumstances that, together, are responsible for an outcome. This fact means that every behavior, belief, and mood has more than one combination of genes and circumstances that could have produced it.

A Psychological Outcome Can Have Many Origins

Some adults maintain a cheery mood despite frustrations because of their childhood history; others are equally cheery because they inherited a gene that allowed a molecule to activate the brain's receptors for cannabinoids (found in marijuana) for a longer time. A vulnerability to depression can also be the product of different genes. Some individuals inherit a DNA sequence in the promoter region of a gene whose protein product results in the molecule serotonin remaining in the synapse for a longer time. Individuals with this mutation appear to experience the bodily sensations that give rise to feelings more easily. If the event is humorous, they are apt to laugh or smile more than others. If the event is aversive, they are likely to experience more distress. Some scientists have reported that individuals with this mutation who also remember being victims of childhood maltreatment are at a higher risk for repeated bouts of depression. It is possible that these adults are prone to exaggerate the severity of an experience that others encountered, but the former either ignored the event or treated it as unimportant. The genetic contribution to depression in these adults must be distinguished from the variety of mutations that raised the risk of a depression in others.

The symptoms of a mental illness illustrate the complexity of the causal cascades that combine genes and experience. A depression, characterized by apathy, fatigue, insomnia, loss of appetite, and a failure to extract pleasure from experiences that had been sources of joy, can be the result of different cascades. Hence, depressed patients should not be pooled into one category. Benjamin Lahey of the University of Chicago, with colleagues, found that some patients diagnosed as depressed on one occasion were classified three years later as having social phobia. A psychiatric diagnosis reflects the symptom(s) that happens to be the most salient at a particular time. Water can assume the form of a cloud, fog, rain, snow, or icicles depending on local conditions.

The genetic heterogeneity of depression is only one example of the principle that the more common the symptom, the more likely it has different origins. A team led by Sarah Karalunas at the Oregon Health and Science University discovered that children diagnosed with attention-deficit-hyperactivity disorder (ADHD) belong to at least three different categories. One group was inattentive; a second was excessively assertive; and the most distinctive group was irritable, prone to temper tantrums, and impulsive. Phobic patients, too, belong to distinct groups defined by different combinations of genes and life experiences. One group is afraid of crowds and strangers; another fears animals and injury to the body; a third is fearful of blood and injections; and a final group feels anxious in closed places.

Even the less common diagnosis of autism is due to a large number of distinctive cascades. Children are classified as autistic if they display serious difficulty communicating and interacting with others. The number of biological conditions capable of generating these symptoms is probably as large as the number of causes of headaches. A small number of autistic children have seizures, disorders of the gut, impaired hearing, or an autoimmune disorder that affects the brain. Christopher McDougle of Massachusetts General Hospital notes that Leo Kanner, the physician who invented the diagnosis of autism in 1943, noticed the prevalence of autoimmune disorders, such as type I diabetes, in the parents or siblings of his original sample. But his theoretical biases led him to disregard these facts and emphasize the mother's behavior with the child.

About 5 Percent of children categorized as autistic possess Fragile X syndrome. This disease, more common in boys, is characterized by many repeats of the trio of bases CGG (cytosine-guanine-guanine) in the regulatory region of a coding gene on the X chromosome that interfere with the production of a protein required for normal brain development. Rett syndrome, rarer than Fragile X and affecting mainly girls, is caused by a mutation in a coding gene on the X chromosome that, in healthy children, is the basis of a protein that adds a methyl group to cytosine that silences a particular gene.

Some 5 percent of autistic patients possess rare, novel mutations that prevent the synthesis of proteins required for synapse formation, receptor function, or epigenetic marks. Most of these mutations occurred spontaneously during the development of the embryo or fetus and were not inherited. A team at the Hospital for Sick Children in Toronto studied families in which two siblings were diagnosed with autism. Close to 70 percent of the siblings in these families had different mutations that occurred spontaneously during fetal development. These facts explain why there are different mutations in autistic patients with low compared with high IQ scores. There is even evidence suggesting that dissimilar genetic abnormalities contribute to autism in males and females.

Although there are a very large number of biological cascades that lead to a diagnosis of autism, the psychological development of these children follows a smaller number of paths. A team led by Peter Szatmari of the University of Toronto found that about 30 percent of three- to four-year-olds diagnosed with autism are very impaired and become more impaired as they develop. Close to 50 percent are only moderately impaired and remain stable over time. And 20 percent are minimally impaired and improve with age. This last group has more girls than boys; the first group has more boys than girls.

Unfortunately, many clinicians continue to diagnose all children with the defining symptoms as belonging to a single autistic spectrum. Oncologists, by contrast, give distinctive names to cancers with different causes and do not assign all patients to a cancer spectrum. To make matters worse, clinicians from different regions within the United States do not use the same criteria when diagnosing autism. Clinicians in Los Angeles County assign this diagnosis more often to children born to foreign born, black, or Vietnamese mothers than to middle-class white children. Clinicians in other states use the category autistic for white children without a serious intellectual impairment and for black children with serious cognitive retardation. For reasons that are not understood, a diagnosis of autism is more common for American children from well-educated families than for European children born to families with the same class and ethnic composition.

The Need for New Signs

Instead of searching for the genes that contribute to each mental illness, scientists would profit from looking for biological properties that are associated with an illness but are under firmer genetic control. Some examples are eye and hair color, the shape of the face and body, subtle abnormalities in the hands, hair, or face, ratio of the length of the index and ring finger, eye blink rate, and variability of heart rate. Each of these features is correlated with one or more traits that are related to an illness but these features are more closely controlled by genes than the symptoms defining the illness.

Although the color of the skin, hair, or iris is controlled by many genes, the final color is the result of a balance between two pigments, called eumelanin and pheomelanin, produced by cells called melanocytes whose surface is covered with receptors. When the receptors react to a specific hormone, the melanocyte makes eumelanin, resulting in a darker skin, hair, or eyes. If the receptors are insensitive to the hormone due to one or more mutations, the melanocytes make pheomelanin and the person will have red hair, a fairer complexion, or light-colored eyes. Only 1 to 2 percent of the world's population have red hair, with Scotland having the highest proportion at 13 percent.

When the melanocytes make less of both kinds of melanin the person will have light blond hair and light blue eyes, features found most often in northern Europeans, who are more likely than Africans or Asians to possess a mutation that is a risk factor for skin cancer. Because the receptors on the melanocytes are also found in the brain and immune system, the genes that control the sensitivity of these receptors might place a person at risk for one or more compromises in psychological function.

Tourette's syndrome, characterized by uncontrollable motor tics, and Parkinson's disease, characterized by motor tremors, are two examples. Caucasians with either disease are a little more likely than the average Caucasian to have red hair. Owners of cocker spaniels with a red coat color say they are more "nervous" than the more common dark-colored spaniels. Eighteenth-century manuals addressed to European mothers of infants advised them to avoid hiring redheaded wet nurses because their irascible personality rendered their breast milk dangerous. The controversial poet Ezra Pound, the narcissistic English king Henry VIII, and the emotionally labile American presidents Andrew Jackson and U. S. Grant had red hair.

Adults who blink more often than the average person under nonstressful circumstances—they display as many as twenty-five to thirty blinks per minute—have higher than normal levels of dopamine activity in brain structures that contribute to motor actions. Patients with Parkinson's disease, who secrete less dopamine, blink less frequently. Obsessive-compulsive patients blink more frequently than the average person. The average female has a higher level of dopamine activity in several brain sites than the average male and, not surprisingly, women blink more often than men.

The average interval between successive heartbeats while a person is sitting quietly varies across individuals, due partly to genes that influence the autonomic nervous system. Those with low heart rate variability maintain roughly the same beat-to-beat interval, say, 1.3 seconds, over several minutes. Those with high heart rate variability display dissimilar beat-to-beat intervals. Adults with less variable heart rates are more likely to report unpleasant social interactions during a typical day; Marines who developed post-traumatic stress disorder after a combat mission had less variable heart rates before the mission. By contrast, more adults with highly variable heart rates report more pleasant interactions than those with minimally variable heart rates. Asian infants have a less variable heart rate than African infants; Caucasian infants have a less variable heart rate than African American infants.

A small proportion of Caucasian male adolescents in one of my studies combined a highly variable heart rate, low levels of uncertainty to challenges, and an easy sociability. Most of these boys also possessed a broad face, a prominent chin, and index fingers that were slightly shorter than their ring fingers. These three anatomical properties are due, in part, to variation in secretion of the male sex hormone and the density of its receptors. Investigators interested in the genetic contributions to a mental illness or a personality trait might profit from searching for the genes that affect variation in eye, hair, and skin color, blink rate, heart rate variability, finger ratios, facial width, and prominence of the chin.

The current hyping of genes by the media persuades the public that genes trump life experiences in most cases of mental illness and invites scientists to ignore the experiential contribution to symptoms, skills, moods, and behaviors. Yes, it is true that without genes humans would be nothing. But because no genes code for water, it is equally true that we would be nothing if we were only genes. The pattern of traits and talents that emerges from a blend of genes and life history can be likened to a blanket composed of thin black-and-white threads woven so closely the two colors are invisible in the homogeneously gray fabric.

Can Brain Explain Mind?

Historical eras are marked by a small number of questions that recruit the most intense curiosity. The reason for the seasons, the symptoms of tuberculosis, and the structure of the gene were at the top of the stack during earlier eras until each was eventually resolved. A preliminary understanding of how any psychological phenomenon emerges from the brain activity that is its necessary origin is the puzzle currently resting at the top of the stack. Those who resolve critical parts of this puzzle will receive the admiration that Newton, Darwin, and Einstein enjoy.

This question could not have achieved its current prominence without the help of elegant machines that permit measurement of brain activity. Although this effort is still in an early phase, most neuroscientists are confident that eventually measures of the brain will permit prediction and explanation of the perception of a face, the memory of yesterday's dinner, sadness on hearing of the death of a friend, an intention to embrace a child, a bout of depression, addiction to cocaine, and difficulty in learning to read.

The Need for Two Vocabularies

Although all psychological outcomes require a brain—I am not a Cartesian dualist—mental events emerge from brain activity and, therefore, possess properties that require a vocabulary different from the one that describes brain processes. Many natural phenomena possess properties that are missing from the elementary forms from which they emerge. The property of opacity, characteristic of a dense fog, is missing from the properties of atoms of hydrogen and oxygen in the water molecules that are the fog's constituents. Iron atoms can be shaped into a wheel, knife, or frying pan. The functions of these objects—rolling, slicing, and cooking food—are not inherent in the iron atoms. A student at Stony Brook University created an unambiguous image of a cat on a wall by directing a light at a certain angle at a jerry-built structure composed of a soda bottle, eyeglasses, Scotch tape, and a ping-pong ball.

The final shape of a protein provides the best analogy. The distinctive shape of each of the estimated one hundred thousand different proteins in the human body is constrained by its particular sequence of amino acids. But two proteins composed of exactly the same amino acid sequence can assume different final shapes because of forces operating during the brief folding process. As a result, the final shape cannot be predicted from the amino acid sequence. Moreover, the words that describe the protein's shape and functions cannot be translated into the vocabulary that is appropriate for the amino acids. Analogously, although a particular brain state constrains the range of thoughts, emotions, or actions that are likely to occur to an event, the outcome that emerges cannot be predicted with certainty from the brain state nor described with the words appropriate for that state.

There is abundant evidence for this conclusion. Lorina Naci of the University of Western Ontario and colleagues recorded the brain activity of adults watching the same eight-minute segment of an Alfred Hitchcock film. Each person's verbal descriptions of the scenes were far more similar than their brain patterns. A team at Harvard University confirmed this observation in adults classifying words. Some brain patterns were so different, no expert would suspect they were generated by individuals engaged in exactly the same task.

Furthermore, the thoughts that emerge from one brain state are often the origin of a different brain state. Mariela Rance of Heidelberg University asked adults who were experiencing an imposed pain in a finger to reduce the level of brain activity in sites the scientist knew mediated the pain. The fact that many were able to do so by thinking of something else implies that thoughts generated by one circuit can affect brain activity in a different circuit.

Not surprisingly, adults who agreed to wear a cast that covered their forearm and wrist for four weeks experienced reduced strength in these muscles. However, Brian Clark of Ohio University found that the loss of muscle strength over the month was less if these volunteers imagined flexing these muscles each day. Apparently, the mental activity involved in imagining muscle movement altered sites in the motor cortex that maintain tone in these muscles.

Although the molecule oxytocin can change the level of activity in brain sites that are involved in emotions such as empathy, a person's thoughts have the power to enhance or reduce that activity. Scientists usually increase the level of oxytocin in the brain by spraying the nose of a participant with this molecule. Two groups of Dutch students under the influence of oxytocin heard the recorded sound of a crying infant. One group was told that the infant was ill, the other that it was bored. Only the students who believed the infant was ill displayed increased neural activity in a site known to mediate empathy even though both groups had been administered the oxytocin.

Xu Chen of Emory University, with colleagues, provided a more convincing example of the dissociation between brain and mind. Men and women who did not know whether they had been sprayed with oxytocin or an inert molecule played a game, called Prisoner's Dilemma, against either a human partner they never saw or a computer program. Those who received oxytocin showed reduced activity in a brain structure—the amygdala—that alters heart rate and muscle tension. However, the oxytocin had no effect on their behaviors or reported feelings during the game. These facts challenge the belief in a determinant relation between an altered brain state and a psychological outcome.

Thoughts explain the power of placebos, which are inert substances that have a beneficial effect because the person believes he or she has received a pill or procedure that has been proven to improve his or her mental or physical state. Anne Schienle and colleagues at the University of Graz found that women who believed that the pill they had ingested would mute feelings of disgust showed reduced activation in a site, called the insula, that is usually responsive to disgusting events and also reported less disgust in response to pictures of dirty toilets and rotting corpses. A similar phenomenon occurred in sixty-year-olds with Parkinson's disease who underwent a sham operation but believed that the surgery would be beneficial. These patients showed a reduction in symptoms and relevant changes in the brain. One could not ask for more persuasive proof of the power of thoughts to alter the brain by promoting the secretion of molecules, such as dopamine, that facilitate motor function.

If Western scientists had not decided that material substances were the foundations of all events, there would have been no need to invent the word *placebo*. This term is needed to explain why immaterial thoughts can have beneficial consequences on the body or mood. Only those who believe that the water they are drinking has a sacred power benefit from drinking it. This is the message L. Frank Baum intended when his Wizard of Oz gave symbols of education, generosity, and courage to the straw man, tin man, and lion. It is odd that neither a college degree nor the Purple Heart is called a placebo, even though their receipt generates thoughts that enhance the recipient's mood.

The evolutionary biologist Bernd Rosslenbroich wrote in *On the Origin of Autonomy* that one of the most significant changes in the evolutionary narrative from bacteria to humans was the ability to cope with more varied environments. The enhanced independence of psychological processes from the brain states that are their foundation represents one of the most significant changes from worms to humans.

A. N. Whitehead noted in a 1937 lecture that human mental processes are a distinctive class of phenomena that cannot be translated into the vocabulary of physics, chemistry, or biology. Close to seventy years later, the distinguished theoretical physicist Bernard d'Espagnat wrote in *Physics and Philosophy* that matter and mind were equally basic entities. Edward Frenkel, the author of *Love and Math*, echoed this position by arguing that physical phenomena, mental events, and mathematics are three separate domains. The mathematical equations that define quarks cannot be replaced with sentences describing the brain activity of Murray Gell-Mann, the man who invented the concept of quarks. Moreover, a description of Gell-Mann's brain patterns while he was working on this problem would be unable to explain how he arrived at those equations. At present, no scientist is close to understanding how the brain of a three-year-old represents the mother's reply "That's a lemon" when the child points to a yellow object on a kitchen counter and asks, "What's that?"

The Distrust of Thought

The neuroscientist's reflex distrust of invisible, immaterial processes makes it easy to regard thoughts as epiphenomena that one day will be explained and understood as derivatives of the brain. Scientists holding executive positions at the National Institutes of Health revealed this prejudice when they instructed the psychologists asked to develop tests of varied cognitive skills that the full battery should take no longer than twenty minutes to administer. These officials would never impose a similar time restriction on a battery of brain measures. It takes more than twenty minutes to prepare a person for an evaluation of brain activity.

Many college students assume that explanations of behavior that include some facts about the brain are more likely to be correct than accounts that mention only thoughts or experience, even if the brain facts are irrelevant. Villanova University students judged explanations that contained superfluous neuroscience information superior to explanations that did not mention the brain. Americans are more receptive to headlines describing the contribution of the brain to a mental illness than articles that emphasize experience, even when the facts demand the opposite conclusion.

Freud's initial conception of neurotic symptoms awarded power to the materialistic processes that accompanied the buildup of sexual excitation, often through masturbation, that was not fully discharged through an orgasm attained during sexual intercourse. Freud may have read about a seventeenth-century devout Jew who became melancholic when he left his wife in Istanbul to assume the position of governor in an Egyptian province. When the man sought medical advice he was told that his sexual abstinence had led to a buildup of semen, which created vapors that rose to his brain and heart. The cure was to take a second wife who could provide the occasions for the discharge of the excess semen.

Too many papers in neuroscience journals read as if any reference to thinking was a politically incorrect obscenity that must not be acknowledged explicitly. A team from the University of Wisconsin led by Julian Motzkin studied four patients with lesions of the ventromedial prefrontal cortex. These rare individuals could have provided important information on the mood changes, if any, that accompany this compromise in brain function. Yet the authors reported only patterns of blood flow and heart rate and said nothing about the patients' thoughts or emotions, even though they admitted they were interested in depression and anxiety.

The conclusions of a research team at the University of Denver provide another example of the neuroscientists' reluctance to acknowledge the contributions of thought. Adults who spent their childhood in poverty showed a pattern of brain activity when regulating emotion that differed from the pattern displayed by those who grew up in advantaged families. Rather than conclude that the childhood experiences associated with growing up poor generated thoughts that motivated special ways to cope with the task, the investigators declared that the brain state created during childhood was preserved through the adult years. There was no acknowledgment of the ideas and feelings that chronic poverty generates.

The writings of Hans Selye, who in the 1950s replaced the traditional definition of stress as an event or a mental state with a pattern of brain activity, reflect this bias. Selye's position is inconsistent with the fact that many events regarded as stressors were not experienced as such at the time they occurred but emerged later as a product of reflection. A German policeman who, with others, obeyed an order from a superior to murder Jewish civilians in a Polish town in 1942 reported many years later, "Truthfully I must say that at the time we didn't any of us become truly conscious of what had happened then. . . . Only later did it first occur to me that [it] had not been right."

Free Will Is No Illusion

Scientists who claim that every action, thought, and feeling is determined by a brain state that is the product of a person's genes, past history, and current setting are treating the subjective state of free will as if it were an all-or-none dichotomy—free will or no free will. Free will, like the ability to remember the past, is graded. I am unable to implement many actions due to my age, temperament, and past history. I do not believe, for example, that I would be able to put on a parachute and jump from a plane at an altitude of ten thousand feet. Neither could I kill a person unless in self-defense. But there are many thousands of behaviors, some familiar and some never executed, that I can choose to display or to inhibit.

I remember my surprise at the affirmative answer of an eminent neuroscientist when I asked him whether he could, with complete knowledge of my brain at that moment, predict that I was thinking of crawling under the table at which we were sitting. The following event should quiet those who insist that free will must be an illusion. I had never crawled under the desk in my study, dialed 411 on my cell phone, and asked the operator for the telephone number of the State Department in Washington. Yet I performed those actions, despite the fact that nothing in my past experience or genes would have forced me to implement that odd sequence of behaviors. The only reasonable conclusion is that I, like everyone else, have the ability to select a new action, suppress many well-practiced ones, and generate novel thoughts that cannot be predicted in advance from the most extensive measures of my brain.

If a behavior required the coordination of a collection of neurons, and each neuron responded in a determinate way 999 out of every 1,000 times, the many occasions when the coordination failed leave open the possibility of an outcome that could not be predicted in advance. This fact invites an affirmative reply to the question: Are humans capable of acting in ways that could not be predicted from knowledge of their brain a fraction of a second before a thought or action occurred?

The current belief in a deeply dependent relation between a brain state and a psychological outcome has had the unfortunate consequence of implying that sane adults could, under some circumstances, be unable to control their behavior. A young resident in psychiatry surprised me by insisting that a physician who had sex with a patient was not always responsible for a failure of will because sexual urges can, under some conditions, be so overwhelming no one can regulate them. The resident's premise is not only false, it is dangerous.

I like Colin McGinn's commonsense approach to the philosophers' discussions of free will. He reminds us that few adults would say to a friend, "I decided that free will is an illusion" or "My actions are determined by fixed causal sequences." Rather, they say, "Johnny decided to get up from his chair and go to the gym to exercise."

I agree with neuroscientists who believe that future investigators will be able to use a brain profile to infer that a person is staring at a photo of a face, about to move the eyes to a new location, searching memory for a name, or planning to grab an object. But it is less likely they will be able to specify whose face is being studied, the target of the shifting eyes, the name being remembered, or the object about to be seized. Phrased differently, every brain state generates more than one possible psychological outcome. The setting, the immediate past, and the person's history, acting together, select one outcome from the larger set the brain proposes.

Emilio Bizzi of the Massachusetts Institute of Technology describes the brain changes that accompany the learning of a new motor response—say, how to use the rudder of a sailboat. The perfection of the behavior is accompanied by changes in the tiny spines that sit on the dendrites of neurons and are believed to be the foundation of the brain's representation of the new habit. Although the new spines that grew as the habit was being learned were replaced or eliminated every few months, the response remained unchanged. My ability to ride a bicycle remains intact, even though I have not been on one in thirty years and the spines that were formed when I learned this skill sixty years ago are no longer present. This situation resembles the paradox of asking whether a ship whose planks have been completely replaced is still the same ship.

Maarten Kamermans of the Netherlands Institute of Neuroscience reminds us that my eyes send my brain two different neural codes when I look out the window of my study at midday, when the sun is bright, and at dusk, when the light is dim. But I see the same tall spruce tree on the lawn at noon and at dusk. My perception of a cup, memory of my mother's name, and the way I hold a pen do not change from day to day, despite continuous variation in my brain state.

The Need for a Language for Brain Activity

Thoughts, actions, and feelings possess properties, such as valence, potency, and intrusiveness, that are denied to brains. Neuroscientists ignored this possibility when they borrowed the words psychologists use to describe humans or animals engaged in mental or physical acts instead of inventing a vocabulary appropriate for neuronal activity. Many neuroscientists write that neurons at certain brain sites "select" a response. *Select*, I suggest, is an inappropriate verb for neurons because this word implies the conscious weighing of alternatives. Only animals and humans can select one of several actions. I, not my brain, selected the word I just typed into this document. Geneticists are more careful when they select verbs that describe what genes do. Genes mutate, transpose, and duplicate, but they do not secrete, beat, or synchronize. I confess to a moment of surprise when I read a paper by three European biologists in the journal *Current Biology* that used the terms *divorce* and *infidelity* to describe the behaviors of birds.

The psychological concept of reward provides an example of the confusing consequences that follow the borrowing of a psychological word to describe a brain pattern. Early twentieth-century psychologists used this word to name the events that animals would expend energy to obtain. Because these events were so varied—a pellet of food, a sexual partner, or the opportunity to peek into a room containing novel objects—psychologists were unable to discover an objective feature that all rewarding events shared. This frustration was exacerbated by the fact that the relative desirability of an experience depended on the setting and the person's psychological and biological state.

As a result, psychologists settled for a functional definition. A reward, they wrote, was any event that an animal would work to obtain. The problem with functional definitions is that scientists want to know the inherent properties of events that belong to a concept. Defining ice as a substance that cools liquids is unsatisfactory. Some neuroscientists have decided that brain profiles can provide the inherent properties of rewards. I am not certain this move will work. Rewards are events that animals or humans like to experience. The brain state that accompanies these experiences depends on the object that is liked, whether cookies, a friend, a holiday, an embrace, a prize, a song, a painkiller, or church attendance. There is no evidence, at least at present, to support the idea that one distinctive brain profile accompanies the receipt of food when hungry, praise after completing a task, a raise in salary, and sexual intimacy with a beloved.

Mathematicians agree that a concept is ambiguous if it has a consistent meaning within each of two systems but an inconsistent meaning across the systems. The concept of infinity is an example. The concepts select, evaluate, code, integrate, know, and reward are also ambiguous because each has one meaning within neuroscience, based on brain measures, and a different meaning within psychology, based on behavioral or self-report measures.

The concept of number is ambiguous because it, too, has different meanings in neuroscience, psychology, and mathematics. Although some neuroscientists claim that select brain sites represent the concept of number, Belgian scientists found no overlap in the pattern of brain activity in adults looking at two, four, six, or eight black circles, on the one hand, and the Arabic numbers 2, 4, 6, or 8 on the other. If a brain site could register number, it should have shown similar profiles to four circles and the number 4. Yale psychologists reported different brain profiles to three equally spaced objects and an array in which two of the objects were close to each other but the third was distant from the pair, even though both arrays had three objects.

Scientists who claim that the brains of animals—monkeys or crows—can recognize the number of black dots in an array fail to consider the possibility that the brains of these animals are responding to the physical features of the array. For example, two crows were able to learn to peck at a screen containing one or two black dots but it was difficult to train them to peck at three dots.

The mathematician's concept of the number 3 equates a collection of a fork, scissors, and ball with one of a plum, tomato, and cookie. The brain's reaction to these two collections, however, would be palpably different. Thus, the meaning of "number" in the writings of neuroscientists is not the meaning mathematicians understand.

A description of the functions of the hippocampus provides a final example of the special meanings of many terms used by neuroscientists.

Neurons in my hippocampus that were unconnected before I moved into my current home many years ago became connected because the locations of the objects in my bedroom, the stairs I walk down to get breakfast, and the objects in the kitchen, as well as the sequence of behaviors I display from the time I awake until I finish breakfast, were repeated many times. As a result, distinctive patterns of neurons now fire when I am in the bedroom, on the stairs, in the kitchen, and during each of the actions in the sequence from waking to putting my coffee cup in the sink. Some neuroscientists rephrase the above description by writing that my hippocampal neurons code spatial and temporal relations.

A Nobel Prize was awarded in 2014 to John O'Keefe, who discovered neurons in the hippocampus of rats that display specific patterns when the animal is in a particular location in an alley in a room. There are two ways to describe this fact. O'Keefe, along with other scientists, concluded that these neurons registered the rat's spatial location in the alley. It is equally reasonable, however, to write that these neurons registered the pattern of visual, tactile, and olfactory features at that place because each change in location was accompanied by a different sensory pattern. This argument is supported by the fact that if the rat stands on his hind feet and looks up, but remains in exactly the same location, the neuronal activity changes.

The hippocampus of an American journalist who is captured by ISIS, blindfolded, and brought to a square room containing two pine tables and an upholstered chair for six months will develop a set of distinctive brain patterns to this scene. These brain patterns will be replaced with very different ones when he is transferred to a narrow room with one oak table and a single plastic chair two hundred miles away, even though neither he nor his brain knows the location of either room.

The main point of this discussion is that the meaning of every concept rests with its particular web of observations and premises. Neuroscientists who borrow terms from psychology or mathematics and apply them to brain profiles are changing the meanings of these words. The meaning of time in Einstein's theory of general relativity is contained in the equations of that theory. This meaning differs from the meaning of time in the sentence "The time between two successive heartbeats in most adults at rest ranges between

1.25 and 1.80 seconds" as well its meaning in the sentence "The estimated time between the Big Bang and the present is 13.7 billion years." I noted in the essay on words that the meaning of a word depends on the sentence in which it occurs. The meaning of a theoretical concept depends on the network in which it is embedded. The belief that a word has only one meaning is characteristic of young children learning their first language.

The Specificity of Brain-Mind Relations

The investigators searching for relations between brain patterns, on the one hand, and emotions, moral judgments, or psychiatric symptoms are not acknowledging that the psychological processes are far removed from the brain's functions. The evidence points to extremely specific relations between a brain state and a psychological outcome.

The case of a fifty-year-old man who suffered a stroke in the temporal and occipital lobes of the left hemisphere affirms this specificity. Alena Stasenko of the University of Rochester discovered that he could perceive and name the colors of a variety of manufactured objects, such as tools and cars, but had difficulty retrieving the names for the colors of select fruits and vegetables, even though he could perceive their color. That is, he could retrieve the correct color word when looking at a picture of a red car but not when he was looking at a red beet. This observation implies that the neurons at the site of the stroke mediated the ability to recall the color names of objects for which color is a distinctive feature: this fact applies to lemons, limes, beets, and broccoli but not cars, houses, dresses, or boxes.

Thomas Busigny of the Catholic University of Louvain described an equally specific deficit in a man with damage to the anterior part of the temporal lobe of the left hemisphere. This patient had difficulty retrieving the names of famous persons, even though he had no trouble describing their profession, gender, and nationality, and could name common objects. A name, like the yellow color of lemons, is a distinctive property of a person. As a result, there is a strong link between the picture of a familiar person and his or her name.

The task facing those who believe that one day measures of the brain will both predict and explain many psychological phenomena is daunting. Let us assume, as many do, that the pattern of firing in a network of connected neurons is the basic building block from which perceptions, acts, words, thoughts, and feelings emerge. The task is to translate a vocabulary for temporal changes in the level of activity in a network's neurons into a vocabulary that describes the goal of a motor action, meaning of a sentence, unpleasantness of a feeling, accuracy of a perception, intrusiveness of a thought, vividness of an image, remembering the first day at school, and the guilt over betraying a friend.

A concrete example may help readers appreciate how difficult it will be to understand the relations between the two vocabularies. The brain profile that allows me to see a streak of lightning began as an alteration in the shape of pigment cells in my retina which, in turn, generated electric impulses that were transferred in phases from the retina to the brain. Future scientists have to find a way to relate my perception of the lightning to the changes in the chemical structure of the pigment cells that occurred a fraction of a second earlier.

The twin principles that a particular brain state can be followed by more than one psychological outcome and that a particular psychological outcome can emerge from more than one brain profile apply equally well to the ten thousand neurons in the larvae of fruit flies and the estimated 86 billion neurons in the human brain. Some of the rare children who were born with minimal connections between the left and right hemispheres develop normal intellectual abilities. When these children solve a language problem they rely on a brain circuit that differs from the one used by normal children, even though both kinds of children arrive at the same answer. That is why Luiz Pessoa urges his neuroscientist colleagues to entertain the possibility of dissociations between the events of brain and those of mind.

Excitation and Inhibition

One reason why it is difficult to infer mental processes from brain measures is that the outcome of every brain profile is influenced by a blend of excitatory and inhibitory forces. The molecule glutamate usually excites neurons; the molecule GABA inhibits them. Therefore, a particular level of activity in the circuit that allows a person to reach for a piece of cake could be due to increased excitation of the circuit that accompanies the anticipation of a sweet taste or a decrease in the inhibitory forces that control the eating of too many sweet foods.

The central nucleus of the amygdala, which projects to the targets that produce the vigilance and sympathetic arousal that accompany fear, receives both excitatory and inhibitory inputs. Therefore, the brain pattern to a feared event, say, a dark alley in a city, could be due to increased excitation or decreased inhibition of this site in the amygdala.

Many scientists claim that activity in a site called the nucleus accumbens is the foundation of the state of "pleasure" that accompanies receipt of a rewarding event, say, a pellet of food, because animals with a damaged nucleus accumbens make no attempt to obtain food or sex when these rewards are available. Stan Floresco of the University of British Columbia offers a different interpretation of this fact that emphasizes the balance between excitatory and inhibitory influences within the accumbens. The neurons of the nucleus accumbens project to the motor centers that allow an animal to approach food or a sexual partner. In effect, these neurons connect to the motor sites that are necessary for implementing the action that leads to a rewarding experience. The inputs to the nucleus accumbens from many brain sites affect the balance between excitation and inhibition in the accumbens which, in turn, determines which action is likely to occur. Animals with a damaged accumbens fail to approach food or a mating partner because they have lost the neurons required for the appropriate behavior, whether striking a lever to receive a pellet of food or approaching a mate with the proper posture. This interpretation requires no assumptions about pleasure.

A major airport provides an analogy. The number of passengers arriving from and departing to various cities determines the actions that the employees at different terminals and gates display. The terminal receiving international flights requires customs officials; the gates associated with long flights require food vendors. No customs officials would be present and doing their tasks if the international terminal were damaged and not receiving passengers. But that fact does not imply that the customs officials enjoy performing their activities.

Michel de Montaigne understood that every source of pleasure contained a potential for harm if it was not regulated. "Moderation, above all" was one of his mantras. For reasons that are unclear, Western scholars have emphasized the excitatory forces over the inhibitory ones. This suggestion is supported by Google's archive of the differential prevalence of the members of select word pairs in books published in English between 1800 and 2000. *Forward* occurs more often than *backward*, *force* more than *resistance*, *gain* more than *lose*, *open* more than *closed*, *active* more than *passive*, and *go* more than *stop*.

The Need for Details

I have read a number of books by distinguished neuroscientists who have tried to make the leap from the certain facts about the brain, many based on studies of rats or mice who have fewer than 60 million neurons, to psychological phenomena in humans, whose brains at maturity have, on average, 86 billion neurons. Most of these texts follow a similar plan. The author first summarizes what has been learned about sensory and motor systems and, in the final chapters, proposes that these facts, when added to new ones yet to be discovered, will eventually account for all psychological events.

These authors fail to explain how these future victories will be attained. An author who writes that select neuronal collections represent a child's perception of a red ball on a carpet does not tell readers the brain events that allowed that perception. Collections of air and water molecules are the elements of a tornado, but that fact does not explain how a tornado emerges from the collection. Specifying the constituents of a phenomenon does not explain how it is formed. The recipes in a cookbook are silent on the details of the processes that occur when the ingredients combine under heat to produce the final product. That is why I am skeptical of Michio Kaku's bold prediction that one day a woman will record on a disc the activity of her brain during her seven-day honeymoon so that, years later, her daughter can reexperience the pleasures of that interlude by playing the disc and receiving the signals her mother's brain produced.

Asking the Right Question

Every scientist knows that posing the right question is a critical requirement for an important discovery. Finding the brain patterns that represent the perception of six vertical black lines on a white background moving from left to right is a good question. Finding the brain pattern that corresponds to the thoughts of adults watching the opening ten minutes of the 2012 film *Argo* is not. An example of the sharp disagreements over the most fruitful questions is seen in papers by two sophisticated neuroscientists. Ralph Adolphs of the California Institute of Technology believes that discovering how neurons compute is a pressing question. Moshe Gur of the Israel Institute of Technology, who rejects the computer as an inappropriate model for neurons, argues that the verb *compute* should not be used in sentences in which neurons are the noun.

Although this essay urges scientists to acknowledge the power of thought, many reliable brain-action relations do not involve thought. Infants display many actions that represent relatively fixed properties of the brain. Neurons in the visual cortex respond to the changes in illumination that define a boundary, such as a thick black line on a white background, leading newborns to automatically focus their eyes on such lines. The brain contains specialized neurons that respond to movement, and infants as well as adults automatically direct their gaze toward a moving object. Other neurons are selectively responsive to curvature, and infants look longer at curved designs than at those composed of straight lines.

The brain is also prepared to link events from different sensory modalities that share a sensory property. Intensity is an example, for the brain treats a tone increasing in loudness as similar to a light increasing in brightness. It also links similar temporal and spatial patterns. For example, the brain treats a pattern of three tones in which the first two are a quarter-second apart and the third tone occurs a second later as sharing a property with a pattern of three circles in which two are close to each other and the third is two inches from this pair.

The punctate nature of an event, meaning the speed with which it reaches peak intensity, is another property the brain is prepared to respond to in a special way. A scream, the taste of pepper, the onset of a bright light, and the smell of sulfur are punctate experiences. The sound of a breeze blowing through the leaves of a tree, the taste of a banana, the light of a full moon falling on a lawn, and the smell of an autumn forest reach peak intensity more slowly and are regarded as gradual events.

The Meaning of Blood Flow

Most conclusions about the relations between brain activity and psychological outcomes in humans are based on only one measure of neuronal activity, called the BOLD signal, that reflects the pattern of blood flow in the brain of a person lying supine in a magnetic scanner. The BOLD signal is the product of the different rates of decay in the magnetic fields of oxygenated and deoxygenated hemoglobin following an event that generated a surge of blood to the brain. Because the BOLD signal is an indirect index of neuronal activity, it is useful to consider the many factors that influence this popular measure.

The brain state implied by blood flow to the event scientists present to their subjects, called state E, is influenced by the person's usual brain state (state U), which varies with his or her mood, mental set, and brain physiology at the time. The latter property can vary with the time of year. Megan Miller and colleagues at the University of Pittsburgh discovered that the volume of the hippocampus is slightly larger in the summer, when there are many hours of sunlight, than the winter. The density of the receptors for the molecule serotonin, which influences neuronal excitability, also varies with the hours of sunlight. Male embryos conceived in early spring, when the hours of sunlight are increasing, experience a larger than normal surge of testosterone during the summer when the hours of daylight are the longest. One consequence of this fact is a greater slowing of the growth of the left hemisphere. Most neuroscientists do not worry about the effect on blood flow of a subject's month of birth or the season of the year when they were assessed.

Participants who are unusually anxious over the prospect of having their brain measured are apt to secrete one or more molecules that affect the blood flow pattern. Esther Keulers and colleagues at Maastricht University found that adolescents who secreted cortisol prior to being placed in the scanner, perhaps because they were anxious, showed less blood flow to certain sites. The more than 100 trillion microbes that occupy the human gut secrete a variety of molecules that influence a person's brain state. Future neuroscientists studying blood flow may decide to gather information on each person's cortisol level and gut bacteria in order to better understand their results.

Each participant's guess about the purpose of the study affects the brain response. For examples, subjects who assumed that the scientist was evaluating their intelligence by having them read words varying in emotionality would activate brain sites that might not correspond to the sites activated by subjects who thought the experimenter was interested in assessing their mental health.

State E, which incorporates state U, is also sensitive to the context of an incentive event. Every neuroscientist knows that the brain integrates information from a circuit that registers the identity of an object with information from another circuit that registers where in space the object is located. Nonetheless, scientists often present adults with an angry or a fearful face that is devoid of any background and assume that the brain's reaction to this unusual stimulus would resemble the reaction that would occur if the same person encountered a stranger on the street with an angry or fearful face. This assumption is probably incorrect. Brains do not react to faces with angry expressions. Rather, brains respond to an unfamiliar (or familiar) male (or female) face with an angry expression in a photograph that lacks a background while their owners are lying in a magnetic scanner in a laboratory. The resulting pattern of blood flow is unlikely to resemble the pattern that would occur if the same person saw a friend assume an angry expression while both of them were sitting at a table in a restaurant. Many paragraphs in books would be confusing to a reader who did not know the context of the material. That is why Daniel Ames of Princeton University found that two brain sites showed more similar activations to an ambiguous narrative when the adults had seen a picture that specified the context of the sentences.

Equally important, the physical features of an event, independent of its meaning, are the bases for the brain's initial reaction to every event. These features include the contours, colors, patterns of light and dark of varied objects, number of objects in a scene, pitch and loudness of sounds, smoothness of textures, and sweetness, saltiness, bitterness, or sourness of tastes.

Most neuroscientists ignore the fact that the subject's eyes make small, reflexive movements, called saccades, to the salient features in a scene. Scenes with more salient features evoke more saccades. These small eye movements are mediated by a circuit that includes a site in the parietal cortex (called the lateral intraparietal cortex). Hence, there will be increased blood flow to this site whenever subjects make many scans of a scene, independent of the scene's meaning. Faces and tall buildings evoke primarily vertical saccades; houses and meadows provoke horizontal saccades. The direction of the saccades can influence the pattern of brain activity in ways that have nothing to do with the category to which the object belongs. Roger Tootell and colleagues at Harvard Medical School discovered that a site called the parahippocampal place area is sensitive to the presence of right angles in a scene. This feature is common because many objects—trees, standing lamps, and flagpoles—form a right angle with the earth's flat surface.

Most adults devote the most attention to the eyes of fearful faces but the mouth area of happy faces. The eyes possess a degree of contour contrast between the dark pupil and the white sclera that is far less for the mouth area. Because select neurons in the amygdala are activated by the eye's contour contrast, the blood flow to the amygdala in subjects looking at fearful faces reflects, in part, the fact that the amygdala as well as other brain sites are especially responsive to this physical feature. Indeed, the amygdala is equally responsive to a pair of eyes, without any other facial elements, that display the enlarged sclera of a fearful face. These observations imply that the enhanced contrast between the larger sclera and pupil, not the subject's emotional state, is a critical cause of amygdala activation to fearful faces.

Jonathan Freeman of New York University and his colleagues failed to acknowledge the influence of the shape of the mouth in photographs of faces when they claimed that the amygdala can detect the "trustworthiness" of a face. The lips in most of the faces the subjects judged untrustworthy were turned down, as they would be in a frown. None of the "trustworthy" faces contained this feature. Hence, the difference in amygdalar activity was probably reflecting the brain's response to the different mouth contours, not the trustworthiness of the face! I assume these investigators would not conclude that the amygdala, or any brain site, could detect the difference between Christianity and Islam if they found that pictures of churches and mosques evoked different patterns of blood flow

Because most scientists present pictures of single objects without a background, an event that rarely occurs in everyday experience, many participants try to name the object. This mental set activates sites that mediate language, which belong to a circuit called the ventral stream. By contrast, there are many occasions in the home or at work when the person wants to know where an object is or how it is used. This mental set activates a circuit in the dorsal stream. A person looking at a picture of a hammer without a context while lying in a scanner should display a large surge of blood flow to the ventral stream; whereas the surge of blood flow (if it could be measured) would be larger to the dorsal stream if the same person were searching for a hammer and found it lying in a drawer. I might be uncertain whether the small object on my arm is a mosquito or a bee, but the speed and accuracy of my slapping it are affected by my brain's ability to specify its location, not by my uncertainty over its identity.

A person's confidence about what he or she saw or heard affects brain activity, independent of the event's meaning. Individuals looking at a face with wide-open eyes and mouth but no information about the person's posture or the setting are often not sure whether the face reflects fear or surprise. A person who is unsure of the correct emotion invests mental effort which, in turn, increases blood flow to varied sites.

E. M. Aminoff of Carnegie Mellon University provides stunning support for this last suggestion. Adults who were unsure whether they had seen a particular face or word that might have been presented earlier showed greater blood flow to both the prefrontal and parietal cortex than when they were confident. This observation implies that the surges of blood flow were measuring the mental effort the subjects expended in order to avoid making a mistake rather than the memorial processes involved in retrieving the face or word. Uncertainty over the identity of an event usually generates more blood flow than the confident perception of the same event.

State E is always affected by the person's expectation of what he or she might see, hear, smell, or taste because the patterns of activity to unexpected events, especially if they are unfamiliar, differ from the patterns shown to familiar or expected ones. The former are typically accompanied by increased blood flow to the amygdala. Obviously, expectations are affected by the individual's life history. Jasmin Cloutier of the University of Chicago, with colleagues, found that white adults who had frequent exposure to black children during their childhood showed less amygdala activation to black faces than whites who had rarely interacted with black children.

Manuel Calvo of the University of La Laguna in Spain asked students to record the occurrence of different facial expressions in the places they visited over a ninety-day period. Happy faces, usually accompanied by a smile, had the highest frequency; fearful faces, with wide eyes and an open mouth, had the lowest. It is likely that smiling faces are more common than fearful faces in most communities. Because a face with a fearful expression is unexpected, it usually evokes increased blood flow to the amygdala. This activation reflects surprise rather than fear.

Because most investigators do not tell participants what they are going to see or hear and because unpleasant events are generally less frequent than pleasant or neutral ones, subjects are more likely to be surprised by unpleasant than by pleasant events. That is why investigators usually find greater blood flow to the amygdala in response to pictures of bloodied bodies, revolvers, and dangerous animals than to scenes of babies, toys, and food.

When adults know they are going to see unpleasant pictures they show reduced activation of the amygdala. Even mice show less activation of the amygdala in reaction to an expected electric shock than to one that is unexpected. Many events called rewards—a film, vacation, or book that is more satisfying than the person anticipated—are unexpected experiences. Some brain sites that are responsive to rewarding events also respond to unexpected ones. Because scientists cannot know all the expectations of the persons whose brains they measure, they cannot always be certain of the meaning of the pattern of activity they record.

The automatic associations evoked by an event generate a brain state, called A for associations, that follows the initial response. Seeing a wineglass, cell phone, or pineapple activates sites that register tactile input because of the acquired associations between the sight of these objects and holding them. The experimenter's instructions can bias a person's associations. A team of French scientists measured the pattern of blood flow prompted by four different odors, each preceded by slightly different verbal descriptions. The examiner told the participants either the source of the odor ("This smell comes from a peach") or where the odor was used ("This smell is used in body lotion"). The same odor generated different blood flow patterns depending on which instructions were given. Elizabeth Musz of the University of Pennsylvania found that words that are read or heard frequently, such as *cup* or *bench*, generate a larger number of associations, and more varied patterns of blood flow, than words that are heard or read infrequently, such as *asparagus* or *binoculars*. This fact implies that blood flow in response to a common event might reflect the number and variety of the associations to a picture, sound, smell, or word.

This phenomenon poses a problem for the correct interpretation of the blood flow profile evoked by the face of a famous movie star because the face typically activates associations to scenes from the actor's films. As a result, the scenes cause increased blood flow to sites that have nothing to do with the actor's face. Scenes that have strong associations with an unpleasant emotion, especially fear, sadness, or anger, generate stronger activation of the right hemisphere and, therefore, a bias to look toward the left. The left side of the face is more revealing of an unpleasant emotion than the right because the muscles of the left cheek and mouth are controlled by the right hemisphere.

Art critics have noted that premodern European painters were more likely to show the left side of the face rather than the right when the person depicted was sad, angry, anxious, or in pain. Lealani Acosta of Vanderbilt University, with colleagues, found that most paintings (86 percent) of the Crucifixion showed the left rather than the right side of Christ's face. By contrast, only 49 percent of the paintings of the Resurrection showed the left side of his face.

The Basis for Inference

The brain state that is the usual basis of the scientist's inference about a person's psychological state, called F for final, is the pattern of blood flow to a variety of sites recorded about six seconds after the event of interest appeared. This long delay poses a problem because the brain responds to a human face in less than a quarter of a second, more than five seconds before state F is measured. This means that state F is the result of a cascade of prior events, including states U, E, and A, which varies among persons. If state F were preceded by only two different states, scientists brooding on the average state F in one hundred adults could not know the pattern of prior activity that was responsible for the outcome they recorded.

The foundation of a perception, feeling, or thought is the timing of the firing of many neurons composing a network. State F does not reveal the pattern of timing. State F is analogous to the average pitch and loudness of all the notes that occur during the first six seconds of a song. If Gyorgy Buzsaki of New York University cannot understand the relation between activity in two connected sites within the hippocampus of a mouse, despite having precise, direct measurements of neuronal activity in each site, it seems unlikely that scientists examining state F across the entire hippocampus can be certain of their inferences.

State F invites more than one inference when a site that does not make an important contribution to a psychological outcome happens to receive a large surge of blood flow because it is the recipient of inputs from many sites that are important for the outcome. For example, sites in the visual cortex are always activated when subjects read obscene words or see disgusting scenes, even though the activity in the visual cortex is not the basis for an emotional reaction to the words or scenes. An observer who knew nothing about the movements that were essential for walking might conclude that the motions of the arms and head were necessary for forward locomotion. On the other hand, a site that does make a significant contribution to an outcome may not receive a large surge of blood flow simply because it has fewer neurons than the sites to which it sends information.

Other problems trail the inferences based on state F. If a site that contributes to a psychological outcome happens to be close to a vein, the BOLD measure will be larger than if an equally relevant site were located away from a vein and near an artery. The reason is that the BOLD signal is based on a change in the concentration of the molecule deoxyhemoglobin, which is greater in veins than in arteries.

A person's usual heart rate is a factor because each time the heart beats a surge of blood is sent to the brain. A person whose average heart rate is one hundred beats per minute will send a surge of blood to many sites, including the amygdala, six thousand times each hour, compared with only forty-two hundred surges for someone with a heart rate of seventy beats per minute. Because the amygdala projects to sites that generate feelings often interpreted as anxiety or fear, those with a higher heart rate should be more vulnerable to these feelings.

Heart rate variability, which is regulated by the balance between activity in the sympathetic and parasympathetic nervous systems, also affects state F. The sympathetic system constricts the brain's blood vessels, leading to a higher, less variable heart rate and less blood flow; the parasympathetic system dilates the vessels, leading to a lower, more variable heart rate and more blood flow. Although some individuals show large surges of blood flow simply because they inherited a dominant parasympathetic system, most investigators ignore this contribution to state F.

Because blood is always flowing to all parts of the brain, investigators have to subtract the blood flow that occurred to an event of interest from the flow during some prior state, called the baseline state. This requirement poses a problem when a site that contributes to a significant psychological outcome also received a lot of blood during the baseline state. Under these conditions the relevant site might not show a significant increase in blood flow. Consider an analogy. If scientists treated muscle activity in the legs during walking as a baseline condition and subtracted this value from the muscle activity when the same person was playing golf, they might conclude that the legs made no contribution to playing golf.

Because all conclusions about the meaning of state F are dependent on the baseline state chosen, the choice of baseline takes on significance. For example, at least eight different conclusions could be drawn from increased blood flow to an angry male face if the baseline event is a male or a female face showing happiness, fear, disgust, or a neutral expression. Conclusions about the weight of twenty-year-olds provides an analogy. If we subtracted the weight of one hundred children (the baseline) from the weight of one hundred twenty-year-olds, we would conclude that the adults are heavier. But if we subtracted the weight of the twenty-year-olds from one hundred sixty-year-olds, we would conclude that the twenty-year-olds are lighter.

The person's posture in the scanner poses a potential problem because participants are required to lie on their back. The brain's physiology in this unusual posture differs from the physiology recorded when individuals are standing upright or sitting. The additional requirement to lie perfectly still activates the cerebellum, whose projections to many cortical sites can enhance or suppress activity in that site. It is useful to repeat Niels Bohr's insight that the features of the setting in which evidence is gathered are essential components of the cascade that produces the observations.

Three additional facts exacerbate the frustrations of those who rely on blood flow to measure brain activity. Studies that find a significant relation between a brain profile and a psychological process are more likely to be published than those that find nothing or uncover evidence inconsistent with published results.

The BOLD signal is influenced by the activity of brain cells called astrocytes, whose filaments wrap around the neuron and its blood supply. Vincent Schmithorst of the Cincinnati Children's Hospital, with colleagues, found that this influence on the BOLD signal increases from childhood through adolescence. This means that the greater blood flow to cognitive tasks in older compared with younger children could be partly due to the greater coupling of astrocytes and neurons.

Finally, scientists base their inferences on the blood flow to a collection of tiny sites, one millimeter on each side, called voxels. The size of the collection usually ranges from several hundred to several thousand voxels. Investigators have to decide which of the large number of collections that received a surge of blood made the critical contributions to the outcome they cared about and which can be ignored. This decision is made with the understanding that most collections contribute to more than one psychological outcome. This assignment resembles the challenge of figuring out the form of Leonardo da Vinci's *Mona Lisa* from a scrambled collection of thousands of one-millimeter squares cut from the painting.

The many influences on blood flow imply that this measure may be unable to detect every psychological product. Aesthetic judgments may belong to this category. Adults were asked to categorize scenes of beaches, city streets, forests, highways, mountains, and offices as either aesthetically good or bad examples of the category. A good image of a highway is a long stretch of open road receding into the distance. Although the participants showed excellent agreement in their conscious judgments of good and bad scenes, the blood flow patterns to relevant brain sites (the visual and parahippocampal cortex) distinguished between good and bad scenes only about 25 percent of the time.

Blood flow patterns also fail to provide a sensitive measure of a person's moral beliefs or related emotions. Adults read one set of vignettes describing immoral actions, for example, acts of dishonesty as well as behaviors that harmed another, and a second set of neutral vignettes. Although the BOLD signals to the two kinds of vignette differed, the blood flow profiles failed to distinguish between the immoral narratives that a person judged as wrong and the immoral acts judged to be acceptable. Apparently, the blood flow patterns were measuring each person's associations to the immoral vignettes rather than his or her evaluation of or emotional reaction to the behaviors described.

Neuroscientists should be troubled by a study finding that the blood flow profiles in adults watching films of 1,705 different objects or actions failed to reveal any evidence that the subjects were activating networks for the antonym pair good-bad. This result is surprising because children and adults from all cultures regularly activate the semantic networks for these terms, sometimes outside consciousness, to most events. Although the mind is always primed to categorize an experience as good or bad, this universal habit escapes being detected with blood flow measures.

Some thoughts about the self may also lie outside the reach of blood flow evidence. German scientists recorded blood flow in an eminent opera singer while she was listening to recordings of her own voice compared with the voice of another talented woman singing the same songs. The only differences between the two conditions involved blood flow to sites that are not regarded as major contributors to self-awareness (the cerebellum, visual cortex, and thalamus).

The evidence and arguments in this essay invite the conclusion that a complete understanding of brain is not synonymous with a full understanding of mind. Martha Farah, a sophisticated psychologist who appreciates the problems surrounding the meaning of blood flow, is more optimistic than I about the contributions this method has made and will make. I hope she is right.

Biology Is the Better Model

Scientists who study the relation between brain and mind have been too admiring of physics and its assumption that all observations can, in principle, be reduced to material things and forces. Unlike inanimate matter, which preserves its defining features indefinitely, life-forms change. The properties of oxygen have not changed since this atom appeared billions of years ago. The genomes, anatomies, and physiologies of insects, fish, lizard, birds, and mammals, however, have changed over a much shorter interval.

The elegant mathematics that describe physical phenomena are impotent when faced with most biological phenomena. The developmental relation between changes in brain and acquisition of knowledge, for example, is counterintuitive. As children learn new skills and facts, their brains lose more synapses than they gain. It is as if the Wikipedia Web site began with several trillion randomly arranged letters and each time someone added information about a topic some letters were deleted until the contemporary set of meaningful Web pages appeared.

Biological phenomena are replete with exceptions that frustrate investigators searching for general principles that apply across species and ecologies. Chimpanzees are social but their close relatives the orangutans are not; geese pair-bond but hawks do not. The extreme particularity of biological phenomena is in sharp contrast to the broad generality of physical laws, such as E = mc². Scientists who study the relation between brain and behavior should take Niels Bohr rather than Albert Einstein as a model. Even though Bohr was a physicist, he recognized the need to tolerate ambiguity, accept the principle that we can be certain only of what the evidence reveals, and to appreciate that all inferences from evidence depend on the procedure used and the setting in which data were gathered.

At the moment the sentences that might bridge the yawning gap between what is happening in the brain and what is happening in its emergent product, the mind, have not been invented. This gap will be narrowed in the future. Karl Deisseroth and others have discovered a method that allows more accurate measurement of neuronal activity than blood flow. Briefly, these investigators attach a gene whose protein product responds to the light of a given frequency to a virus and inject this unit into individual neurons. If light of the proper frequency is shone on these neurons, they become active and this activity can be measured.

Although this elegant method will illuminate our understanding of many puzzles, I suspect that the gap between brain and mind cannot be closed completely for the same reason that the words *roll, slice,* and *cook* will never be replaced with words that describe the properties of the atoms that compose the instruments performing these actions. The verbs *know, perceive, regulate, remember, feel, plan, compute, judge, act,* and *understand* require a person or animal, not a brain site, as the noun.

Yes, the brain is the foundation of all psychological phenomena, as the sun is the foundation of all life on earth. Biologists accept the sun's significance and proceed to fill in the details that might explain how cells divide and embryos grow without ever mentioning the sun. Neuroscientists have to do more than write that thoughts, feelings, and actions originate in a brain. They have to explain how my brain generated the perception of many points of moving light on a section of sea lit by a full moon on a cloudless night.

Neuroscientists have to acknowledge that, on occasion, the brain is only one element in a cascade that includes the immune system, gut, hormones, transmitters, and outside events. Although most investigators emphasize the action of the molecule serotonin in the brain, 95 percent of the body's serotonin is secreted by the gut and only 5 percent by the brain. One of serotonin's many effects is to relax the muscles of the intestine, which facilitates regularity. This fact implies that perhaps the reports of a better mood by depressed patients who are taking Prozac or Fluoxetine, drugs that prolong the activity of serotonin, might be partly due to the fact that they are no longer constipated.

A bout of depression in a forty-year-old woman could have its origin in an immune response to a flu infection which activated brain sites that, in turn, provoked a fatigue the woman interpreted as depression because she was feeling guilty over not doing more to help her daughter cope with a drug addiction. In this scenario, the brain is one element in a cascade that began with a bout of the flu. There will be many surprises in the attempts to pinpoint the correspondences between brain and mind.

A joke invites a bit more humility among those who believe that one day all mental phenomena will be explained by brain activity. The rabbi of Krakow interrupted his sermon to tell the congregation he had just had a vision that the rabbi of Warsaw had died moments earlier. The congregation was duly impressed with the rabbi's remarkable powers. Several weeks later a few Krakow residents visiting Warsaw saw that the rabbi there was alive and reported this fact to their friends when they returned home. When some Krakow Jews began to snicker about their rabbi's error, his ardent defenders noted that although his prophecy might have been wrong, one must admit that it was a marvelous vision.

The Family's Contribution

When a social arrangement survives across several hundred generations in varied cultures, it is likely that biological processes are contributing to its preservation. Although political, economic, judicial, and educational institutions have undergone major changes over the past ten thousand years, the family, until recently composed of a man, a woman, and their children, remains the fundamental unit in at least 80 percent of human societies, compared with fewer than 25 percent of nonhuman primate species.

The Conditions Favoring a Family

At least three conditions contribute to the persistence of the family as a fundamental legal and social unit. The most obvious is that infants cannot survive without adult care. This brute fact means that every society must decide who is responsible for rearing the young child. A society could assign this task to the entire community, the birth mother, her relatives, or hired caretakers, which is the choice of those living on Israeli kibbutzim. Because humans are biased to assign responsibility for an outcome to its cause, most societies award the burden of care to the couple who conceived or adopted the child.

A strong sense of possession, present as early as the second birthday, renders adults resistant to sharing a source of pleasure with a stranger. Contemporary Israeli mothers living on a kibbutz have become more reluctant than earlier generations to leave all the daily care of their children to hired caretakers. Even two-year-olds complain when another child seizes one of their toys.

Most individuals regard their partner's sexual favors as a valued possession not to be shared with others. One of the rare exceptions to this rule is found in some regions of Nigeria where young unmarried men are allowed to sleep with the wife of a member of the same family. This practice has the advantage of reducing the likelihood that a young man will disrupt community harmony by having sex with a woman from a different family.

The effort required to maintain a household with children is a heavy burden for one person without relatives living nearby or the resources to hire servants. Hence, an arrangement in which two people share the tasks is attractive. These three facts help to explain the robustness of the family as a social arrangement.

Historical Changes

The medieval church enhanced a European woman's position in marriage by declaring that no woman should be forced to marry a man she did not desire. The empowerment of women, which surged in Europe and North America following industrialization, gradually diluted an earlier complementarity between married partners. The eighteenth-century man who married believed he was gaining the gentleness and innocence of a woman. In taking a husband, the woman assumed she had gained protection from the competitive harshness of the world of work as well as the possibility of a vicarious pride in her husband's status and worldliness. Each member of the dyad enjoyed the belief that each had obtained a desired resource that they lacked. These complementary gratifications are missing from many contemporary marriages in which both partners are educated, hold interesting, high-paying jobs, and have personal sexual histories. A professional woman does not need her husband's status; her husband is deprived of a woman's gentle innocence. This state of affairs leaves companionship, sexual pleasures, and children as the glue holding the pair together.

When the ideal of an egalitarian marriage was wedded to the technological advances that brought cars, electric appliances, telephones, laundries, frozen foods, takeout meals, and supermarkets, the burden of maintaining a home with one or two children became manageable and each partner recognized that he or she could, if necessary, survive without a spouse. With that recognition came the freedom to ask whether one was "happy" in the marriage. If the private answer was no, one might entertain dissolving the marital bond. It is not a coincidence that the divorce rate is highest in the United States, Denmark, and the United Kingdom, countries in which women enjoy equal rights with men. Latin American countries, which allow men to dominate women, have lower rates.

Despite the homogenizing effect of an information technology that unites the world, a number of European nations retain a few features of family life that distinguish them from their neighbors. France celebrates the family more than Britain; Italy is distinguished by an unusually intense relation between a mother and her son; Scandinavians tolerate the state's intrusion into family life; and Spain continues to promote a hierarchical family with the husband as its head.

The social pressure to marry and establish a family is weaker in 2015 than it was in the past. The decline in the attractiveness of marriage is due partly to the fact that unmarried adults in many communities are no longer marginalized. More important, many young adults have raised the bar on the satisfactions that a marital bond ought to provide. Most twenty-five-year-olds expect more pleasure from a marriage than their grandparents and therefore are more easily frustrated by any deficiency in a partner.

More recent Hollywood films depicting unhappy couples support a skeptical attitude toward marital bliss. *The War of the Roses* and *Who's Afraid of Virginia Woolf?* are examples. A pair of sociologists who studied a typical midwestern American town in the 1920s found a far more idealistic view of marriage.

A Trio of Challenges

There are at least three additional sources of unhappiness in contemporary marriages in developed societies. The first involves envy. The partners in many dyads were equally accomplished the day they married, but a decade later one partner holds a higher-status job, has more friends, or enjoys greater community respect. This asymmetry, which rubs against the ideal of equality, occasionally provokes resentment toward the more accomplished partner. This feeling, if maintained, is followed by guilt over a jealousy or anger that the envious partner cannot justify. As a result, the spouse attempts to dilute the guilt through excessive demands, frequent criticisms, or bursts of undisguised hostility in the hope of provoking a retaliation that would rationalize the unreasonable behavior toward the partner.

The novel *The Kite Runner* captures this dynamic in the relation between Amir and Hassan, two boys who have been close friends for years. Amir is dealing with a corrosive guilt brought on by his failure to rescue Hassan from a harsh attack by several older boys. Amir tries to dilute his guilt by pummeling Hassan's face with pomegranates and demanding a retaliation. Hassan frustrates his friend by doing nothing, which only serves to exacerbate Amir's guilt.

Although the unique pleasures of sexual intimacies potentiate the marital bond, these pleasures have assumed a prominence over the past forty years that makes it easy for one or both partners to become dissatisfied with the sexual gratification the other provides. This belief is the basis of a second threat to contemporary marriages. A number of novels, films, television dramas, and documentaries imply, or on occasion suggest explicitly, that a marriage ought to dissolve if the partners do not enjoy mutual orgasms on a regular schedule. In the film *House of Sand and Fog* a middle-aged husband says to his wife after sexual intimacy, "We are blessed." Shereen El Feki in *Sex and the Citadel* describes contemporary Egyptian women who worry continually over their ability to satisfy their husbands and married men who have been persuaded that a certain number of orgasms each day is necessary for optimal health.

Pascal Bruckner writes in *Has Marriage for Love Failed?* that "we expect everything from love which has become the secular form of salvation." If men and women adopted an equally high standard for food, no one would eat at McDonald's. A column by Gretchen Reynolds in the June 26, 2015, issue of the *New York Times* devoted to the relation between the frequency of marital sex and happiness revealed that even scientists have been persuaded of the possible truth of this relation. The social scientists who asked married couples to increase their sexual encounters found out what they should have known. No, more sex does not make people happier.

I could not suppress a laugh while reading an essay in the February 6, 2014, issue of the *New York Times* in which the author warned couples in an egalitarian marriage that they were probably experiencing 1.5 fewer sexual intimacies each month, compared with husbands and wives in less egalitarian marriages. I wondered whether this author would warn youths who study for examinations rather than party with friends that they will miss 1.8 pizzas and 2.3 beers each month. The suggestion that an extra 1.5 orgasms per month trumps the pleasure derived from an egalitarian relationship reveals a view of sex that might surprise even Sigmund Freud.

Psychiatrists cooperated with the public's new assumption regarding the significance of sexual joy by treating weak sexual desire or an inability to have orgasms during most intimacies as signs of a mental illness. This decision, which transforms an invented community value into a disease, may have persuaded physically disabled adults that they, too, ought to enjoy frequent orgasms. Switzerland, Germany, and Denmark have legal sex surrogates who provide these pleasures for a fee, typically around $130. A number of nursing homes have set aside a special room that can be used for an hour or so by older residents who wish to be intimate. The caption of a *New Yorker* cartoon illustrating a secretary reading her boss a telephone message reads, "Your wife called to remind you not to have sex with anyone on your way home."

The conditions of contemporary life in developed societies, which place much of the responsibility for joyful moments on the marital bond, were conducive to making sexual pleasures an imperative. When history removed sources of pleasure outside the home, orgasms that blew both partners out of bed became a more significant feature of a stable marriage. Married men and women before the Second World War used to participate in a variety of recreations with same-sex friends. Weekly gatherings to play poker, bridge, mahjong, or attend meetings at the local Mason lodges or Jane Austen societies have vanished in many cities and towns, leaving the marriage to pick up the lost moments of joy through better and more frequent sex.

A cartoon in the May 2014 *New Yorker* titled "The Bluebird of Nothing-ness" illustrates a bluebird on a windowsill telling an older man lying in bed, "There is no essential self. The universe is silent. Man's condition is absurd." Anyone who reflected on this message, even briefly, might be tempted to adopt a philosophy of "Go for it now." If no metaphysical power is watching and neighbors do not care what one does, it seems foolish to deny the self what is advertised as life's greatest pleasure and supremely clever to get as much sex as possible before the gauge on the store of libidi-nal energy moves closer to empty.

A temptation to blame a partner for frustrations that originate in the workplace is a third contribution to the fragility of an unknown number of contemporary marriages. Family and work are the primary sources of gratification for a majority of adults in developed societies. Because it is hard to detect the difference between a feeling of frustration that arises in each setting, it is easy to attribute to the marriage a disappointment whose origin lies in the workplace. The unhappiness over work conditions cannot be changed; the frustrations of the marriage can—through separation or divorce.

The generation entering high school in the fall of 2015 may make a stronger commitment to marriage than their parents. As the proportion of divorced or unmarried adults rises, a successful marriage becomes a symbol of an accomplishment that can be a source of pride. Marriage promises to dilute the loneliness and mistrust that pervade modern societies. Equally important, the members of each generation are prone to blame their current angst on the practices of their parents, leading to a silent vow to do it differ-ently when it is their turn.

This dynamic may have begun. The divorce rate in America over the past ten years is slightly lower than the rate from 1970 to 1990, perhaps because well-educated women are marrying in their thirties rather than their twen-ties. If these trends continue, they will affirm the intuition that a sustained relationship between two adults with a child living under the same roof generates unique pleasures. The family is not about to disappear. Indeed, marriage may regain, at least for some, the sacramental properties the church endowed it with nine centuries earlier.

Family Effects on Children

Although few experts deny that parents exert a profound influence on their children, it is easy to find serious disagreements over the nature and magnitude of that influence. Early twentieth-century experts, influenced by behaviorism, told parents that their children's development depended primarily on the actions they rewarded and punished. Freud's writings persuaded American parents to award their children more autonomy and to replace physical punishments with threats of love withdrawal. John Bowlby's books on the significance of the attachment bond between infant and parent made parental love for the child as necessary as food and water.

The idea that a parent's love for a child—I prefer the verb *value* to *love*—trumps all other influences enjoys a remarkable degree of consensus across developed societies. Parental love, according to most experts, requires physical affection combined with behaviors that persuade children that their personhood is valued. A small number of middle-class parents treat each child as a prince or princess entitled to immediate satisfaction of every wish.

Young children understand the meanings of good and bad. Because things that are valued are also good, children want to believe they are valued. Western experts warn parents that if they fail to establish this belief early in their children's lives, they will suffer the consequences of an adolescent or adult who forms superficial friendships, abuses alcohol or drugs, is unable to love another, or develops anxiety, depression, or a criminal career.

A child's perception of his or her value depends on the interpretation of the parents' behaviors, rather than the action a camera would record. A $20 gift from a father who is unemployed is interpreted as an act of love. An afternoon outing has the same value for a child whose wealthy father works twelve-hour days and is rarely home on weekends.

About 140 million children in 2015 do not have at least one parent caring for them. Some are in institutions that provide neither intellectual stimulation nor signs of their value. Children can tolerate one or, at the most, two years of this form of rearing and still retain the ability to recover normal functioning if adopted by an affectionate family. Children who remain in these settings for more than two years find it difficult to erase the damage these compromising environments generated.

It is important to distinguish between the experience of spending the first two years in a depriving institution and being a victim of physical or sexual abuse in a family setting because children impose different interpretations on these experiences. Cathy Widom of the City University of New York found that adults who, as children, had been physically abused but not sexually abused or neglected were not more likely than others from the same social class to abuse their children. Parents are most likely to physically abuse a child when he or she disobeys them. Children who interpret the harsh punishment for disobedience as deserved, rather than as a sign of parental hostility, appear to escape serious emotional harm if most parents in that society are also harsh.

An equally benign interpretation is impossible when a parent sexually abuses a child because that act is interpreted as a betrayal of the parent's moral obligation. This conclusion is far more toxic to the child's sense of self than harsh punishments for misdemeanors. The main point is that the consequences of most parental practices are not determined by the specific actions but by the interpretation the child imposes on them.

Children growing up in seventeenth-century colonial New England experienced parental harshness that contemporary observers would classify as physical abuse. But because these behaviors were the dominant style in Puritan families, children did not interpret their parents' actions as reflecting hostility or rejection. The Mehinaku Indians of central Brazil indulge their infants but respond to an older child's disobedience by sloshing water on his legs and scarifying the calves and thighs with a fish-tooth scraper as the child screams in pain. Because this punishment is expected and perceived as just, these children do not become adults who are unduly aggressive or depressed.

Sir Peter Mansfield, a Nobel laureate in physiology, was a young child during the Blitz in London. His parents sent him away on two occasions to live with strangers in order to protect him from harm. Mansfield did not interpret these separations as implying parental rejection. The childhood memories of a prominent Japanese physician and novelist capture the importance of the child's interpretation. "My father was an awesome, fright-ening being. . . . When I overheard my father reprimand somebody . . . a cold shiver used to run down my spine . . . and yet he was truly a support as I grew up."

Of course, each child's temperamental biases have some influence on the consequences of parental behaviors. A fair number of infants inherit a temperament that protects them from crippling anxiety in response to harsh punishment, divorce, or other unpleasant experiences. Others are born with a biology that renders them especially vulnerable to an anxious reaction to the same experiences.

Variation in Rearing Practices

The anthropologists Robert and Sarah LeVine, who have spent their careers studying the extraordinary variation in parental practices across cultures, remind us that the dominant patterns of parental behavior in the contempo-rary United States and Europe are not replicated in most settings in Africa, South America, the Far East, India, or Indonesia because each cultural setting presents a special set of challenges. Parents living in rural Tanzania know that their children have to learn how to raise corn, wheat, and pigs and acquire the personality traits that are adaptive in a small, stable commu-nity if they want to gain economic security and respect from others. As a result, they implement socialization practices they believe will be most effective in establishing these properties.

American and European parents hold a different understanding of the traits their children need to acquire. Children must do well in school in order to gain admission to a good college where they will acquire the skills and values linked to success in contemporary technological societies. These requirements lead most middle-class parents to encourage a level of autonomy, language skills, and competitiveness that Kikuyu mothers living near Lake Victoria would regard as maladaptive. Gusii mothers of south-western Kenya see no need to talk to or praise their child and often tell a five- or six-year-old daughter to care for her infant sibling for most of the day. Psychologists who believe in the power of infant attachment would regard mothers who behaved this way as insensitive and assume their infants were insecurely attached.

Members of Western cultures often use the adjective *unresponsive* to describe a mother who does not praise or play with her child. But all children do not interpret the absence of praise or play as implying a lack of parental interest in their development. The absence of praise or reciprocal play is a risk factor for an undesirable outcome only in societies where children interpret these behaviors as indifference. The important point is that there are no parental actions, excluding sexual abuse or extreme neglect, that have the same effect on all children independent of the meaning imposed on them. The consequences of what parents do must be viewed against a background of the cultural premises in which they occur. Most parents do what they believe is in the best interest of their child.

The Significance of Identifications

A child's pattern of identifications represents a different but equally significant influence on development. Young children cannot help but recognize some similarities between their own features and those of one or both parents. They notice the same last name as well as similar skin color and select features of face or body. Some older children learn about the unusual accomplishments of present or past family members. Although they know little or nothing about genes, children sense that they share a material essence with those who conceived them. This belief in invisible essences comes easily to children. That is why they insist that a dog who lost its tail, ears, and four legs would still be a dog. The less than conscious premise that the biologically related members of a family share fundamental properties expands, in time, to become the conscious realization that the child is a member of a unique category.

Once this belief is in place, most children go one step further and entertain the less rational notion that perhaps they possess some traits of a family member for which objective evidence is lacking. A girl who notices that her mother becomes frightened when she sees a mouse assumes that she, too, may possess the same propensity. A girl who knows that her mother is well liked by her friends toys with the notion that she, too, is likely to be popular with her peers.

Amos Oz, a celebrated Israeli writer, remembers the day his father, also a respected writer, told his six-year-old son he could place his childhood books on the shelf holding the father's volumes. This sharing of a distinctive feature with a parent who regarded books as sacred objects contributed to the boy's inference that perhaps he, too, had the talent to become a great writer. Marcia Davenport's identification with her mother, the famous singer Alma Gluck, tempted the daughter to assume she had special talents that would bring her a measure of fame. The self-confidence her identification bred allowed Marcia, at age twenty-seven, to decide to write a biography of Mozart without any knowledge of German or the technical details of musical composition.

The belief that one shares distinctive features with another is usually, but not always, accompanied by a vicarious emotion, typically pride or shame, when the person with whom the features are shared has a particular experience. A child is said to be identified with a person or a group when the experience of vicarious emotions is added to the recognition that one shares distinctive features with another. Both conditions must be satisfied. A girl knows she shares features with other females but she may not experience a vicarious emotion when a female wins a Nobel Prize or is accused of multiple murders.

Marcia Davenport felt vicarious pride when her mother was praised for her singing because she assumed that others would regard her as belonging to the same category as her parent. Vicarious pride often protects children from high-achieving or elite families from the debilitating anxiety that accompanies a rejecting or harsh childhood. Winston Churchill suffered from parental indifference, John Maynard Keynes from a harsh socialization. One reason neither was defeated by these experiences is, I suggest, due to their identification with an elite British family.

A few families that maintain an elite status over many generations have an uncommon surname that makes it easier for the children of successive generations to identify with their family pedigree. Gregory Clark notes in *The Son Also Rises* that the surname Gyllenstjerna in Sweden and Gu in

China are uncommon names whose members enjoyed an elite position for more than three hundred years. Rockefeller and Roosevelt are uncommon names in the United States, and many members of these two families attained positions of importance during the twentieth century.

Vicarious shame occurs when a family member has violated an ethical norm and the child assumes that others will judge him as they judge the family member. Alice Munro, who won the 2013 Nobel Prize in literature, told an interviewer that she was ashamed to be with her mother in public because the parent had Parkinson's disease. It is possible that young Osama bin Laden felt vicarious shame when his mother, one of the father's many wives, suffered the stigma of a divorce. The boy's shame may have blended with anger when his mother remarried and young Osama felt marginalized in his new home with many siblings who were the natural offspring of his stepfather.

The occurrence of vicarious pride or shame with a group depends on the child's understanding of the community's evaluation of that group. Pride is likely if the group enjoys a reputation for possessing praiseworthy features. If the group's features are undesirable, vicarious shame will be the dominant emotion. Members of a respected ethnic or religious group are protected from shame when another member misbehaves. Buddhists, a respected minority in America, are unlikely to feel to vicarious shame when a Buddhist behaves inappropriately. Mexican society used to hold an unfavorable view of its Indian citizens, leading Indian children to hide their ethnicity. When Mexicans became more tolerant of Indians, more of these children experienced vicarious pride in their ethnic heritage.

The strength of an identification with a family, ethnic, religious, or national group always depends on the distinctiveness of the group's features. Asian Americans who were born and live in Hawaii represent the majority ethnic group; Asian Americans who grew up in California are a minority. The latter appear to have a stronger identification with their ethnic group than the former because they are more distinctive in their setting.

Turkish Muslims who emigrated to Germany experience more intense prejudice than Turkish Muslims who chose to live in the Netherlands. As a result, the Muslims in Germany possess a stronger identification with their religion and a weaker identification with their adopted nation. Stanley Lieberson of Harvard University discovered that soon after the passing of civil rights legislation in the 1960s, African American parents began to give their children distinctive names, such as Rasha and Kareem, presumably to enhance an identification with their ethnic group.

Members of a vocation possessing distinctive features that the community views as praiseworthy usually develop an identification with the category that generates vicarious pride. Many Americans who are paid firefighters, rather than volunteers, possess such an identification because they represent a small proportion of the workforce, often have a parent or grandparent who chose the same career, put their lives on the line to serve their community, and are rarely accused of immoral behavior.

The Japanese have a strong national identification because they live on an island of ethnically homogeneous citizens. Chinese youths find it easy to develop a strong identification with their nation because China has the oldest continuous civilization, covers a large landmass, and has the largest population in the world. The fact that the proportion of non-Hispanic whites in the United States has dropped from 90 percent in 1950 to 63 percent in 2014 has made some white citizens, especially those living in the South and California, more conscious of their ethnicity.

I suggested in the essay on words that each symbolic network contains a core term that has associations of varying strength with other words and schemata. Everyone possesses a network in which the self is the core term, with links to the physical and psychological features and properties of self and family members. When a person learns that a family member has done something praiseworthy or despicable, the network for self adds the desirable or undesirable feature. When Franklin Roosevelt learned that he was related to Teddy Roosevelt, he added the latter's talent and fame to his network for self. That addition implied that he possessed a potential for greatness.

An identification with a family member does not require direct contact. Many German adolescents born long after the end of World War II felt vicarious shame when they learned that a relative they had never met had been a Nazi. Rainer Hoess, as mentioned earlier, fell into a depression and attempted suicide when, at age twelve, he learned that his grandfather, the commandant at the Auschwitz concentration camp, was responsible for the deaths of more than a million people. On the other hand, Jean-Paul Sartre felt vicarious pride when he discovered that his grandfather had been a famous writer.

Children resist acknowledging undesirable qualities in family members, for such an admission implies that they, too, might possess a hidden flaw. I once interviewed a fourteen-year-old girl whose mentally ill mother had locked her, as an infant, with an older sister in a bedroom until both were rescued and adopted three years later. When I asked her why her mother behaved abnormally she defended the parent saying, "Well, Mama had many children and her life was made a little easier by putting us in the bedroom." She would not admit that the mother was mentally disturbed.

Sherwin Nuland, a respected writer and surgeon at Yale University, grew up in a poor neighborhood in New York City with an extremely cruel father. He described in his memoir *Lost in America* his childhood anger at and fear of his uneducated father, who generated vicarious shame in the young Sherwin when he was with the father in public. But at the end of the memoir, written when Nuland was in his seventies, he confesses his love for his father, now deceased. It is hard for adults, as it is for children, to accept the possibility that they were the offspring of a bad person.

Identifications with a family are not altered easily. Adults can change their name, hair, and facial features but not their membership in this unique group. This fact explains why many adults who had been adopted as young children want to find their biological parents or at least learn more about them. Some boys who learn that their birth was the result of a premarital tryst, followed by the father's abandonment of both mother and child, try to dilute the shame provoked by an identification with an unreliable father through extraordinary accomplishments. The psychoanalyst Erik Erikson, Barack Obama, and Jeff Bezos, the founder of Amazon, are possible examples of this dynamic.

Asti Hustvedt notes that some of the Catholic women who were patients in the Pitié-Salpêtrière hospital in the 1880s diagnosed with hysteria tried to identify, albeit momentarily, with Christ's suffering by harming their bodies

in order to mute their guilt over being a participant in several past seduc-
tions or rapes. The early Christian disciples singled out a restraint on carnal
lust, rather than greed or hate, as a requirement for salvation. The new
recruits to Christianity identified with the slaves wealthy Romans used for
sexual pleasures. Since they, too, were victims of Roman domination, it was
easy to be persuaded of the evil of carnal sex.

Children are most likely to identify with the ethnic, religious, class, or
national category to which they belong when the group has distinctive
features. A poor Muslim boy growing up in a Muslim country such as Qatar,
which has many wealthy families and few poor ones, might have a stronger
identification with his social class than his religion. A poor Muslim boy
growing up in Jakarta, which has many poor Muslims, is likely to have a
stronger identification with his nation than with his religion.

An ethnic group is distinctive if it is a minority in the society, a target of
prejudice, possesses some salient physical features, or many members are
either accomplished or disreputable. Many Jews identify with their ethnic
group because the category meets all four of the above criteria. I know
several Jews in their eighties, still strongly identified with their ethnic group,
who continue to feel a blend of anger and shame created by the experience
of an intense anti-Semitism during their youth.

Sigmund Freud, who identified with his Jewish pedigree, held a dark
view of society because he lived in an anti-Semitic society. Norbert Wiener,
one of the twentieth century's most acclaimed mathematicians, described
the self-doubt he felt as a child because of his mother's open shame of being
Jewish. He wrote in his memoir *I Am a Mathematician* that the recognition
of his ethnicity "forced on me a sense of inferiority which contributed
greatly to my insecurity." Michael McDonald, born in South Boston in 1967
to a poor Irish family, described in *All Souls* his anger upon learning
that middle-class Bostonians regarded members of his ethnic group as
"white niggers."

Disadvantaged youths and adults who live in a society with a high level
of inequality find it easier to identify with the underdog. Laura Hillenbrand,
author of *Seabiscuit*, notes that millions of Americans who were out of work
during the Depression of the 1930s identified with a horse who, experts

predicted, would be a loser because he did not possess the elegant bodily form of winning Thoroughbreds such as War Admiral. The public enjoyed a moment of vicarious pride whenever Seabiscuit, the topic of more lines of print in the nation's newspapers in 1938 than any American, including Franklin Roosevelt, won a race.

I was born in 1929 into a family that was also struggling to survive during that cruel decade. I remember cheering for the Brooklyn Dodgers because they were an underdog team. This identification retains some strength today, seventy-five years after my support for the Dodgers, for I continue to root for the underdog when I watch a sports event on television. A colleague who grew up in a poor Jewish family in New York City regularly defended psychologists who advocated unpopular scientific ideas, even if he did not believe in them. He explained his behavior by arguing that someone had to stand up for a perspective that a majority dismissed. Larry Tye suggests that the comic book character Superman was more popular in 1938 than Buck Rogers, Dick Tracy, or Tarzan because, despite the shy posture character-istic of the underdog, he was able to transform himself into a superhero.

The brothers responsible for the Boston Marathon bombings in 2013 were born in the Caucasus and came to the United States in 2002. The deci-sion to bomb the site at the end of the marathon may have been precipitated by the anger of Tamerlan Tsarnaev, the older brother, when the Immigration Service denied his request to apply for citizenship. Because Tamerlan Tsarnaev felt marginalized, he was susceptible to radicalization when he felt he was being treated unfairly.

On the other hand, others who identify with a victimized group feel uncomfortable when their group assumes a position of dominance. The Shia have traditionally seen themselves as victims of the larger Sunni popu-lations in many nations. When the Shia are victorious, as they were in Iran in the late 1970s, Hamid Dabashi suggests they become susceptible to a feeling of confusion because victims are not supposed to succeed.

An identification with one's nation is more probable when a majority of the citizens share the same language, ethnicity, and religion. National identifications are making it difficult for European political leaders to create one political entity with which all Europeans—French, German, Spanish,

Scandinavian, Greek, and British citizens—can identify If nineteenth-century Americans had been less strongly identified with their region and more firmly identified with their nation, the Civil War might have been avoided. The balance between the strength of a regional versus a national identification shifted in favor of the latter during the twentieth century because a host of events allowed Americans in different parts of the country to recognize that they shared a number of distinctive features. These features included the rise of national brands of consumable goods (Coca-Cola, Wrigley's gum, Kodak film, Heinz ketchup), national television shows, films, and radio programs, the creation of interstate highways that made it easy to migrate to distant parts of the country, and federal legislation establishing the Internal Revenue Service, Social Security Administration, and the Federal Reserve.

Demagogues find it easier to gain control of societies that once enjoyed, but lost, a position of respect or power. The yearning for a return to the earlier period of greatness helps to explain why Hitler, Mussolini, and Franco were able to gain despotic control of their societies, and why Putin enjoys popularity among Russians. Equally ambitious twentieth-century European politicians in Finland, Switzerland, or Ireland would have found it harder to seize the same degree of power.

The philosopher Pascal Bruckner suggests that French citizens who are strongly identified with their nation feel a measure of vicarious guilt over their grandparents' collaborations with the Nazis. The harsh attacks by the French press on the Israeli treatment of Palestinians appears to be an attempt to dilute that guilt. By depicting the Jews of Israel as villains, they are able to reduce the guilt linked to their grandparents' actions in the 1940s.

Americans born before 1940 were proud of America's role in accepting millions of European immigrants, saving the world from the Nazis and Japan, helping Europe rebuild, and establishing more world-class universities than any other nation. Those born after 1980 experience slightly less pride. Some may even feel a little shame over the wars in Vietnam, Iraq, and Afghanistan, the decay of urban public schools, rising income inequality, the greed of corporate executives, and an incarceration rate larger than Russia's and ten times the rate in Scandinavia.

Historians use the layers of the sea as a metaphor for a society. The surface features of the sea are due mainly to the wind, whereas the properties at deeper levels are more dependent on its history. The surface features of a society are more easily altered than the deeper layers. The products of each person's identifications occupy the deepest layers of their character. Because identifications are difficult to measure, most psychologists study the effects of parental practices which, although easier to quantify, do not reflect the pattern of identifications. Social scientists would gain profound insights if they developed sensitive measures of this process.

A Summary

Cultures vary in the pattern of abilities, values, and personalities youths must acquire if they wish to adapt to their setting. A majority of parents possess a relatively accurate intuition of the needed qualities and an implicit theory of socialization that is supposed to create the desired traits. The extraordinary variation in parental practices across the world is a product of the different theories. Hence, the answer to the question "What is the best way to raise children?" varies with the setting and historical era. There is no "best" set of practices for all societies at all times.

The child's interpretations of a parent's actions are far more important than the actions a camera might record. An insightful child who senses that a mother's impulsive tirades are due to her painful illness and do not reflect anger with or devaluation of the child will be protected from the undesirable outcomes that befall a less reflective child.

Finally, the lack of research on the consequences of children's identifications with their family pedigree as well as their ethnic, religious, or national group is a serious lacuna in explanations of development. It is impossible to understand the adult personality of Winston Churchill, who lived with indifferent parents having adulterous affairs during his formative years, without recognizing the strengths young Winston exploited from his identification with an elite family. I suspect that Charles Darwin's willingness to publish a theory he knew would anger so many members of his society was made easier by his identification with a distinguished family pedigree.

It is impossible to explain the disproportionate prevalence of academic failure, incarceration, and teenage pregnancies among African Americans by citing only the practices of their parents, poverty, or the inadequacy of urban schools. The consequences of identifying with a group that is reminded regularly of its failure to adapt to society's demands and believes it is a target of hostility by the majority population must be added to the mix of other conditions. Hopefully, the next cohort of social scientists will repair this gaping hole in our understanding of the course of each person's developmental journey.

Each child's pattern of identifications is blended with a set of temperamental biases, family practices, sibling position, cultural setting, and historical era to generate a profile that becomes harder, but not impossible, to change after the twentieth birthday. It is not possible to assign a number that parades as an estimate of the separate influence of each condition because all the circumstances come together to create a unique itinerary for each traveler.

On Spruce Trees and Cats

There are two ways to think about experience. Our senses tell us that the world is composed of qualitatively discrete things—stones, cows, cats, mosquitoes, flowers, trees, rivers, and clouds. A spruce tree is so unlike a cat it is counterintuitive to toy with the idea that they differ only quantitatively because they share different combinations of the same basic elements. Yet, that is exactly what the ancient Greeks assumed when they invented a hypothetical world of invisible substances that gave rise to a world of seemingly distinctive things. Two thousand years later scientists affirmed the Greek intuition that everything we see, touch, smell, and hear is a product of a blending of the three hypothetical entities called leptons, quarks, and bosons.

Einstein's theory of general relativity, which made mass and energy interchangeable, supported the physicists' conviction that a smooth quantitative variation in invisible substances was the foundation of all events. This principle, however, does not rule out the possibility that the objects or processes that emerge from the underlying blends of energies are qualitatively distinct. The male and female sex hormones—testosterone and estradiol—share more than 90 percent of the same atoms, but the spatial arrangement of the atoms, and their effects on body and brain, are qualitatively distinct.

The essay on genes noted that the regulatory DNA sequences called enhancers determine where and when a coding gene will be expressed. The genes that are the bases for the proteins in heart muscle are transcribed only in the cells responsible for building the heart and are silenced in the cells of liver and brain. There is no blurring of boundaries. A heart is qualitatively different from a liver and a brain.

The decision to treat an object or process as belonging to a discrete category or as part of a quantitative continuum depends on the features a person chooses for classification. That choice is not inherent in the object but varies with the classifier's purpose. Biologists emphasize the quantitative differences in the physiology of cows and camels. Commodity traders on Wall Street regard cows and camels as qualitatively different categories because Americans do not eat camel meat. The number of genes shared by edible and poisonous mushrooms varies quantitatively, but consumers care about the qualitative difference in the power of the two species to cause illness. The IQ scores of one thousand children form a continuous distribution. But children with low IQs who were born with the chromosomal abnormality that causes Down syndrome differ qualitatively from genetically normal children with the same or similar IQs whose scores are due to deprivation. Two recordings of a symphony can be experienced as identical, even though one was heard on an old vinyl record that registered sounds varying continuously in pitch and loudness and the other was heard on a CD that registered discrete values.

The natural scientist's fondness for quantitative differences among events is sustained, in part, by the desire to impose numbers that vary in magnitude on all observations, despite Einstein's warning that "not everything that counts can be counted and not everything that can be counted counts." This desire biases investigators searching for relations between two phenomena—say, a brain measure and a psychological trait—to reject the possibility that the relation might be restricted to the small number of subjects who have extreme values on the two measures because that strategy would imply qualitatively different kinds of people. Tennis fans regard Federer, Djokovic, and Nadal as possessing skills that are qualitatively superior to those of most players in a tournament. A mathematician who once wrote that all physicists are intelligent, some are geniuses, but only a rare few are magicians regarded Richard Feynman as a magician.

Most neuroscientists relying on blood flow as an index of neuronal activation measure the average increase in blood flow across large numbers of

voxels (remember, a voxel is one cubic millimeter of brain tissue) in particular brain locations. One team was disappointed to find that the average
activation across hundreds of voxels in a particular site did not differentiate
among pictures of faces, bodies, scenes, and objects. However, additional
examination of the evidence revealed that the patterns of blood flow to the
ten voxels within this site that received the largest increases in blood flow
did differentiate among the four types of pictures. Extreme values contained
information that the average did not reveal.

Psychologists have cycled in their preference for discrete types of people
compared with continuous variation in traits. Are extraverts qualitatively
different from introverts, as Carl Jung believed? Or do each of these personality traits belong to a quantitatively varying continuum? The nineteenth-
century concept of hysteria was treated as a qualitative category. Contemporary
psychologists regard generalized anxiety, which was a salient property of
hysterics, as a continuous trait. The quantitative position is in closer accord
with the egalitarian assumption that individuals are born with similar propen-
sities to develop any of a variety of traits. Each person's life experiences sculpt
quantitative differences in personality profiles. Psychologists prefer to study
properties that vary continuously and are less interested in the small number
who have an extraordinary ability to remember the past, suffer intensely from
a fear of heights, or cannot regulate their anger.

The controversies surrounding the choice between quantitative variation
and qualitative categories assume many forms in contemporary science.
This essay considers two of these forms. One centers on the variation among
species. The second is concerned with the relation between the acquired
traits of infants and young children, on the one hand, and their adult properties. Are some early childhood traits preserved indefinitely or is the collection of adult traits qualitatively different from the earlier profile?

Evolution's Contribution

Charles Darwin contributed to the attractiveness of quantitative variation
by assuming an unbroken, albeit twisted, trail from the first life-forms, about
3.5 billion years ago, to modern humans. The generations of biologists who

followed recognized, but minimized, the obvious discontinuities that emerge when one species displays a novel feature. Examples include the first single cell with a nucleus and the first animal with eyes, a backbone, wings, internal fertilization, or a convoluted rather than smooth cortex. Biologists who study the bacterium E. coli, the tiny worm C. elegans, the fruit fly Drosophila, or the zebra fish hold the confident belief that a small number of basic human properties are present in some form in these species. An eminent biologist's comment, "What's true for E. coli is true for elephants. What's not true for E. coli is not true," reveals the faith in an unbroken thread from bacteria to humans.

A team of Louisiana scientists argued that the zebra fish, which is only 1.6 inches long and has a genome one-fourth the size of humans, is a good model for understanding attention-deficit-hyperactivity disorder, post-traumatic stress disorder, and addiction to alcohol or drugs in our species. Marion Thomas of the University of Strasbourg notes that nineteenth-century French naturalists claimed that the behaviors of wasps could illuminate the bases of human maternal behavior. I was surprised by reading, in separate papers, that fish can feel lonely and lions can be individualistic. These two words were intended to apply only to humans and possess a different meaning when applied to fish or lions. I do not believe that fish are able to feel the quality of loneliness experienced by an adult who has moved to a new city and has no friends. I doubt that lions can reflect on the alternative possibilities of pursuing additional food resources or leaving them for other members of the pride.

The commitment to continuities among species motivates investigators who study primates to try to demonstrate that humans have very few, if any, unique features. One team claimed that the processes that lead humans to wage war share basic features with the processes that lead male chimpanzees to kill another chimp. Neuroscientists minimize the contribution of the unique cells and circuits in the human brain that are missing from the brains of mice and rats. The neuroscientist Todd Preuss is troubled by the resistance his colleagues show to any suggestion that the human brain possesses some important properties denied to apes. In a personal communication he wrote, "When I've pressed neuroscientists on this issue, their usual answer is, 'Yes, there must be differences between humans and apes, but not in the part of the brain that I study.'"

The human genome contains about 45 million DNA sequences, excluding deletions and insertions, that are missing from the chimpanzee genome. These sequences contribute to a larger and better-connected brain, little bodily hair, many sweat glands, downward-pointing nostrils, an upright posture and, in females, a fatty breast and a clitoris located outside and above a vagina that is tipped forward.

The monkey and human behaviors that appear similar on the surface are often the product of qualitatively different cascades. Although both monkeys and humans can learn to discriminate between pictures of fruits and animals, the two species rely on different mechanisms to do so. Humans solve the problem quickly by naming each of the categories. Monkeys, who rely on a different strategy, take much longer to master the same task. Federica Amici of the Max Planck Institute in Leipzig found that neither chimps, bonobos, orangutans, nor gorillas display any behavior that she could interpret as reflecting a sense of obligation to an animal who had been kind to them in the past.

Margaret Livingstone of Harvard Medical School invested considerable effort training monkeys to solve simple addition problems, such as 2 + 4, that school-age children solve quickly. Despite months of training and many thousands of trials, she could not teach the monkeys to solve these problems because they did not assign numerical symbols to arrays containing different numbers of black circles. I suspect that Livingstone and her colleagues would not have initiated this time-consuming experiment if they did not wish to prove that monkeys could add.

Etienne Meunier of Rutgers University received permission to attend weekly gatherings in a New York City apartment where groups of about a hundred gay men engaged in multiple acts of oral and anal sex with strangers over the course of several hours. It is impossible to imagine a group of male chimpanzees displaying behaviors even remotely similar to those Meunier observed.

Psychologists and biologists who use animal behaviors to explain human traits do not always acknowledge that the dominant societal concerns of their historical era influence the traits they choose to study. Eighteenth- and nineteenth-century scholars, who believed that a competitive spirit was adaptive, argued that this human trait was a derivative of behaviors observed in monkeys and chimpanzees. Because many contemporary adults are troubled by an excessively competitive individualism, more scientists in 2015 study cooperation in these and other species. In both cases the scientists assumed, without firm evidence, that the mechanisms leading to competition or cooperation in animals were essentially the same as or similar to those operating in humans.

Frank Beach, my mentor at Yale when I was a graduate student in the 1950s, used Lewis Carroll's poem "The Hunting of the Snark" to convey his skeptical view of the premise that any species was as good as any other when searching for psychological principles. Although most snarks are harmless, a few are boojums who can destroy a hunter trying to capture them. Beach was suggesting that psychologists who studied white rats, the most popular animal in psychological research at that time, to discover a fact applicable to humans were in danger of spending many years searching for what they believed was a snark but turned out to be a boojum. Thomas Insel, a distinguished biologist and current director of the National Institute of Mental Health, warned colleagues in 2014: "Failure to attend to species differences not only ignores the opportunity for understanding mechanisms of diversity, it will doom anyone who wants to make facile comparisons."

Continuity in Human Development

Humans are addicted to wondering about the origins of events. As early as the third birthday children ask "why" and, by age six, they automatically assume that a current event was caused by an earlier one. The origins of the universe, the first life-forms, and each person's collection of psychological traits have usually been at the top of the scientist's list of questions. Although the variation in adult psychological profiles is the result of a blending of temperamental biases, the interpretations imposed on encounters in and outside the family, and local circumstances, European and American scholars since the eighteenth century have had a special interest in proving that select traits in infants are preserved indefinitely and exert an influence on the adult's moods, ideas, and actions.

Once one accepts the premise of unbroken threads from infant to adult, it is easy to be persuaded that six-month-olds can be angry, sad, or anxious; add numbers; and infer the intended goal of an adult's action. Nineteenth-century experts were convinced that the newborn's automatic grasping of a pencil placed in the palm was an early form of adult greed. Freud persuaded millions of intelligent readers that the feelings that led a nursing infant to bite the mother's nipple were transformed into sarcasm in the adult.

The psychiatrist John Bowlby was certain that an infant's experiences with the mother during the first two years created an emotional state, which he called a secure or insecure attachment, that might be preserved for a lifetime. This bold idea implied that a bout of depression in a twenty-five-year-old man who lost a gratifying relationship with a woman might be traced to experiences with his mother twenty-four years earlier. In this account the man's current employment, income, health, and friendships are of less relevance than his infant attachment.

Evidence gathered by Cathryn Booth-LaForce of the University of Washington and Glenn Roisman of the University of Minnesota challenges Bowlby's assumption. An infant's security of attachment at fifteen months, measured with a standard procedure called the Strange Situation, was unrelated to the attachment status of eighteen-year-olds, based on their replies to the Adult Attachment Interview. The social class of the adolescent's family was a better predictor of each adolescent's current attachment status than their infant attachment category. It is not surprising that those who had been securely attached at fifteen months but were classified as insecurely attached as adolescents grew up in homes with less income and, according to the evidence in essay 4, more life stress.

A team at the University of Maryland confirmed this fact, finding no difference between securely and insecurely attached infants in level of anxiety during adolescence. One reason is that some of the infants classified as insecurely attached were born with a temperament that protected them from intense distress to unexpected events. A mother who suddenly gets up from her chair and, without explanation, walks out the door of an unfamiliar room, leaving the infant alone, is such an unexpected experience. Because these infants did not cry when the mother left and continued playing when the mother returned three minutes later, attachment theorists believe these behaviors reflect an insecure attachment. It is equally plausible to argue that these infants behaved this way because their temperament muted a state of fear to this sequence.

Bowlby's decision to award formative power to the experiences of the first two years continued a tradition that had begun two centuries earlier when ministers told their congregations that the mother's treatment of her infant laid the foundation of the child's future character, an idea amplified by Sigmund Freud and Erik Erikson. All three men, products of Western culture, assumed, without definitive evidence, that the first experiences had to exert a profound effect on a child's future. Their conception of an infant brain resembled John Locke's understanding of mind as a blank surface ready to be permanently altered by experience or an engineer's image of the hard disc of a new computer.

A hard disc is a flawed metaphor for the brain because neurons that are changed by an experience often revert to their original form if the experience is not repeated. The infant's brain turns out to be remarkably resilient. A team of Brazilian scientists discovered that the brains of the rare children born with no connections between the two hemispheres managed to establish alternative connections as they grew. Adolescents and adults born with cataracts that had rendered them blind since birth developed a remarkable ability to solve problems requiring spatial reasoning after their cataracts were removed. More persuasive are the results of an experiment with cats. Scientists at Wake Forest University deactivated a brain site in one hemisphere of three-week-old kittens that contributes to the animal's ability to move toward a light. Although the behaviors of one-year-old cats were abnormal, surprisingly, by age four, these cats had attained a level of skill found in normal cats. The earlier deficiency was no longer detectable.

Most adolescents or adults cannot remember any events that occurred before their third birthday, especially the times and locations of salient personal experiences. This phenomenon, called infantile amnesia, might be attributable to the absence of three processes that are mediated by the hippocampus, a structure that does not approach an adult level of maturity until children are about four years old. A mature hippocampus binds a salient event to its setting to create a unified representation. This structure also connects a schema for an event, which in infants resembles a single snapshot without semantic meaning, with a network of words. Because the early schemata were not tagged with a word, older children find it difficult retrieving an event that occurred in their second year. Finally, it is possible that the immature hippocampus does not transfer most early experiences to sites in the cortex that hold long-term memories.

The absence of these three processes during the first three years, which would explain infantile amnesia, implies that many experiences before the third birthday, excluding traumata, have a minimal effect on the actions, beliefs, and emotions of adolescents or adults. This suggestion accords well with the fact that the personality traits of most three-year-olds are poor predictors of adult traits as well as the observation that prediction improves after the sixth birthday. These facts, along with many others, are inconsistent with a position that awards special significance to the events of the first year. The accumulating evidence pointing to serious discontinuities between infancy and later childhood has shifted the burden of proof to those who still believe in the indefinite preservation of infant traits.

Maturation of Psychological Properties

The brain changes that occur in all healthy children over the first fifteen to eighteen years, along with those in the hippocampus, are accompanied by the emergence of new mental abilities and emotions that are denied to young infants. Important changes occur between eight and twelve months, one and two years, three and four years, five and seven years, and eleven and fifteen years.

Infants older than seven or eight months are able to hold two events in working memory for five to ten seconds. This ability allows them to relate a present event to one that happened seconds earlier. One sign of this new ability is the sudden cry many infants display when their mother leaves them alone in an unfamiliar place. The infant cries because she is able to retrieve a schema of the mother's presence moments earlier along with a schema for the present moment, which contains no mother, but is unable to relate the two schemata. This inability is accompanied by a state of uncertainty, which evokes the crying. The uncertainty and subsequent crying could not occur until the infant had reached an age where a firmer connectivity between sites in the temporal and frontal cortex allowed her to hold schemata of past and present in working memory. An adult with an impaired connectivity between these sites, perhaps due to a stroke, brain infection, or Alzheimer's disease, is unable to relate the odd sound of a plane's engines to schemata of the normal sound acquired during many past flights. As a result the unusual sound does not generate anxiety.

The second year witnesses the emergence of a quartet of novel abilities that radically alter the child's view of the world and permanently separate the psychological properties of humans from those of apes. These talents are a symbolic language, an initial appreciation of right and wrong, a capacity for inference, and consciousness. Children now begin to speak and to understand a large number of words and short sentences. Two-year-olds say "All gone" in response to the disappearance of a cookie. Some reveal a curiosity about names when they point at an object and ask, "Wha's that?"

Two-year-olds also possess an early appreciation of right and wrong actions. Michael Tomasello, a psychologist at the Max Planck Institute in Leipzig, and his wife recorded their daughter's speech during the second year. The toddler's sentences revealed an understanding of prohibited acts, for she would say, "Sorry, baby doll" (when she caught a hairbrush in the doll's hair), "Wipe this off there" (when she had mud on her shoes), and "No" (when she spilled milk). The early recognition of improper acts is the initial phase of what will become the older child's conscience.

The abilities to infer some of the thoughts and feelings of others and to be consciously aware of some of one's feelings, intentions, and actions round out the quartet of talents. Two-year-olds infer that a parent is in pain, a stranger needs help, or an infant sibling is hungry. They are also aware of select intentions, motives, and feelings and may describe some of them. Michael Tomasello's daughter said, "Eyes hurt," "Scared of man," and "Do it self" before she was two years old. Some two-year-olds reveal their newly discovered consciousness by describing their behaviors as they are happening, as in "Mary eat," "Mary climb," and "Mary sit."

The fact that all four properties appear in an early form in all healthy children between fourteen and twenty-four months wherever they live, whether a city, isolated village, jungle, mountainside, seaside, or desert, implies that maturational changes in the brain, especially enhanced connectivity between the right and left hemispheres, combined with a richer corpus of acquired knowledge generate psychological processes that are unique to our species. No observer has ever seen a young ape respond to an unexpected event (say, a tree falling suddenly) by displaying a gesture or vocal sound that has the same meaning a child intends when she asks, "Why tree fall, Mommy?" One twenty-seven-month-old, noticing that it had just begun to rain, asked her mother, "Why is it raining?" No chimpanzee, young or old, would show any sign of puzzlement at the sudden onset of a shower because apes do not automatically infer that every event has a prior cause.

The ability to integrate a sequence of past events that occurred earlier and to relate them to the present improves significantly between three and four years. As a result, four-year-olds are better able to anticipate the end of a sentence when they hear a verb. For example, if, while sitting at the breakfast table picking at scrambled eggs with his fingers, a child hears a parent say, "Please eat with a . . .," he anticipates that the next word will be "fork." Four-year-olds are able to recall events that occurred days earlier and relate them to the present. As a result, they automatically link a current event, say, waving to a parent taking a taxi to an airport, to the parent's return three days later. The consistent habit of attributing an event to its origin renders four-year-olds vulnerable to moments of guilt. A boy who accidentally knocked a vase from a table because he ran too fast recognizes that his carelessness was the reason for the broken vase and is vulnerable to self-blame and perhaps a moment of shame or guilt.

Five significant psychological properties are added between the fifth and seventh birthdays in children growing up in developed societies. This transition occurs a few years later in children living in poor, isolated communities without adequate, compulsory schooling. The new talents are accompanied by the left hemisphere attaining dominance over the right as well as an enhanced reliance on language to register experience.

Children now understand that an object, person, or event can belong to more than one semantic category. A woman can be a mother, lawyer, and wife, and each role comes with a distinct package of responsibilities. Seven-year-olds recognize that they, too, belong to a variety of semantic categories. They are girls or boys, Catholic or Protestant, Hispanic or black, rich or poor. Each category is linked to a set of values that children feel obligated to honor. Many boys believe they ought to be brave and fearless. Hence, a timid boy tries to alter his persona to fit his understanding of the ideal by suppressing the display of shy, avoidant behavior. This is the interval when identifications with family as well as ethnic, religious, and class groups emerge as important determinants of moods, expectations, and self-confidence.

The realization that an event can have more than one meaning allows six-year-olds to discriminate between the literal and sarcastic meaning of a sentence. An adult who intends to be sarcastic usually utters the final word of a sentence in a lower pitch. If a father, upon seeing a baseball player on television drop a fly ball, says, "Nice catch," his six-year-old son sitting beside him uses the pitch of the last word to decide whether the father's comment was intended to be taken literally or as sarcastic.

Children younger than five can detect the fact that two objects share the same color or shape. But they are less able to appreciate that physically different events might share the same relation. For example, the relation between a small and a large ball is the same as the relation between a small and large dog. The relation between parent and child resembles the relation between teacher and child and both call for obedience to the older person.

The ability to pause before acting in order to reflect on alternative behaviors is a third competence that emerges during this interval. Most societies, past and present, have recognized this maturational achievement and usually wait until children are six or seven before requiring formal schooling.

Finally, six-year-olds are less likely than they had been earlier to activate schemata upon hearing a word. For example, the verbal free associations of four-year-olds are rich with schemata. They say bark to the word *dog*, shine to *sun*, and work to *daddy*. Seven-year-olds are apt to respond to *dog* with cat, to *sun* with moon, and to *daddy* with mommy. The occasional stripping of schemata from emotional words means that the child can say she is mad, sad, afraid, or happy without experiencing a relevant feeling.

The brain changes of puberty introduce a quartet of new competences. Adolescents understand that some problems have a definite answer if logic is applied to the evidence presented, independent of any correspondence with actual experience. Seven-year-olds do not understand the difference between problems that do or do not have this feature. They rely on what they have learned is true rather than the facts belonging to a hypothetical question. Youths, by contrast, can reason correctly about hypothetical events. For example, adolescents acknowledge the correctness of the conclusion in sentence 3 that follows from the initial two premises:

1. All things that have wings can fly.
2. Watermelons have wings.
3. Therefore, watermelons can fly.

Younger children reject this conclusion because it conflicts with their past experience.

Youths understand a variety of metaphors because they are able to detect a relation between the primary feature of one concept, say, a gorilla's ability to harm people, and a secondary feature of another, say, boys, and therefore appreciate that "Boys are the school's gorillas" is a clever metaphor. Six-year-olds are apt to be confused because they treat the sentence literally.

The confident belief that all the possible solutions to a problem have been considered is a third competence of this era. A teen who cannot tell her parents she is pregnant, does not know where the father is, and does not have the money for an abortion is vulnerable to a depression because she is certain she has examined all the possible solutions to her problem and none is feasible.

The automatic detection of a semantic inconsistency in a set of beliefs, combined with a need to resolve it, completes the quartet. Adolescents with a father who is kind to them but unreasonably harsh with the mother face an inconsistency in their evaluation of the father. They feel an urge to resolve the inconsistency and decide, once and for all, whether their father is a good or a bad person. Adolescent girls who have been sexually molested by their father face an excruciating conflict. They have to decide whether their father is bad because he betrayed a basic trust or whether they are partly responsible because they were passive and should have resisted.

Many contemporary youths are trying to resolve four inconsistencies. If males and females should be treated equally, why are males more often in leadership roles? If I am supposed look out for myself first, when should I care more about the welfare of others? If enhanced status is an empty idea, why should I work hard to attain an ascent in status? Why, if God loves humans and is all powerful, is there so much human misery?

Implications

The sequence of talents described transforms or, in some cases, eliminates many of the products of early childhood. The increased prevalence of depression among adolescent girls who had shown no evidence of a depressed mood during childhood is an example. Young girls who had been sexually abused do not usually show serious depressive symptoms until their adolescent or early adult years rather than immediately following the abuse. The later ruminations, which persuade the adolescent that she may bear some responsibility for the abuse, make a critical contribution to the symptoms.

The six-year-old girl being molested by her father is likely to be afraid when he enters her bedroom because she is unsure of her ability to prevent the parent's actions. Reflecting on these experiences twenty years later, she is more likely to feel shame over being a partner in a polluting event, anger at the father for betraying her trust, and guilt over not resisting his abusive behaviors. The emotions of shame and guilt, which are interpretations imposed on the past, generate the depression. The main point is that the primary cause of subsequent behaviors and moods is a later interpretation of the experience not the experience as it unfolded at the time.

Jewish children who were forced to leave Germany or Austria between 1937 and 1941 to avoid being killed or imprisoned by the Nazis developed different ideologies because of later reflections. Some never overcame the feeling that they were outsiders in their host country. A second group could not conquer the guilt of being a survivor. Others remained angry, and still others decided to devote their lives to making the world a better place.

All children experience some events that most observers would regard as stressful. The child's interpretation of the event and subsequent emotions shape the psychological outcome. The current generation is exposed to vivid images of impending catastrophes that include rising sea levels that will flood cities, tectonic plates moving under the Pacific Ocean that may cause massive earthquakes, and rogue actors exploding nuclear weapons. This knowledge may be generating a conception of the future that is more uncertain than the one held by their parents or grandparents.

Neglect of the Recent Past and Present

Given the evidence pointing to major changes in brains, genes, values, word meanings, and institutions as children move toward adult status, it is reasonable to ask why some scientists continue to award a great deal of formative power to the deep past while ignoring the recent past and present circumstances. Jared Diamond, for example, asks readers to believe that the current practices of hunter-gatherer groups in Botswana resemble the behaviors of their ancestors one hundred thousand years ago. This speculation assumes that the events of the past one hundred thousand years have had little influence on present behaviors. Diamond might reflect on the fact that the current sites in Iraq that were the locations of three important cities in ancient civilizations about five thousand years ago—Uruk, Ur, and Babylon—are among the least developed urban areas in the modern world.

Scientists dislike explanations of phenomena whose causes cannot be observed. This prejudice may be one reason why psychologists prioritize, even eroticize the past. Psychologists find it more attractive to assume that a parent's neglect or permissive socialization of her child, which can be observed, is a better explanation of the high levels of binge drinking, permissive sexuality, or antisocial behavior in adolescents than the influence of the Internet, the media, and the recent economic necessity of two working parents on the thoughts of youths because thoughts are difficult to measure.

If the events of the first three years had less power than experts assume, psychologists would devote more attention to the influences of recent experiences and current circumstances. These investigators would profit from reading the work of Peter and Rosemary Grant, who discovered that unpredictable climatic events were responsible for alterations in the shape and size of the beaks of three species of finch living on the small Galápagos island of Daphne Major. The shapes and sizes of the beaks of each species, measured during the first year of the Grants' observations, were unrelated to the values they observed thirty years later because unpredictable droughts and intervals of heavy rain caused by an El Niño changed the nature of the island's food supply. As a result, the beak shape that was optimal for feeding from flowers and seeds that varied in hardness changed over time. The past was a poor harbinger of the future.

Joseph Stalin, who was responsible for as many murders as Adolf Hitler, had been at age fifteen a conscientious, conforming seminary student with high grades who looked forward to becoming a priest. His unhappy experiences with particular monks at the seminary and the presence of a student group opposing the tsar, both unpredictable, radicalized Stalin and started him on the path to his adult personality.

If Herbert Hoover had not lost both parents when he was a child living in a small town in Iowa, he would not have been sent to live with his uncle in Oregon and would not have met a high school teacher who suggested he attend the recently established Stanford University. If he had not gone to Stanford, he would not have taken a course with an influential faculty member who recommended the young Herbert for the position of manager of a new gold mine in Australia despite his inexperience. Hoover's acceptance of this assignment made him rich enough to retire when he was a young man. He decided to go to Washington and pursue a second career in governmental affairs. Without this sequence of unpredictable events over five decades, Herbert Hoover would not have become president of the United States.

If an older psychologist had not turned down an offer to lead a project at the Fels Research Institute in Yellow Springs, Ohio, in 1956, I would not have been hired a year later to direct the project, which resulted in the book *Birth to Maturity*, which led, in turn, to an invitation to join the Harvard faculty. If I had not been invited to be a member of a National Institutes of Health committee evaluating a proposal for research on nutrition in Guatemala, I would not have studied development in the small village of San Marcos La Laguna on Lake Atitlán in 1972 and might not have changed my mind about the determinism of the infant years. And if a Boston political group had not stopped a research project on the effects of day care on African American infants, my colleagues and I would not have enrolled Chinese infants and I would not have initiated productive work on human temperaments. If any one of these unpredictable events had not occurred over a thirty-year interval, my scientific research would have followed a different path.

A desire for a few transcendental truths provides an important reason for the attractiveness of infant determinism. God, the beauty of knowledge, and the sanctity of the marriage bond, which met this criterion in earlier centuries, have lost some of their glow. The sacredness of the bond between the biological mother and her infant is at risk as more mothers place their infants in surrogate care. The insistence on the significance of this relationship is due, in part, to a stubborn reluctance to relinquish this beautiful idea. If the consequences of a love relationship between the biological mother and her infant do not constitute transcendental truths, Americans and Europeans fear that they will be alone on a flimsy raft in a very rough sea.

Recent and Prolonged Cascades

Some events have a short history, others a longer one. The dramatic rise in the size of the Chinese gross domestic product had its origin in political decisions in Beijing less than thirty years ago. The United States was the most admired nation in the world in the 1950s. Many contemporary politicians in Germany, France, and England are now accusing American businesses and media of being a cause of moral decay in their nations. This fall from grace occurred in only two generations. The dramatic increase in the average human life span and the proportion of the world's population that is younger than ten or older than seventy years are also relatively sudden events whose causes can be traced to medical advances that occurred less than one hundred years earlier in a species that is more than one hundred thousand years old.

Other phenomena require a longer history. Taggart Murphy, in *Japan and the Shackles of the Past,* describes the preservation over several centuries of the Japanese respect for authority, sense of distinctiveness, strong national identification, and ability to accept contradictions. Physicists hold the title for believers in the continuity of events that began in the deep past. They are certain that their radio telescopes have detected remnants of the energy present moments after the Big Bang 13.7 billion years ago.

The inability to predict the traits of a majority of adults from their profiles at the end of the third year is a stubborn fact. Prediction improves a little after age seven, in part because of the quality of the schools attended and identifications with gender, ethnic, class, and religious groups. In addition, later experiences can sculpt reactions that are either congruent or inconsistent with the child's initial temperamental biases. Some children born with a temperament that renders them vulnerable to intense uncertainty when unfamiliar events occur become passive, timid adolescents; others with the same infant temperament acquire a dominating posture. Evidence from my own laboratory as well as that of Nathan Fox affirms that many children with the same temperament change behavioral profiles as they develop. For example, only 15 to 20 percent of very shy, timid two-year-olds maintained that profile over the next four years, and at least 40 percent of two-year-olds who were confident and sociable developed a more reticent style over time. Adults who, as children, had a temperamental bias favoring a bold approach to challenge might, depending on their life settings, select a career in business, trial law, surgery, politics, managing a hedge fund, or smuggling.

Identifications with family, ethnic, class, or religious groups, which exert their force after age five or six, affect the balance between confidence and doubt over future choices. A twenty-year-old woman reflecting on her father's abandonment of the family could decide that men are unreliable and vow not to marry, or she might marry in order to prove a happy marriage is possible. Some adolescent victims of bullying decide that those in positions of power who dominate others are undesirable as role models. That conclusion could lead them to avoid assuming positions of responsibility, for the adoption of such roles would transform them into the kind of individual they did not want to become.

A giant pinball machine provides a metaphor for life journeys that cannot be predicted from the psychological profile on the second birthday. The obstacles in the machine represent the sequence of challenges that a ball could encounter; the size and weight of each ball symbolize the child's temperamental biases; and the ball's location at the top of the machine stands for the class and cultural setting in which a life begins. That is why an understanding of a person's profile at a particular moment requires a narrative that begins with the present and proceeds backward in time.

What Is Education For?

The availability of college courses to anyone with access to the Internet has provoked a discussion, long overdue, of the meaning of a college degree and, more broadly, the purposes of formal education in this young century. One observation is so obvious it borders on the banal. Youths must learn some of the skills that the economy of their society requires. The historical evolution from the self-sufficiency of families in an agricultural society to an increasingly technological modern economy requiring workers with particular talents meant that institutions had to supply the instruction. Those who fail to take advantage of the training find themselves adrift. The unemployment rate among Americans aged twenty-five to thirty-four who did not graduate high school was 14 percent in 2014, compared with 2 percent for those with a college degree.

The Rise of Universities

Several conditions in eleventh-century Europe led to the creation of the continent's first universities: a growth in population, more cities with artisan guilds, an increased demand for doctors and lawyers, and literate men, many from Catholic monasteries, wanting to transmit their knowledge to the next generation. The male students, typically between seven and fifteen years, were taught grammar, composition, law, and medicine either in the tutors' lodgings or in hostels where the students lived. As the numbers grew—there were about ten thousand students in Bologna in 1200—monarchs recognized the need for rules that governed the administration and evaluation of examinations so that those who acquired the skills entitling them to the titles of doctor, lawyer, or priest could be distinguished from those who lacked sufficient discipline or talent. In time, the collections of teachers and students in Bologna, Salerno, Paris, Oxford, and Hamburg were called universities. Although admittance to these centers of learning was open to any male, most students came from a wealthy family that could pay their son's room and board and, if necessary, provide a salary for the teachers.

Graduation from a respected university automatically enhanced the status of the graduate. An anticipated rise in class position was a primary motive for a majority of the young men who matriculated at Harvard, Yale, or William & Mary, the first three colleges established in the American colonies. Roger Geiger's excellent history of higher education in America notes that most students at these colleges were the sons of ministers, merchants, or farmers who wanted at least one member of their family to have the trappings of a gentleman. The faculty taught logic, ethics, literature, and rhetoric, all in Latin, not English. Although Benjamin Franklin's curriculum added gardening, mechanics, and arithmetic, widespread instruction in science, engineering, and agriculture had to wait until the 1870s, when industrialization and the growing population of the West required a workforce with more practical skills.

The notion that every person had a right to a college education that promised a well-paying job and a measure of respect was an heir of the egalitarian ethos that swept across Europe during the eighteenth century, but did not have a serious influence on America's institutions until the twentieth. The United States in 2015 has about five thousand postsecondary institutions enrolling more than 18 million students. About one-half are nonprofit, four-year colleges; the rest are either two-year community colleges or for-profit institutions, such as the University of Phoenix. The availability of student loans was a critical cause of the increased proportion of Americans with a postsecondary degree to more than 40 percent.

A better-educated public is one reason for the lower level of corruption in America's cities over the past century. Lincoln Steffens's investigative articles in *McClure's* magazine in 1903 described the widespread bribery and voter fraud in the nation's six largest cities. Although no American city in 2015 is free of corruption, contemporary politicians are saints compared with the mayors and city council members in St. Louis, Minneapolis, Pittsburgh, Philadelphia, Chicago, and New York in 1903.

A Mismatch

Western culture has traditionally awarded enhanced status to those with a liberal arts degree from a four-year college or university. Unfortunately, a slightly lower status is attached to careers that do not require such a degree, although the economy needs them. This fact poses a problem in countries with too few adults who know how to build, operate, or repair computers, televisions, cell phones, cars, planes, appliances, water systems, and electric grids. Many youths who would have enjoyed the tasks and financial security these vocations provide choose instead to major in fields with fewer job openings, leading to a mismatch between the skills of the typical college graduate and those the economy needs. The largest number of American undergraduates major in business; too few concentrate in computer science. Germany is the economic powerhouse in Europe partly because it does have institutions that provide this training.

What Do Schools Do?

Educational institutions have at least five additional functions besides equipping the next generation with the skills needed to make a living. Teachers help students appreciate the history of their own and other cultures, gain familiarity with the fundamental concepts and methods of the sciences, enhance their ability to evaluate information critically, achieve facility in writing and speaking coherently, and articulate the ethical values that a majority regards as consensual. This last assignment is replete with controversy in the United States and Europe because of the sharp disagreements surrounding abortion, religion, the origin of the universe, sexuality, gender roles, individualism, and loyalty to the community.

The divisiveness of these issues combined with the pragmatic bent endemic among Americans bias college courses offered on the Internet to emphasize the factual content of a discipline. Most facts, if not used or rehearsed regularly, are quickly forgotten. Most college seniors can't remember more than 5 percent of the facts they learned from their freshman courses, although they are remarkably accurate in recalling the names and locations of the buildings in which the courses were taught.

The assumption that acquiring facts is the most important function of an education needs critical examination. A room full of facts is a quiet place. The justices of the Supreme Court, the presidents of universities, and the CEOs of large corporations did not acquire their positions because of the facts they learned but because they are able to select the facts that are relevant to a particular problem and to use them appropriately to arrive at a solution. A student's score on a multiple-choice test is the usual way faculty evaluate what a student has learned from a course, even though these answers do not reveal the student's depth of understanding. In one study, the grade students received in a course on evolution based on a multiple-choice test did not match the grade an examiner gave them following an interview designed to determine whether they had acquired a scaffold of principles in which the facts could be placed.

Facts and Scaffolds

It has become so easy to acquire facts on almost any topic that the reason for knowing them has receded in importance. Before the explosion in information technology, most individuals had a question they wanted resolved before they expended the time and energy needed to find the answer. Much of the information available to the public 24/7 does not serve the function of illuminating an important puzzle that is frustrating the reader. A fact that is not placed in a scaffold of assumptions and old facts often has little value. What is the average citizen to do with a headline announcing that one in eighty-eight American children has autism if they have never seen an autistic child and know neither the properties of autistic children nor how physicians arrive at this diagnosis? Because all facts are susceptible to being invalidated, individuals need a collection of premises to help them decide which facts to ignore and which to incorporate into an existing structure, while remaining ready to replace the belief when the evidence demands it.

The current position of privilege awarded to scientific facts, especially those with implications for human health, climate change, or the economy, has been accompanied by a muted interest in a society's ethical premises and history, which are essential elements in a scaffold. The American government's high level of health expenditures cannot be separated from the fact that Americans are living about twenty years longer than their grandparents. Because this trend will continue, citizens have to reflect on the wisdom of maintaining the life of a ninety-year-old with metastatic cancer for six additional months. Adults who do not understand their society's history, demography, and ethics are deprived of a scaffold that places new facts about medical advances designed to prolong the life of eighty-year-olds with cancer or premature infants born with brain damage in a coherent perspective.

Rules of Thought

The acquisition of strategies relevant to the solutions of specific classes of problems supplements the importance of facts. The women enrolled in most chemistry or physics courses receive a slightly lower grade than the men. One reason is that performance in this knowledge domain is aided by an ability to create images that represent the spatial patterns of atoms in a molecule. Men seem to be better than women at imagining how a pattern of atoms looks when it is rotated in various planes. A team at the University of Illinois taught undergraduate women enrolled in a chemistry course the relevant strategies in only three one-hour workshops that combined instruction in generating images with analyzing patterns of molecules into their separate elements. As a result, these women did as well as the men on the final examination. But the ability to imagine the spatial arrangements of atoms does not necessarily facilitate performance in a course on evolution or history.

A fair number of European and North American educators believe that acquiring rules of thought that apply to many domains—from physics to history—should trump the learning of facts. "Teach students to think" is their mantra. I share Emily Grosholz's skeptical view of this premise because a mind must possess the factual content of a discipline before it can apply any rule of thought. Consider the rule "Examine alternative explanations of a phenomenon before settling on one." Darwin could not profitably use that rule until he learned about the selective breeding of dogs and pigeons and had seen the variety of carapaces on the tortoises living on the different islands in the Galápagos.

Moreover, some rules of thought that are useful in physics are not equally helpful in biology. The physicist George Gamow provides a persuasive example of this claim. Gamow had conceived of DNA as a code before Francis Crick and James Watson. But Gamow thought as a physicist when he assumed that it made no difference whether messenger RNA transcribed DNA from right to left or left to right because symmetry is a seminal rule in physics. It turns out that genetic transcription is not symmetrical and messenger RNA transcribes DNA in only one direction.

The enthusiasm for teaching general rules of thought was responsible for a project in 1958 led by mathematicians who spent millions of federal dollars constructing a new strategy for teaching arithmetic to elementary school-children. Christopher Phillips in *The New Math* traces the history of a curriculum that taught second-grade children set theory before they understood the concept of number. The project closed down in 1972, after only a decade of application, because parents and teachers complained it was not accomplishing its aims. The hope of teaching abstract rules of thought that apply to domains ranging from the history of music to particle physics remains as elusive as the hope that life can be prolonged indefinitely.

The Need for a Motive

Discussions of the promise of online courses often ignore student motivation. A person who had little motivation to study in a traditional classroom is unlikely to suddenly develop a strong desire to do the same work just because the information appears on a screen. That is why less than 10 percent of enrollees in Internet courses complete the lectures. Most drop out after a week. As is true of all interventions designed to alter a person's mind or actions, including psychotherapy, clients must want to change their current state and believe that persistent effort will effect that change. If these criteria are not met, no intervention can hope to enjoy widespread success. This fact explains why more than 80 percent of adults from varied countries who took an Internet course in 2013 already had a college degree and wanted to learn a little more about their specialty in order to advance their career.

The Humanities

The current need for more adults with technical skills has had the unfortunate consequence of weakening the position of the humanities in most universities. Historians, novelists, poets, philosophers, and artists are valuable because they remind a society of its contradictions, articulate a public's inchoate feelings, detect the first signs of a change in values, and recognize the significance of the historical setting on a society's ideology. Patrick Modiano made this point in a lecture associated with his receipt of the 2014 Nobel Prize in literature. Historians point to the combination of geographic isolation, perceived outsider status, and increased prosperity and literacy in eighteenth-century Scotland to explain the flowering of new ideas reflected in the influential writings of Adam Smith and David Hume.

The ascendance of science as the ultimate arbiter of truth, a view that accelerated after the end of the Second World War, has been accompanied by the conviction that scientific research will provide a more complete understanding of human emotions such as fear or love than the reflections of philosophers or historians. This premise is flawed because the patterns of properties that define an emotion change with history. The mental state of a sixteenth-century citizen of Geneva who feared an eternity in purgatory is not to be equated with the fear of an American aid worker captured by the Taliban in Afghanistan. The emotion of an Athenian youth in 350 BCE who was sexually aroused when he allowed his tutor to embrace him does not match the emotion of a contemporary adolescent in Los Angeles who adopts the same posture with his high school coach because the Greek adolescent believed he had a moral obligation to suppress all sexual feelings in this setting.

Humanists anticipate nascent ideological movements that the public has not yet articulated. Dostoyevsky's description of Raskolnikov in *Crime and Punishment* captured the conflict generated by a waning piety and a waxing individualism in nineteenth-century Europe. European writers and artists at the end of the First World War helped the public understand the novel ideas the war had spawned. Robert Anderson's 1953 play *Tea and Sympathy* generated a more sympathetic attitude toward adolescent boys coping with anxiety over heterosexual relationships. The memoirs of Frank Kermode, John Updike, and George Kennan described the authors' feeling of "inauthenticity," an emotion that social scientists rarely study.

Humanists remind us that every event occurs in a particular context. The ideas, discoveries, poems, symphonies, and paintings that are judged creative require a public that is psychologically prepared for the original product. Americans were not prepared for the ideas in Herman Melville's *Moby-Dick* when it was published in 1851 and it was a commercial failure. Twentieth-century readers were ready to appreciate this novel. A large number of early twentieth-century Americans were receptive to Freud's hypotheses; residents of Beijing and Delhi were not.

Humanists detect subtle feelings of tension in a society whose surface shines with optimism. North Americans and Europeans in 1958 were enjoying peace and economic prosperity, physicists and engineers were glowing with pride over their contributions to the victory over Germany and Japan, and the public was anticipating the manufacture of the polio vaccine. The surface gleamed with high hopes for the future.

But 1958 was also the year audiences saw an old, disheveled man slip on a banana peel in the opening scene of Samuel Beckett's play *Krapp's Last Tape*, John Kenneth Galbraith lamented the consumerism of Americans, and youths were talking about the power of Jack Kerouac's *On the Road* to evoke nostalgia for a simpler era when most of the town turned out for the July 4 parade and Clark Gable, in the film version of *Gone with the Wind*, was the model for young men wondering how to behave with their dates on Saturday night. Only a few years later young adults were applauding the line in Bob

Dylan's song representing his response to a woman longing for a man to care for her in times of distress: "No, no, no, it ain't me, babe / It ain't me you're lookin' for, babe." Humanists are usually the first to notice the early signs of a pessimism lurking beneath a shiny surface that can help the public shape a more coherent understanding of their historical era.

The profound mood of sadness in T. S. Eliot's *The Waste Land,* published in 1922, reflected a personal blend of anxiety and melancholy that had its origin in his failed marriage, excessive perfectionism, inability to sustain a spontaneous, relaxed persona in social situations, sexual unsureness, embarrassment over his large ears and need to wear a truss, outsider status as an American in London, and financial insecurity. But because Eliot's mood resembled the mood of a society saddened by the loss of the optimism and idealism present before the First World War, the poem helped many adults better articulate their feelings.

Because it is difficult to decide whether the humanists' conclusions are true or false, there is the possibility that the knowledge packaged for digital users will steer clear of these domains, whose answers are often "maybe" or "under some circumstances," and persuade youths that scientific facts are the only ones worth acquiring. I hope that for-profit companies that prepare digitally packaged courses do not exclude domains with less certain facts because they do not want to provoke controversy and loss of market share.

Anthony Grafton and Marina Warner are critical of the British government's plan to reduce the number of faculty in history, classic languages, and philosophy because these disciplines have little relevance for the nation's economy. This decision to use a college graduate's future income as the primary index of the value of a college education, which is a nascent value in the United States as well, equates the totality of a college experience with a set of books that summarize the certain facts of the major disciplines.

Selecting the Chiefs

Educational institutions are charged with designing procedures capable of selecting the minority who will be given responsibility for the health, economic welfare, security, education, and legal rights of the majority. A youth's performance during the first sixteen years of schooling is the usual basis for selection. The premise is simple. The forty-year-olds who are most likely to behave responsibly and wisely when investing another's money, operating on a brain, defending clients in court, designing a bridge, or running an institution are those who had displayed similar traits in the past.

Educators set up a series of obstacles, in the form of tests, papers, and projects, that separate those who have perfected their talents and sustained the motivation needed to meet these demands competently for intervals ranging from sixteen to twenty years from those who have not. This is surely the longest personnel test in human history. The armed forces rely on a similar strategy to choose the few with the courage, personality, and skills to serve as special operation forces.

Graduate students who protest against comprehensive examinations fail to understand that the purpose of the exams is, first, to determine who is conscientious and second, to allow those who worked hard to infuse their degree with symbolic value which, in turn, should motivate them to behave professionally. Students would award little symbolic value to their degree if it was obtained with minimal effort. No pain, no gain.

A New Chapter

America's schools and universities did not regard their multiple assignments as especially burdensome during most of the last century. Millions of children born to European immigrants, many illiterate, were taught to read, write, and calculate and exposed to the values of democracy, equality, and capitalism. Adolescents who were studious gained admission to a college, after which many found a satisfying career. This sequence functioned smoothly for close to sixty years. The percentage of Americans who earned a four-year college degree jumped from one in twenty in 1940 to close to one in three in 2010. Then social conditions changed.

When Americans could no longer ignore the less adequate education of African American children in segregated schools, the Supreme Court acknowledged public sentiment and, for the first time in American history, declared segregated schools unconstitutional. This momentous decision had one unanticipated consequence. Many white parents removed their children from the public schools where black children were matriculating in large numbers, once again creating segregated classrooms in many cities.

At the same time, the continuing empowerment of women led many who would have become talented teachers to pursue careers in medicine, law, science, or business. The exodus of bright, conscientious women from the public schools was not replaced with a teacher cohort equally well trained or motivated to deal with children from homes where academic achievement was not high on the list of values. Teacher morale fell and a fatalism penetrated many urban schools. The presence of guns and knives in middle and high schools and occasional physical attacks on teachers did not help. As a result, the average literacy and numeracy skills of Americans between age sixteen and sixty-five sank to a rank of eleven in a group of twenty-two nations surveyed.

The loss of manufacturing jobs through outsourcing created a sharper class division in the workforce and a more serious imbalance in incomes. The third of American adults who graduated from college were being paid, on average, twice as much as those who had only a high school diploma and close to three times as much as those who did not complete high school. This brute fact led many youths to assume that a degree from any four-year college guaranteed a higher salary. The content that was mastered or the interactions with faculty and peers were deemed less relevant than possession of a diploma. This confounding of a symbol with the experiences the symbol was supposed to represent led the governors of Texas and Florida to pressure their state universities and colleges to create four-year degree programs that cost about $10,000, compared with the $40,000 tuition of most state universities. If the rationale behind this pressure were applied to holidays, then tourists should realize they could save $10,000 by purchasing a DVD travel film of the Galápagos instead of traveling to these islands.

The opening paragraphs of the British government's 2003 white paper on the future of higher education stated that the needs of the British economy should have priority when listing the value of an undergraduate degree. The decision to treat the value of an education with the same economic metric we apply to pizza and shoes is facilitated, in part, by a growing hostility toward all elites, which I described in Essay 4, combined with a larger ratio of applicants to America's best colleges and best jobs. This combination generated a pragmatic philosophy among undergraduates who, sensing the stiff competition for admission to a professional school or a first high-paying job, became narrowly task oriented and less interested in history, anthropology, philosophy, art, and other fields of study that seemed to have little relevance for their career plans. The ideal of the "well-rounded liberal arts graduate" was becoming an antiquated luxury reserved for a small number of privileged youths. Anyone who wished to know the history of the Incas, Monet's early frustrations, or Kant's philosophy could acquire this knowledge by consulting Wikipedia.

Conditions in 2015 support a skeptical posture toward the traditional assumption that the college experience is supposed to persuade youths they are participating in rituals that allow an appreciation of the beauty inherent in the mastery of a domain of knowledge and the meanings of truth. Too often undergraduates feel they are on a bus tour through a beautiful countryside in which the primary aim is to keep the bus on schedule.

Contemporary students at many of America's respected universities resemble guests at a hotel served by a faculty afraid to displease them by giving a grade less than A or A–. Many students, including some with excellent high school records, skip classes to relax at campus recreational facilities that include pools, water slides, lazy rivers with palm trees and, inevitably, a gymnasium. Undergraduates at the University of California, one of America's elite institutions, say that they spend less than one-third of their waking hours on academic work.

Harvey Mansfield, a Harvard professor of government disturbed by this trend, gave each student in his courses in 2014 two grades. One was the official grade of A or A–, the typical grade given to undergraduates in most courses, which he sent to the registrar. An unofficial grade, sent privately to each student and usually lower, was Mansfield's evaluation of that student's level of achievement. The lack of any embarrassment over the hypocrisy of this practice reveals a confusion over the purpose of a college education.

Journalists and faculty are criticizing universities and their executives because they are accomplices to these changes. Ross Douthat, a columnist for the *New York Times*, and Mark Edmundson, a professor of English at the University of Virginia and the author of *Why Teach?*, describe large universities as corporations that are more concerned with their national status, political correctness, and financial integrity than the ambience of the campus and the quality of the instruction. Deans and provosts turn their gaze away from the faculty's willingness to be blackmailed into giving high grades in order to avoid harshly critical evaluations by students more interested in the athletic facilities and lounge areas than the quality of the lectures, reading assignments, and discussions that might force them to examine their premises.

This harsh conclusion is supported by the startling fact that 75 percent of the teaching positions in America's colleges in 2014 were filled by graduate students or adjunct faculty paid by the course or working on an annual contract. These conditions make it hard for students as well as faculty to sustain the illusion that they are participating in a sacred mission that transcends the ordinariness of daily life.

This indictment is confirmed by the surprisingly small gains in knowledge that occur over the four years of courses in a fair number of American colleges. Derek Bok, a former president of Harvard University, notes in *Higher Education in America* that the average American senior attending a four-year college is only a little more proficient than he or she was as a freshman. Less than 10 percent are proficient in critical thinking, mathematics, and writing skills.

Neil Smelser in *Dynamic of the Contemporary University* lists the many reasons for this sad state of affairs. The most relevant are the extraordinary growth in student and faculty populations; the addition of pragmatic demands to contribute to the economy; specialization by faculty, who are more loyal to their discipline than to their institution; students who regard their college years as preparation for a profession rather than an opportunity to broaden their understanding; and an ethos that regards students as guests at a resort entitled to interesting but gentle teachers, tasty food, and elegant recreational facilities. Michael Crow, the president of Arizona State University, estimates that only about 2 to 3 percent of the 18 million students enrolled in an American college—about five hundred thousand—are receiving a first-class education. The majority are not.

Critics of higher education who variously blame students, faculty, or university administrators fail to recognize that all three are caught in a web of values, laws, economic constraints, and demographic changes that contributed to the current state of affairs. Public demands to admit more students from poor and minority families to elite colleges; more applicants for specialized professional degrees than openings; more graduates than jobs commensurate with the graduates' skills; too many with advanced degrees in law, one of the humanities, anthropology, and sociology; and, finally, defensive college administrators worried about students or faculty members ready to sue the institution over their frustrations have created a historically unique ambience. Placing blame for the current problems on students is analogous to blaming the recent recession on those who bought homes they could not afford.

The pragmatic emphasis in higher education is part of a broader rejection of any claim to sacredness for an institution, person, career, or ritual. The demand for equality resulted in legislation that protected students from unjust treatment which, in turn, forced university presidents to hire more administrators to defend the university from litigation. These administrators, wanting to feel useful, began to treat faculty as salaried employees required to submit forms annually describing how they spent their time.

As the number of institutions increased, they began to compete with each other for the best and the brightest. The media fueled the competition by issuing annual rankings of institutions and departments, which, unfortunately, students treated as accurate measures of quality to use when deciding where one wished to study. The university as it was when the young Albert Einstein entered one over a hundred years ago has disappeared along with kerosene lamps, iceboxes, bottles of fresh milk on doorsteps, and a belief that the world is getting better.

Einstein would have been puzzled, or more likely saddened, by a 2014 essay addressed to graduate students in neuroscience advising them to respect their faculty advisor, be polite, abandon a problem after a series of failures, and figure out one's strengths and weaknesses. Missing was any mention of a passion to understand an aspect of nature. Apparently, that mood is a luxury that students in natural science can no longer afford.

Frederick Sanger, a biochemist who died in 2013 at age ninety-five, was one of the rare scientists who won two Nobel Prizes in physiology or medicine. But, as Sydney Brenner noted in an obituary in *Science* magazine, Sanger would not have fared well had he been born after 1980. He published so little of importance between 1952 and 1967 that funding agencies would have regarded him as an unproductive scientist and denied him the money he needed for the discoveries about DNA he made in later years.

Some Needed Reforms

The most constructive suggestions for reform depend on an accurate diagnosis of the problem. I agree with many observers of American society that the two most pressing domestic problems are the growing magnitude of economic inequality and the increasingly impenetrable barrier to social mobility among youths who grew up in less advantaged families. Today's economy requires workers who, at a minimum, have acquired a twelfth-grade proficiency in reading, writing, arithmetic, and operation of a computer. More white than African or Hispanic Americans possess these talents. More disturbing is the fact that, in 2014, close to 40 percent of minority students did not graduate from high school in four years. These troubling facts mean that the barriers to social mobility will remain high for these youths, who will find it difficult to establish financially secure careers.

One benevolent change would be the establishment of more institutions that teach the skills that, traditionally, led to blue-collar jobs. It will be necessary, however, to remove the compromised status of these vocations and award them more dignity. This is not an impossible task if more Americans, especially members of disadvantaged groups, become less sensitive to their social status. Each time an expert makes this proposal, a minority group member stands up in a public meeting claiming that this plan is a plot designed to keep poor minority youths in their proper place. Some American universities might create a new school on campus with a curriculum designed for high school graduates who want a career in plumbing, carpentry, masonry, automobile mechanics, or electrical services. Graduates of such a program would enjoy the status attached to a college degree.

Citizens must be willing to pay higher local taxes for more generous teacher salaries in order to attract back to the public schools the talented men and women who abandoned this profession after 1950. When that happens the status of teachers will rise, because Americans link status with annual income. Many citizens hold the correct intuition that the quality of the relationship between teachers and pupils is the most important basis for improved academic performance. New curricula, charter schools, or computerized instruction are not as effective as men and women who represent flesh-and-blood examples of adults who found a career that combined an adequate income, an opportunity to be useful to others, a measure of dignity, and an opportunity for satisfying moments. Today's youths need to believe that such people exist. Unfortunately, the demand for such changes by a majority of Americans is not yet vocal enough to produce the needed reforms. Too many middle-class parents whose children are in private or suburban public schools are not sufficiently motivated to agitate for change because they are not unhappy with the education of their children.

Many accomplished adults in earlier eras were educated at home by a devoted mother. Thomas Edison, the American credited with the invention of the first commercially successful lightbulb, phonograph, and movie projector, had only three years of formal schooling followed by homeschooling with his mother, who inspired curiosity and a work ethic. This example is not meant to imply that all children should be homeschooled. Rather, it is necessary to understand, as Montaigne did in his essay on education, that the teacher is the central element in the education of a child. He wrote that great care should be "taken in the selection of a guide with a well-formed rather than a well-filled intellect."

The absence of large numbers of admired role models in our schools contributes to the gap between the academic abilities of poor children in urban schools and middle-class children in private ones. A reluctance to acknowledge that face-to-face interactions with a competent, caring teacher are the critical experiences that motivate children and youths to improve their academic talents is obstructing progress.

The efficient functioning of so many machines we have become dependent on tempted many to assume that computers might be as effective as teachers in educating youths. This belief contains some truth for children who are motivated by the educational values their families socialized, but it has less validity for children who failed to receive or incorporate this message. These youths require teachers who can create the desire to acquire relevant intellectual talents. Machines cannot replace humans when children must learn facts and rules that are not demanded by or come easy to their biology and, in addition, require perseverance in the face of frustration and an ability to tolerate the shame that follows occasional failure.

Finally, teachers have to initiate and moderate with their students candid discussions of the competing values that dominate a certain historical moment. These discussions are more meaningful than reading online texts about abortion or gay marriage. Schools and universities, like the police, firefighters, courts, and local elected representatives, serve their societies. Hence, they must remain sensitive to historical changes in values while resisting the temptation to avoid controversy by giving in to those who demand politically correct postures.

I hope that the generation now preparing to have children will be friendly to the suggestions for reform advocated here.

Expectations

The brain is always prepared for the event that is likely to materialize in the next moment. Most of the time the expected outcome occurs. On the infrequent occasions when prediction fails — say, a light does not turn on when the switch is flipped — a number of connected brain sites immediately release a cocktail of molecules that enhance a state of alertness and award the unexpected event a salience that renders it more memorable. Some events can activate a brain that is not in a conscious state. The brains of sleeping newborns, for example, respond when the sound of a bell occurs after a series of identical tones because the bell sound is unexpected.

The detailed features of unexpected events that evoke strong feelings — for example, seeing a plane strike the World Trade Center on September 11, 2001 — are remembered for many years. A team of scientists led by William Hirst studied the preservation of the schemata and thoughts that many Americans formed that day. Although less salient features were lost during the succeeding years, most adults retained remarkably accurate memories of where they were, what they were doing, who they were with, and other details about the falling buildings for as long as ten years. These faithful representations are called "flashbulb" memories.

Unexpected events that are not understood evoke a state of uncertainty in infants long before snakes or spiders generate a similar state. Four-month-olds do not expect to hear a blend of recorded female voices speaking sentences such as "Hello, baby, how are you today?" without a human present. The alert infants stare with a puzzled facial expression at the small speaker that is the source of the sounds. A few cry. The inability to relate an unexpected event to what one knows—that is, to understand it—is a more frequent cause of fear or anxiety in children than the anticipation of being physically harmed. Perhaps that is why the words *who, what, when,* and *why* appear in a child's vocabulary by the fourth birthday

Young children may require exposure to some unexpected events in order to learn how to respond to these experiences. A sizeable number of children who had spent most of their first year lying in a crib in a depriving Romanian orphanage, where they had experienced few surprises, failed to show the appropriate caution as five-year-olds living with a foster family when a stranger knocked on the door and asked them to go with her in order to receive a gift. Family-reared children were less likely to be as trusting of a stranger who made a similar request.

Many rewarding events are unexpected experiences. Animals will learn a new motor response if it is followed by an unexpected, nonaversive change in what they see, hear, feel, or taste. A monkey in a barren room learns to strike a lever if that action is followed by a five-second peek at unfamiliar objects outside the room. Neuroscientists are discovering what commentators on human nature have known for a long time: the desirability of many experiences is enhanced when they are surprises. Unexpected praise from a parent for a high grade is more effective in strengthening a child's motivation than anticipated praise.

Secretion of the molecule dopamine in response to an unexpected event is occasionally accompanied by a pleasant feeling. As humans age, they lose some of the neurons that secrete dopamine. Seventy-year-olds are less motivated than twenty-year-olds to visit a new place, meet a new person, or view a novel artistic production because the intensity of the pleasure is diluted. Not surprisingly, children and adults vary in their attraction to new experiences, partly because they vary in the genes responsible for a larger or a smaller surge of dopamine.

The adjectives *unexpected* and *novel* are not synonyms. Adults expect to see novel events when visiting an unfamiliar part of the world, and a familiar event is unexpected if it occurs at an unfamiliar time or in an unfamiliar location. Examples include a telephone ringing at 3:00 a.m. and a man on a bus brushing his teeth. It is impossible to list the features that define unexpected events because these properties always depend on the person's accumulated knowledge and the setting in which the event occurs. Americans are no longer surprised by television scenes showing bombs destroying homes, large refugee camps, or volcanoes erupting.

The Need to Understand

An unexpected event automatically evokes an attempt to understand its origin and to assign it to a category. When both questions are answered, which happens most of the time, brain and mind return to whatever they were doing before the intrusion. When either answer is not forthcoming, a state of uncertainty may pierce consciousness. Most gray-haired scholars brooding on the characteristics that render humans unique nominated a symbolic language and a moral sense. Few suggested that a need to understand is a third, equally significant property. Psychologists have awarded too much power to the anticipation of physical harm and not enough to the unpleasant feeling that accompanies an inability to understand why things are the way they are.

Feelings toward a parent, spouse, or friend can change dramatically when their actions violate expectations. Arthur Miller captured this phenomenon in *Death of a Salesman* when Biff discovers the father he had idealized in a hotel room with a prostitute. Couples who believe that a happy marriage ought to be free of serious quarrels are susceptible to a bout of anger or sadness when the expectation of continuous harmony is disconfirmed. Couples in arranged marriages are protected from these disappointments because they did not hold this unrealistic conception of the marital experience.

The brain and psychological states created by an unexpected event, called event uncertainty, are not identical to the states evoked by an unsureness over the best action to implement when alternatives exist, called response uncertainty. Event uncertainty is accompanied by vigilance and the implicit question "What is that?" Response uncertainty is accompanied by concern over choosing the wrong response and the question "What should I do?"

The Benevolent Properties of Rituals

Status hierarchies in monkey troops reduce response uncertainty by limiting each member's range of behaviors toward every other member in the troop. The fall of the Roman Empire made the new Christian religion attractive to many members of the empire because adoption of its beliefs and rituals muted the response uncertainty created by the absence of the order the government had provided. Humans spend their days in a narrow corridor bordered on the right by the boredom of near-perfect predictability and on the left by a fear of total unpredictability.

Participation in unfamiliar rituals that the individual expects to be benevolent is accompanied by a surge of opioids that creates a feeling many describe as relaxed. This process helps to explain why the magic rituals of shamans, which consist of unfamiliar actions performed with familiar objects, are infused with power. A popular ritual in ancient Egypt required the shaman to drown a falcon in a bowl of milk taken from a brown cow, wrap the dead falcon in a cloth free of dye, and place the cloth next to fingernails and strands of human hair.

All successful psychotherapies possess some unexpected features. Those who believe in the curative power of the therapy are more likely to evaluate its unfamiliar rituals as helpful. Psychoanalysis, which was introduced to Americans and Europeans early in the last century, required patients to lie on a couch, not look at the therapist, and free-associate. This therapy had a measure of curative power for patients who believed that these unusual actions would relieve their distress. Psychoanalysis had a measure of success for about fifty years, until the rituals lost their novelty and patients were no longer persuaded that this therapy possessed unique healing properties. Some psychoanalysts, too, became less convinced that they were practitioners of a powerful cure. The Chinese had not been receptive to psychoanalysis when it was popular elsewhere because they were unaccustomed to sharing personal matters with strangers. Contemporary Chinese who are friendlier to Freud's ideas and can afford the cost are making appointments with psychoanalysts because of the therapy's novel features.

Many American and European psychotherapists practice cognitive behavioral therapy, or CBT, with anxious or depressed patients. The rituals of CBT include exposure to the objects or situations that evoke anxiety. For example, the therapist often accompanies a patient who is afraid of flying on several flights. As this therapy approaches its fiftieth anniversary it, too, is beginning to lose its earlier effectiveness for the same reason that psychoanalysis lost much of its curative power.

Patients who practice rituals that are novel, such as yoga, meditation, or breathing exercises, report remission of their symptoms because they expected these activities to be helpful. Some depressed patients who spent time on a farm reported feeling happier. So did older adults in a residence home who constructed a simulated garden. Many patients who receive a combination of psychotherapy and a drug feel slightly better than those receiving only one of these treatments because the former assume that two forms of therapy ought to be more effective than one.

The tens of thousands of nineteenth-century Europeans who visited the shrine at Lourdes believed the visit would cure their illness. Even Jean-Martin Charcot, the renowned director of the Pitié-Salpêtrière hospital in Paris who insisted that all cases of hysteria were due to a brain abnormality, acknowledged in 1892, a year before he died, that faith cures were possible.

Patients who have minimal confidence in their therapy, or hold unrealistically high expectations of a rapid cure, are usually disappointed. Investigators at the University of Cologne found that Parkinson's patients who held excessively high expectations of the effectiveness of deep brain stimulation reported little improvement, despite objective evidence of improved functioning. Dour perfectionists who expect to be disappointed usually confirm their own prophecy. When hope of improvement is absent, the power of most therapies dissolves as quickly as the sister of the witch of the East when Dorothy doused her with water. Indeed, if a medicine proven to be effective with an illness is administered to patients without their knowledge, there is a smaller reduction in symptoms.

No form of psychotherapy has proven to be clearly superior to any other when patients are evaluated five years after they began treatment. The relation between the therapist and patient makes a far more important contribution to remission of symptoms than the specific rituals the therapist follows. Although no therapy can help all patients, there is probably one therapy that will help some patients. No lover can arouse romantic feelings in everyone, but there is probably at least one partner for every eager lover.

Effectiveness of Interventions

Many intervention projects designed to help children or youths acquire more adaptive traits usually compare those who received the intervention with a control group that did not. If the former improve, investigators conclude that the intervention was effective. They rarely entertain the possibility that the improvement is due to the fact that the participants expected to be helped. This expectation was missing among the members of the control group.

Many interventions designed to change the child-rearing practices of mothers with less than a high school education fail because most of these parents had little faith either in their ability to change their children or in the intervention ritual. A person, group, or society has to be psychologically prepared for and motivated to take advantage of a therapeutic experience. This fact explains the minimal improvement in the academic achievement of African American children from poor families living in Newark, New Jersey, despite the introduction of large amounts of money into the city's public school system.

A readiness for change or a lack thereof applies to nations. European leaders assumed the rules they imposed on many nations of the European Union would be welcome because they promised to bring greater prosperity to all. However, European voters rejected that premise, electing a large number of representatives to the European Parliament in May 2014 who were opposed to many of these rules. Unlike an ointment applied to the skin to reduce itching, attempts to alter human beliefs, values, or behaviors are unlikely to be successful if the client is not favorably disposed to the recommended ideas or practices. A cartoon in the *New Yorker* shows a monarch butterfly, posing as a psychotherapist, telling a caterpillar patient lying on a couch, "The thing is, you have to really want to change."

Scientists at Stanford University developed virtual reality goggles that allow young adults to see their face morph into the visage of a sixty-five-year-old ready to retire. The hope is that this novel experience will motivate the youths to save money for their retirement years. It is too early to know whether this ritual will have the expected effect. I suspect that once a majority of youths know the purpose of the goggles, its advantages will disappear. It is far too easy to spin optimistic narratives for new machines, medicines, curricula, or inventions.

Evaluations of Self

Unexpected events are, by definition, deviations from some norm. When the norm is a person's understanding of his or her physical and psychological properties, a serious deviation can evoke an unpleasant state. Most twenty-year-olds have a reasonably accurate idea of where they rank with their peers with respect to popularity, wealth, abilities, attractiveness, and status. A deviation from that understanding creates both event and response uncertainty. A scientist who was always in the top 5 percent of her class from kindergarten through her PhD degree will feel threatened at age forty-five if she has unexpectedly fallen to a much lower rank. An adult who was always in the bottom half of his class from elementary school through college and does not understand why, at age forty, he is richer and more respected than his peers may feel his success is undeserved.

The brain and mind accept a modest amount of deviation from the usual because these events are most likely to be understood. When a deviant event passes a tipping point, individuals have a choice of three strategies: maintain their older understanding and ignore the event, acknowledge the event and mount a protection against its implications, or acknowledge the deviation and recalibrate their understanding. Younger adults usually take the third path; older ones prefer the first two. I was in my late fifties when cell phones became as regular a part of one's costume as socks and shoes. I rarely take my cell phone when I leave home, and I have neither a Facebook nor Twitter account. As a result, I see the potential problems that trail the addiction to iPhones. My twenty-four-year-old granddaughter sees only the advantages and pleasures.

History is replete with deviations from a population's expectations that assume the form of wars, civil unrest, natural catastrophes, pandemics, new machines, and novel ideologies. The French Revolution stripped nobles of their privileges; the First World War destroyed the illusion of progress; the wars in Vietnam, Iraq, and Afghanistan turned Americans against war. The future contains the possibility of coastal cities underwater, new viruses causing pandemics, hacking of government and bank computers, and radical groups bombing cities. Those who ruminate on the possibility of these events experience changes in brain and body that prepare them for an exaggerated reaction to the smaller deviations scattered throughout a typical week. A feeling of vitality oscillates in a narrow space of moderate uncertainty. When this state is replaced by either perfect certainty or chronic uncertainty, boredom or vigilance replaces vitality.

Why Support Basic Research?

Public support for basic scientific research whose results have no immediate practical advantages requires a society in which a majority of citizens enjoy a moment of pleasure when they learn a novel scientific fact. The United States has many bridges, schools, tunnels, and highways in need of repair, more than 17 million Americans who go to bed hungry, and a government debt that exceeds $18 trillion. Yet the federal government will probably spend about $20 billion in 2015 on research whose main purpose is to add to our knowledge of the universe. Although the facts that will be learned have no obvious effects on the daily lives of most Americans, a majority approve of public support of this research because they extract some delight from the discoveries. Youths trailed Socrates as he wandered around Athens, and sixteenth-century Europeans paid money to sit in a large hall listening to a scholar read from a text on ethics, theology, mathematics, or philosophy.

What are the bases of the pleasure that accompanies the learning of a new fact? I am excluding the scientists who made the discoveries. Their pleasure is easy to understand. Uncovering a new fact is inherently pleasing and occasionally brings a promotion, a prize, or celebrity. I also exclude the money spent on research on human illness because everyone is concerned with improving health.

Why did I feel a moment of pleasure upon learning that the earth is 4.5 billion years old? I had a similar feeling when a new fact implied an unwanted event in the distant future. The moon has been slowly receding from the earth since it first formed. Scientists believe there will come a time in the very distant future when the moon will be so far from our planet its gravitational force will be too weak to prevent the earth from wobbling in its orbit. Despite the potentially catastrophic consequences for our climate, I confess to more pleasure in knowing this fact than increased worry over the future wobbling of our planet.

Two explanations of an addiction to knowledge seem reasonable. The popular account claims that the learning of a new fact, like mastering a new skill, is inherently pleasant. Three-year-olds are eager to know the names of things and often smile when their pointing at an unfamiliar object is followed by a parent supplying a name. The same smile is occasionally seen on the faces of students in a large lecture hall the moment they understand the point the speaker is trying to make. This smile reflects the moment of understanding. Dissipation of the unpleasant state of "not knowing" is usually followed by a pleasant feeling.

A second explanation assumes that the pleasure of knowing rests on the many past occasions when the acquisition of a fact dispelled an unpleasant feeling. A three-year-old who, while staring at a golf club, asks a parent, "Wha's that?" is in a state of uncertainty. The mother's answer, "That's Mama's new golf club," dissolves the uncertainty and strengthens the state we call curiosity.

A child who broke a valuable glass ornament when no adult was in the room worries about the severity of the imminent punishment. When the punishment occurs, the worry is dissipated. A mother once told me of a pair of incidents that captures the unpleasantness of not knowing and the satisfaction that follows the loss of uncertainty. Her two-year-old son put some freshly ironed clothes in the toilet bowl. When the mother discovered this, she lost her temper and struck the boy harshly. Several days later the boy repeated the same action, but this time he went to his mother immediately, let her know what he had done, and assumed the posture appropriate for a punishment. Why did the boy do this? One answer is that he did not understand the reason for the initial punishment and needed to find out if putting ironed clothes in the toilet bowl had been the cause. His second action was an attempt to find the answer and, having found it, he never again displayed this behavior.

A forty-eight-year-old woman consulted a psychiatrist because her failure to understand why she felt like a man was causing her great distress. When the psychiatrist, who had her genome analyzed, told her she had been born with an abnormality in the sex chromosomes she felt much better, simply because she had learned the reason for her feelings. A large number of adolescent boys who feel tense and uncertain with girls because of their childhood experiences, rather than an inherited biology, stop dating because the encounter is too distressing. In time, a proportion of these young men lose interest in heterosexual romance and begin to wonder why they feel this way. Contemporary society provides an answer—they are gay. Once they accept this fact they feel relieved and may initiate sexual relationships with other males to affirm their newly discovered category.

It is not clear whether the desire for knowledge is a biologically prepared urge or a motive acquired through the past reductions of uncertainty by new facts. In either case, uncertainty and its reduction are seminal processes in both narratives. I am less certain today than I was forty years ago that all knowledge sets humans free. But I am more certain that knowing emerges as a desirable state during childhood and retains its power to satisfy indefinitely. The psychological state that follows reading that the universe has billions of galaxies or that newborn infants react to human voices in a special way can compete with the pragmatic advantage of repairing our bridges, schools, and highways.

The Force of Feelings

Biologists are fond of saying that nothing about living things makes sense without an understanding of evolution. Equally, a great many human psychological properties make no sense without an understanding of feelings. This claim has been unpopular among the Western scientists who celebrate cool, rational thought free of the taint of emotions that pose a threat to civic order. Many societies, including China and Japan, do not regard feelings as dangerous demons.

Feelings as the Bases of Emotions and Moods

The meanings of the related words *feeling* and *emotion* remain controversial. I use the term feeling to name the conscious perception of sensations that originate in body and brain, without claiming this is the best definition or the one most scientists prefer. A feeling can penetrate consciousness when an external event, spontaneous change within the body, or a thought generates activity in heart, gut, lungs, muscles, or the sensory receptors for tastes, smells, touches, heat, pain, sights, or sounds. The detection of a racing heart, warm face, relaxed muscles, sweet taste, or pain generates a feeling. Although events, body sensations, and thoughts alter the existing brain state, not every such change is accompanied by a conscious feeling. Men who did not know they had been given a large dose of the stress hormone cortisol reported no change in feeling, even though the hormone altered their brain state.

The writer Nathan McCall captured the intrusiveness of some feelings. "The heart is a stubborn thing. It don't give a shit what you tell it to do. It does what it wants and it can't be trained to do otherwise." Two strips of cortex in the anterior portion of the brain, called the insula and the cingulate, make significant contributions to feelings. Both regions contain a large number of uniquely shaped cells, called von Economo neurons, found in the cortex of primates, whales, elephants, and humans. Because human brains possess the largest number of these distinctive neurons, it is tempting to suggest that they play an important function in creating an awareness of one's feelings.

Moods

Each person has a dominant feeling that is maintained during most hours of most days. Although this feeling is typically ignored because it is not intrusive, if asked to name it most individuals would choose synonyms of the English words *relaxed, vital, tense, irritable, apathetic, down, apprehensive,* or *vigilant.* These interpretations are moods.

The ancient Greek terms *sanguine, choleric, phlegmatic,* and *melancholic* described moods. Although we do not know all the processes that create dominant moods, the balance between the sympathetic and parasympathetic arms of the autonomic nervous system represents one contribution. A balance that favors the sympathetic arm is accompanied by a high and minimally variable heart rate (meaning little variation in the time between successive heartbeats) and a tense, vigilant mood. A balance favoring the parasympathetic arm is associated with a low, more variable heart rate and a relaxed mood. The balance between the two systems is subject to genetic control and is influenced by the sites containing the von Economo neurons. Relaxed, sociable, fearless adults usually have lower and more variable heart rates than tense, shy, cautious ones.

Life experiences make a significant contribution to moods. Frequent losses, threats of harm, poverty, or many childhood frustrations often generate a melancholic mood. A life marked by security, accomplishment, and an identification with family members who have desirable qualities is likely to create a relaxed mood.

I noted in essay 5 that persistent poverty, abuse, or frequent illness stimulates the production of proteins, called cytokines, that activate brain sites responsible for the fatigue and apathy that accompany an illness. Adults who detect this feeling but do not believe they are ill look for another interpretation. The conclusion that they are depressed is one common solution. The cytokine proteins did not cause the depressed mood directly. Rather, these proteins were the origins of a feeling that was interpreted as depression. American women are more likely than men to attribute this feeling to a lack of close friendships. Men with a similar feeling are biased to blame work problems, loss of money, or failure at an important task.

A small number of highly successful adults are susceptible to an unpleasant feeling they interpret as tension or depression when they are not engaged in something useful. These individuals usually attained their wealth, fame, or status through a persistent work ethic that began when they entered the first grade. Each time they received a high grade, praise, money, a promotion, or a leadership role they attributed the moment of pleasure to their highly disciplined work habits. As a result, the feeling that accompanies working on any challenging assignment is interpreted as pleasant. These "workaholics" feel tense or depressed when they are not engaged in a task they regard as important. Others live with a mood marked by worry over a less than perfect performance on a task that someone might observe and judge. These adults tend to refuse assignments that pose the risk of failure, even when the task is inviting.

Emotions

An emotion, unlike a mood, is an interpretation of a feeling that usually lasts a few seconds but can persist for several minutes, hours, or days if the person ruminates on it. Individuals can assign the origin of these feelings to a thought, an outside event, illness, medicine, or a spontaneous bodily change. The cause selected, which is always dependent on the setting, affects the emotional word the person chooses to describe the feeling. The emotional words *fearful, anxious, excited, sad, depressed, happy, excited, angry, proud, loving, ashamed, guilty, nostalgic, jealous,* and *disgusted* are popular interpretations of feelings.

A perception of increased facial warmth and a rise in heart rate could occur when a person is insulted, spills food in public, or receives unexpected praise. The context and accompanying thoughts determine whether the person selects anger, shame, or pride as the interpretation of the feeling. Some adults who detect a rise in heart rate and tension in the muscles of the chest while preparing to be interviewed for an important job decide they are anxious. Others, with exactly the same feeling, conclude they are excited. Adults who take the drug prednisone to treat asthma but do not know it can generate a mildly unpleasant feeling are prone to interpret the feeling as irritation with a child or spouse or anxiety over an imminent challenge. In one study, the electrical stimulation of neurons in a site near the insula created a feeling that men interpreted in different ways. One man reported feeling like a "football player getting ready to go out and make his first touchdown"; another said he felt sad.

Tony Parker interviewed a large number of convicted criminals who had confessed to a violent crime. One woman who had shot her lover with a revolver and pushed his body over a cliff reported that, as a child, she rarely experienced any feeling when she violated a family or community norm. She interpreted her absence of feeling as implying that she was unable to feel guilty: "I never had a strong sense of sin. . . . I missed out on guilt."

The feeling originating in a thought differs from the feeling generated by experiencing the comparable event. The feeling that follows the accidental spilling of wine on a guest at a dinner party is more intense than the feeling that accompanies reflection on that incident the next day. Anger provides a more persuasive example. The quality and intensity of the feeling that follows being struck across the face by a friend are unlike those of the feeling evoked when the victim reflects on that incident a week later. The person may use the same emotional word, but the feeling is very different.

The words chosen to name a feeling can change over time. The nineteenth-century writer Thomas Hardy was fond of the terms *temerity, muddled,* and *equanimity.* Contemporary authors are more likely to use *apprehensive, confused,* and *serenity* for the same feelings. Some emotional words are novel additions to a language. The English term *anomie* does not appear in books until the 1960s. Czesław Miłosz, a celebrated Polish poet, was unable to suppress an uncomfortable feeling while he was a visiting faculty member at the University of California. He described this feeling in a letter to Thomas Merton written many years after he returned to Europe. "Ten years ago I just escaped from America, being afraid of a life without purpose and of acedia." Miłosz chose *acedia* to describe a feeling that many Americans might call spiritually hollow. The seminal point is that the interpretation of a feeling is the basis of the emotional word chosen.

History alters the feelings, and therefore the emotions, that are probable. The lives of a majority of humans for most of the last one hundred thousand years were marked by frequent loss of a young child or spouse, illness, loss of property, and backbreaking physical work. Thomas Hobbes famously described life as nasty, brutish, and short. A majority of adults expected to experience uncertainty, pain, frustration, and loss. Days that were free of an unpleasant feeling were a cause for joy.

The expected mood began to change at the beginning of the last century when potable water, electricity, medical advances, and machines reduced the frequency of illness, prolonged lives, and replaced muscles with machines for physically demanding tasks. These novelties began to alter the average person's expectations. When some prominent social scientists suggested that happiness was the emotional state nature intended, many were persuaded that if they were not happy most of the time they were probably violating a natural law and something was wrong with them or their society.

This shift in the dominant mood each person was supposed to experience was accompanied by increased scientific and media attention to the concept of stress, defined as a state brought on by illness, loss, poverty, marginalization, victimhood, excessive competitiveness, work pressures, or war. Contemporary adults are biased to interpret a persistent tension, fatigue, or vigilance as the product of stress in their daily lives. The declaration "I feel stressed" has replaced the full sentences of earlier generations specifying the cause of the feeling: "I am worried about my sick infant," "I am ashamed of my poverty," "I feel guilty over my loss of faith in God," "I am jealous of my neighbor's easy life," "I am angry over my husband's infidelity," "I am worried over my inability to support my family," or "I feel frustrated because I cannot meet all my responsibilities." Each of these emotional states is apt to be accompanied by a distinctive brain profile. Collapsing these varied states into one category of stress ignores these differences.

Can Animals Be Afraid, Angry, or Happy?

The scientists who speculate that animals have emotions resembling those of humans believe it is appropriate to use terms such as *fearful, anxious, sad, angry,* or *happy* to describe the psychological states of monkeys, mice, or rats. This practice is questionable because animals do not interpret their bodily sensations. The fact that monkeys and chimps show facial expressions that resemble those observed in humans who report feeling happy, sad, angry, or surprised facilitates this belief. However, the muscular pattern adopted in a smile does not always reflect happiness. Humans smile when they want to inform another that they are not about to become aggressive. Chimpanzees display a similar facial expression under the same conditions.

Scientists have used some of the behavioral consequences of the molecule oxytocin to argue that animals and humans experience similar emotional states. Because oxytocin facilitates the bonding of a male and female pair in a species of rodents called prairie voles, investigators classified this molecule as the basis of emotional bonding between humans or between humans and their pet dogs. However, all oxytocin can do is to alter a brain or bodily state, which can include relaxing muscles and lowering heart rate and blood pressure. These bodily changes usually increase the intensity of the pleasure of an experience, whether making love, eating dinner with a friend, or watching a film. The interpretation of the feeling—and therefore the behavior that might arise from it—depends on the setting. Is the person under the influence of a higher level of oxytocin walking alone in a spring forest full of flowers, making love, petting a puppy, strolling in an art museum, showering after exercise, or watching a humorous film? Oxytocin should be labeled the relaxing molecule, not the bonding molecule.

I do not believe that the psychological state of a monkey who has just lost a piece of food to a larger animal resembles the state of a woman who has just lost her handbag to a youth who seized it from her shoulder. The woman's feeling could invite an interpretation of sadness over the loss, anger at the youth, or the more pleasant emotion of revenge because the handbag was old and contained only a used Kleenex and a broken comb. The monkey's response to the loss of food is more predictable because it is a direct product of the brain's reaction, without the intrusion of thought. Only humans can be angry, sad, or anxious because these words are interpretations of feelings.

Two Dimensions

Psychologists classify emotional words as having a positive or negative valence depending on whether the feeling that is the presumed basis for the emotion is pleasant or unpleasant. The brain honors this distinction through separate circuits for pleasant and unpleasant sensations. Emotions also vary in potency, defined by the intensity or intrusiveness of the underlying feeling. The word *sad* has an unpleasant valence and low potency. *Anger* has an unpleasant valence and high potency. English has more words for unpleasant than pleasant emotions because the feelings that accompany the former states are usually more intense and/or more intrusive. Most unpleasant sensations— pain, bitter tastes, acrid smells, or witnessing an act of cruelty—evoke a larger brain response than most pleasant ones.

Some societies believe that each person is born with a finite amount of vital energy. The men in these societies are vulnerable to a blend of pleasant and unpleasant feelings when they engage in sex because each time they ejaculate they believe they lose vital energy. Americans and East Asians hold divergent views about unpleasant feelings. Americans try to mute them; Asians interpret unpleasant feelings as possessing some desirable features. A favorite Chinese proverb reads, "Pleasure is the seed of pain; pain is the seed of pleasure."

Interpretations Outnumber Words for Feelings

The world's languages contain more words that are interpretations of feelings than names for the sensations that are the bases of feelings. There are several reasons why bodily sensations have a fuzzy quality that is hard to describe. The heart, stomach, lungs, and muscles have fewer sensory receptors than the eyes or ears, and it takes longer for information from the former to get to the brain than information from the eyes, ears, nose, tongue, and skin. In addition, sensations from the heart, stomach, and muscles are more fully elaborated by the right hemisphere, which represents whole patterns rather than detailed features. Languages have more words for a single feature of a feeling, such as *sharp*, *dull*, or *intense*, than terms for the pattern that all the features assume.

Most feelings, like photographs taken out of focus, invite more than one interpretation. The interpretation of the sensation that follows drinking a glass of wine at the end of the day is usually correct. But there is more than one reasonable interpretation of a sudden rise in heart rate while sitting in a chair. Americans and Europeans are biased to interpret this feeling as anxiety if they cannot assign it to illness or something they ate. Adults in other cultures, however, might interpret the same feeling as fatigue. Many middle-aged Yamati women, members of an isolated Australian community living about 420 kilometers north of the city of Perth, interpret the hot flashes and sweating of menopause as an illness rather than as the product of a life stage.

Freud recognized that adults try to avoid interpretations of shame or guilt. A man who does not want to recognize his guilt over failing to repay a friend the money he borrowed might interpret the uncomfortable feeling as anger at the friend for expecting the repayment so soon. An adolescent boy sitting at a table in a school cafeteria who detects a sudden rise in heart rate and tension in his chest muscles might leave the table if he decides he is coming down with a cold. He is likely to say something aggressive, however, if he concludes that the origin of the feeling was seeing a sneer on the face of the boy sitting across from him. And he will finish his lunch quickly and go to a quiet place to study if he interprets the same feeling as provoked by the thought that he is not prepared for an examination that afternoon.

The Inadequacy of Words

The lack of sensitive methods to measure the quality and intensity of feelings forces scientists to assume that the emotional words people use are accurate indexes of conscious feelings. This premise is deeply flawed.

Americans habitually say, "I love you" without experiencing any feeling. If words reflected feelings, non–English speakers using synonyms for the English terms *anxious, happy, angry,* or *lonely* should experience the same feelings. This is not the case. The Utku Eskimo of Hudson Bay have four words that specify the setting in which the feeling English speakers call loneliness occurs. English speakers use the word *angry* or *mad* to describe the different feelings provoked by losing one's keys, reflecting on a silly error made on an exam, being the target of a slur, being caught in traffic, betrayal by a friend, or seeing a neighbor throw garbage on the lawn. Other languages have invented words to distinguish among the feelings accompanying these diverse experiences.

I do not possess a word to describe a novel feeling that lasted for close to thirty minutes after I finished reading Hannah Arendt's book summarizing the 1961 trial of Adolf Eichmann, a Nazi who was responsible for the murder of many Jews. Neither *sad, angry,* nor *disgusted* came close to capturing a feeling that blended a heaviness bearing down on my body with a sense of lost agency. The Japanese have no word to describe the feeling evoked when one learns that a disliked person has suffered a misfortune. The German word for this feeling is *schadenfreude.*

Although the Yucatec language of the Mayan Indians does not contain different words for the feelings that English speakers call anger and disgust, it is likely that these Indians experience distinctive feelings when they are insulted compared with seeing dirt on a dish of food. Residents of Sumatra use the word *malu* to describe how they feel when they make a mistake and when they are in the presence of a person who has much higher status, even though their feelings in these settings are likely to differ.

The evidence invites the conclusion that language is an inadequate vehicle to describe feelings. The sparse vocabulary for feelings can be likened to a palette containing only six pigments belonging to an artist who plans to paint all the flowers in a large garden in May. Humans invented language to communicate facts about the environment, moral rules to follow, and the teaching of skills. Words were not intended to describe feelings because it is not always adaptive to reveal feelings that others might interpret as anger, shame, guilt, jealousy, or lust.

Languages have few words capable of describing a blend of interpretations imposed on a collection of feelings. An unmarried adolescent who is about to drown her newborn infant experiences a blend that combines regret over not using contraception, anger at the boy who abandoned her, and guilt over the murder she is planning. Americans who reflect on the events of the past century are susceptible to a blend of interpretations of feelings generated by a suspicion of strangers, confusion over the meaning of their lives, and uncertainty over the moral values that demand unquestioned loyalty. English has not yet invented a name for this emotion, although Miłosz's *acedia* is a candidate. Minds favor a single best word for a feeling. Blends mar the beauty of the idea that there is a small number of basic emotions, each having a single, best name.

Happiness

Most Americans say they want to be happy, and hope the same for their children. They do not mean the brief sensation that accompanies eating a tasty meal when hungry, entering a warm house on a cold day, or an orgasm. If questioned further about the conditions for happiness, most would say they want to feel satisfied with the life they have led up to that point. When people are asked what they must do to attain this state, there is often a prolonged silence because of an unsureness over the actions that would guarantee this prize. It is surely odd that so many yearn for a psychological state they do not know how to obtain.

Two different cascades, accompanied by different brain profiles, allow individuals to move closer to two feelings that happen to have the same English name: happiness. One path requires the possession of a temperamental bias that mutes the intensity of the feelings that accompany frustration, danger, insult, loss, or violation of a personal moral standard. Those born with this biology say they are happy because they are protected from excessive anger, anxiety, sadness, or guilt when they are insulted, diagnosed with cancer, lose money, or miss an appointment with a friend.

Humans have more control over the second path to a somewhat different happiness, which is the feeling that accompanies attaining some of the important goals one had invented earlier as signs of having led a good life. These goals vary, but among the most common are performing actions that contribute to the welfare of others, perfecting a talent, raising happy children, maintaining a mutually gratifying marriage, or acquiring a resource the society admires. A 2012 Pew Foundation poll found that Americans are more likely than Europeans to believe that hard work usually leads to the success that allows one to feel satisfied with the way one's life played out. Social scientists call this state subjective well-being.

The poet Wallace Stevens understood that each person must invent the goals he or she decides are worth pursuing. "The final belief is to believe in a fiction, there being nothing else. The exquisite truth is to know that it is a fiction and that you believe in it willingly." Stevens may have read a comment by the Marquise du Châtelet, the mistress of Voltaire, who wrote, "To be happy one must be susceptible to illusions for it is to illusions that we owe the majority of our pleasures. Unhappy is the one who has lost them."

All judgments of well-being are necessarily based on comparisons. Information technologies allow adults living in societies with high levels of poverty, disease, corruption, and crime, such as Haiti or Somalia, to compare their circumstances with those living in more advantaged nations. This comparison can dilute the subjective well-being of the accomplished adults in these poor, corrupt societies. Adults who move from a poorer nation to a wealthier one can compare their new circumstances with those of the impoverished friends they left behind or the wealthier acquaintances they meet. An eleventh-century Chinese scholar, Shao Yong, explained why he felt happy: "I am a human and not an animal, a male and not a female, a Chinese and not a barbarian, and because I live in Luoyang, the most wonderful city in the world."

I suspect, but cannot prove, that many white, middle-class Americans born between 1950 and 1980 are less happy than those born between 1880 and the onset of the First World War because the former are more likely to question the claim by political candidates that the United States is the most moral, democratic, egalitarian, optimistic, and productive nation on earth. Members of the earlier generation found it easier to experience a vicarious pride when they reflected on the American Revolution, the Emancipation Proclamation, the bravery at the Alamo, and America's contribution to the defeat of the

Nazis and Japanese in 1945. Those born between 1950 and 1980 are reminded of the harsh treatment of slaves in the antebellum South, the slaughter of Native Americans, the greedy robber barons who exploited European immigrants huddled in tenements, the murder of innocent civilians in Vietnam, Iraq, and Afghanistan, the millions of high school graduates who cannot read a newspaper, teenage girls fellating boys they just met, school massacres, priests sexually abusing children, physicians taking money from drug companies in exchange for touting the qualities of the firm's medicines, and the federal government giving billions of dollars to banks, insurance firms, and automobile companies to rescue them from the consequences of excessively risky decisions while doing less to help the millions of citizens who lost their homes because of a foolish decision to buy a house they could not afford.

Most adults behave as if the wisest strategy is to pursue a few praiseworthy goals while maintaining the hope that one morning the elusive state of well-being will unexpectedly pierce consciousness. The many thousands of scientists working seventy-hour weeks recognize that the probability they will make a significant discovery is very low. But they also appreciate the meaning Camus intended in *The Myth of Sisyphus*. If they stopped doing research they would miss the happiness that is an intimate partner of the pursuit of all prized goals. Jean-Paul Sartre, Samuel Beckett, and Albert Camus acknowledged that life was absurd and without a special meaning. But instead of giving up and crumbling in a heap, their advice was to invent a meaning and pursue its implied goals as the most adaptive response to the puzzle of human existence.

Feelings and the Sexes

Although the evidence for sex differences in moods and acute emotions is too weak for any strong conclusions, the slightly different genomes, physiologies, and brain anatomy of males and females could generate subtle differences in the likelihood of particular bodily feelings. Observations of young boys and girls from diverse cultures imply that a feeling that blends high energy, frustration over restraints on movement, and automatic urges to approach new settings is a little more common in males. Young boys often climb into small cabinets, jump from heights, and approach unfamiliar objects or places with minimal caution. Young girls prefer quieter play with other children and are usually more cautious in dangerous or novel settings. A visit to any day care center or nursery school in any part of the world affirms these claims. Juvenile male monkeys prefer to play with objects that move when manipulated. Young female monkeys like to play with small objects that have soft surfaces.

Parents in most cultures are more permissive of vigorous activity, attempts to dominate others, and aggression in their sons. These experiences contribute to a susceptibility in boys and men to an unpleasant feeling when they believe they are in a subordinate position. The stubborn fact that men commit far more murders than women made it reasonable for Shakespeare to have Lady Macbeth plead, "Unsex me" on the evening she planned to encourage her husband to murder the king.

By contrast, females are more vulnerable to an unpleasant feeling when their relationships with others are threatened. Kenneth Kendler, reflecting on the results of many studies, confirmed that loss of a close relationship is more distressing to women than men. In cases in which only one member of a brother-sister twin pair developed a serious depression, the women reported an unsatisfying marital relationship, insufficient parental affection, or minimal social support from friends. The depressed brother was more likely to report work failure or financial problems.

Hong Kong adolescent females who inflicted self-harm said they wanted to relieve feelings of apathy. The adolescent boys who injured themselves said they wanted to prove they had the self-control required to cut their skin. François Jacob and Rita Levi-Montalcini, twentieth-century Nobel laureates in physiology, both wrote memoirs. Jacob's prose emphasized the solitary, highly competitive ambience of research; Levi-Montalcini's autobiography elaborated on her collegial, cooperative relationships with other scientists.

Gender and Career Choice

Sarah-Jane Leslie of Princeton University, with the help of colleagues, examined the recipients of PhD degrees awarded by American universities in 2011. Women were more likely to receive degrees in fields where most investigators work with others on a problem related to human welfare—for example, biology, psychology, and education. Women were underrepresented in fields where the investigator works alone on problems with less obvious relevance for human welfare—for example, physics, mathematics, and philosophy. Close to 60 percent of PhDs in molecular biology in 2011 were awarded to women, compared with 15 percent in physics and 30 percent in philosophy. Because most females possess exceptional talent in language, one would expect more women to choose philosophy as a life career. The fact that they do not implies that they do not like working alone on arcane problems of logic or meaning. Men are more likely to choose these careers because the solitary work setting provides protection from domination or intimidation by other men.

A wise society accommodates to a person's preferences. The strident claim that gender prejudice is operating when there are unequal proportions of males and females in a certain vocation ignores the different motives of men and women. I am certain that there are millions of women who are as capable as men of becoming brilliant physicists or philosophers. They just don't prefer those specialties. No one contends that gender prejudice explains why, in 2015, more women than men occupy senior faculty positions in developmental psychology in American universities, when fifty years earlier the ratio favored men. Unequal sex ratios in a vocation do not always imply gender prejudice.

Biological Contributions to Gender

Select genes on the Y chromosome, combined with the balance of the sex hormones and their receptors, are likely to contribute to sex differences in moods and emotions. Only the male fetus secretes testosterone three to five months after conception and for a brief interval right after birth. This hormone activates two kinds of estrogen receptors. One is responsible for masculinizing the brain; the other prevents the formation of some feminine features, such as a rounder face and thicker lips.

Because the surge of male hormone slows the growth of the left hemisphere, a dominant right hemisphere and left-handedness are more common in males. A site in the parietal cortex of the right hemisphere facilitates the ability to mentally manipulate complex shapes, a skill called spatial reasoning. Although the average scores of males and females on tests of spatial reasoning are equal, more males have scores that place them in the top 1 percent of the distribution.

The surge in the male sex hormone contributes to a variety of subtle anatomical differences. The distance between the anal opening and the genital is one example. Males are born with a slightly longer distance than females. The sexes also differ in the ratio of the lengths of the index and ring fingers. Males have a slightly shorter index than ring finger, whereas these two fingers are of roughly equal length in females. The ratio of the length of the index over the ring finger, called the 2D:4D ratio, is usually between .95 and .97 in males but between .98 and 1.00 for females. Although the ratio is the result of several factors, the magnitude of the surge in fetal testosterone is one of them.

Because the finger ratio is an easier and less intrusive measure than the anal-genital distance, most research has used this feature. The finger ratio is correlated with a variety of physical and psychological properties. For example, men with very masculine ratios, typically less than .97, are more likely to have a muscular body build, prominent chin, broader face, engage in high-risk activities, and display greater stamina, speed, and competitiveness in athletic activities than men with ratios greater than .97.

Social scientists at the University of Cambridge studied forty-three men who were high-frequency traders at an investment firm. The three men who made the most money for their clients had more masculine ratios than the men with feminine ratios who made the least money. It is likely that the former were better able to cope with the pressure accompanying the need to make hundreds of decisions involving large amounts of money many times during a typical workday.

Men with broad faces, who are also likely to possess a masculine finger ratio, more often hold executive positions. British psychologists at the University of Sussex measured facial breadth (the ratio of the width at the upper cheekbone divided by the distance between the upper lip and the top of the eyelid) in men who were chief executives of leading British businesses as well as men of the same age who did not hold such positions. Not only did the CEOs have significantly broader faces but students (who did not know the men personally) looking at their photos rated these men as more successful than men with narrower faces. A team from the University of Wisconsin studying firms with a simple leadership structure found that the CEOs with the broadest faces made more money than those with narrower faces. Scientists at Leeds University in Great Britain who observed the behavior of capuchin monkeys at three different sites found that the males with the broadest faces were the most assertive and likely to be the alpha male in their troop.

The minority of women with masculine finger ratios are more likely to engage in competitive athletics, choose a "masculine" vocation, have a better sense of direction, are more reflective when solving problems, and are less likely to develop cervical cancer or an eating disorder. Psychologists at Umeå University found that the women attending a feminist conference in Sweden had more masculine ratios than the average Swedish woman.

A tiny proportion of newborn infants are genetic males (they are born with one X and one Y chromosome) but possess female genitals because the receptors for male sex hormone were dysfunctional. Although these children were raised as girls, they quickly developed masculine interests if given injections of testosterone when they reached adolescence. The rapid acquisition of male psychological traits, despite a dozen years of socialization as a girl, affirms the biological foundations for differences in the moods of males and females.

The genes that infants inherit from their mother make an important contribution to the growth of brain sites responsible for thought, suggesting that Athena, not Venus, is the more appropriate symbol for women. The genes children inherit from the father make a more significant contribution to the formation of the hypothalamus, which controls feelings, moods, and especially ease of sexual arousal. Despite the permissiveness surrounding the sexual behavior of unmarried young adults in America in 2015, college-age women continue to use the degrading term *slut* to describe a female who sleeps with many men. There is no comparable term of insult for a male who has frequent sex with many women.

A team at the University of Pennsylvania may have discovered one basis for expecting sex differences in feelings, moods, or specific abilities. Males possess more tracts connecting sites within the left or the right hemisphere. Because the right hemisphere elaborates images, men should find it easier to manipulate images free of semantic networks. Females, by contrast, possess more tracts that connect the two hemispheres. This anatomy should make it easier to combine the semantic networks of the left hemisphere with the feelings and images elaborated by the right. The cerebellum, a large structure in the posterior part of the brain that coordinates motor activities, is an exception to the above rule, for males possess greater connectivity between the left and right cerebellum. This arrangement should be accompanied by better coordination of large muscle movements.

I noted that young boys display a stronger attraction to new experiences that entail a risk of harm than do girls. The anticipation as well as the attainment of an improbable but desired goal is accompanied by a surge of dopamine that contributes to a feeling youths and adults interpret as pleasant. Sex differences in the brain's concentration of the molecule dopamine may contribute to the male's attraction to risky behaviors. A large increase in the level of dopamine in the prefrontal cortex following a new experience, compared with the usual level prior to the event, is accompanied by an enhanced brain response. The usual level of dopamine activity in many brain sites is slightly lower in males than females, partly because the female sex hormone estradiol facilitates the secretion of dopamine and interferes with a molecule that absorbs excess dopamine from the brain's synapses.

Because most male brains are operating at a lower level of dopamine activity, the proportionate increase in dopamine to an improbable experience, not the absolute increase, will be larger in boys and men, and therefore the pleasant feeling should be more intense. For example, an increase in dopamine from a usual level of five to a level of eight represents a 60 percent increase in dopamine activity. By contrast, an absolute increase of three from a level of eight to eleven represents only a 37 percent increase. A sweet food, such as chocolate, generates a more pleasant feeling when one is hungry and blood glucose levels are low than when one has just eaten dinner.

These facts imply that more males than females experience a more intense high following the attainment of a desired but improbable goal. This claim could explain why males are attracted to high-risk activities, such as high-stakes gambling, investing large amounts of money in a precarious enterprise, sport parachuting, climbing glacier-covered mountains, drag racing, and sexual intimacies with many new partners.

Two additional observations are relevant. A team at the University of Virginia led by Meghan Puglia found that, among Caucasians, women were more likely than men to possess an epigenetic mark on the gene for the oxytocin receptor that silences the gene and therefore reduces oxytocin activity. Because oxytocin creates a relaxed feeling marked by low tension, this observation implies that men find it easier to experience a relaxed mood. This speculation is supported by the fact that estradiol suppresses the molecule GABA, which reduces neuronal excitability in many sites, while enhancing activity of the molecule glutamate, which adds to neuronal excitability. Testosterone, by contrast, enhances GABA activity and, as a result, a slightly less excited brain.

All the evidence invites the suggestion that the female brain, from puberty to menopause, is slightly more susceptible than the male brain to creating a feeling that adults are likely to interpret as tension, worry, or sadness, depending on the context. It may not be a coincidence, therefore, that the increased levels of anxiety and depression that occur soon after puberty are more prevalent in girls than boys. Adolescence brings new challenges that create uncertainty. If select sites in the female brain are vulnerable to being aroused by such experiences, interpretations of the resulting feelings as worry or sadness are likely.

Males and females, across varied cultural settings, give different replies to the question: how should I relate to others? More females than males try to establish emotionally close, more egalitarian relationships with others; more males prefer relationships in which they are in a position of dominance. Females worry over losing close relationships; males worry over a threat to their ability to be psychologically potent. Male gangs are far more common than female gangs because belonging to a group enhances each member's potency. Experts suggest that young Muslim men who feel marginalized in the United States or Europe are susceptible to joining ISIS because membership in a group that seems to possess power brings an enhanced feeling of potency.

Sigmund Freud and Alfred Adler were Jews who hungered for the respect enjoyed by the majority in their anti-Semitic Christian societies. Both asserted that envy of those with power was a major cause of anxiety. Freud believed that young boys envied the father's command of the mother's love; Adler wrote that the second born was jealous of the privileged position of the first born. Carl Jung, like most Christian psychiatrists and psychologists active during this era, rejected Freud's argument.

None of the women who were attracted to psychoanalytic theory early in the last century considered a frustrated wish for power a significant cause of human anxiety. Helene Deutsch emphasized the significance of identification; Melanie Klein awarded importance to aggression; and Freud's daughter, Anna, believed that the mental mechanisms of projection, rationalization, and denial were far more influential than a feeling interpreted as a compromised sense of potency.

The Bases of Decisions

Decisions that claim to be based on a logical argument often draw their strength from a feeling. Many Supreme Court decisions are coherent, semantic arguments constructed to legitimize a feeling that the justices recognize is shared by a majority of Americans. The decisions to desegregate schools and to legalize abortion and gay marriage are three examples. During the Cold War, from 1945 through the 1980s, an influential collection of scholars persuaded America's political leaders that they could come up with a set of logical rules that would dictate the most rational responses by the leaders of the Soviet Union and the United States. The feelings of the leaders were ignored. These logical analyses failed to predict the fall of the Berlin Wall as well as the unexpected demise of the Soviet Union. No rational analysis would have predicted the fall of the Tunisian regime in 2011 nor the Arab Spring that followed. Three lines by the poet e. e. cummings reflect his delight in the ease with which feelings trump reason.

Who pays any attention
To the syntax of things
Will never wholly kiss you.

What Have We Learned?

Psychologists lack a compelling theory of emotions because they continue to rely mainly on words as evidence, despite the fact that the words people use are not accurate interpretations of the feelings that are the essential properties of emotions. It will prove more profitable to probe the properties of feelings in a context rather than ask people what they think they are feeling. The words people use to name their feeling states, unlike the terms *animal, plant,* and *mineral,* do not cut nature at its joints.

Investigators would profit from studying the relations between feelings that vary in salience, origin, expectedness, and familiarity, on the one hand, and settings, actions, and/or brain profiles on the other. Scientists who claim that brain measures are sensitive indexes of an emotional state, especially when the person denies any change in feeling, are relying on a unique definition of emotion. The range of interpretations that people can impose on a feeling is not captured by the current list of popular emotional words. The time has come to declare a moratorium on the use of the contextually naked terms *happy, sad, fearful, anxious, angry,* and *disgusted* and instead to write full sentences that do not require readers or listeners to figure out who, whom, why, and what.

Does a Moral Person Behave Morally?

E very known society is deeply concerned with stipulating which actions are right and which wrong and classifying each member of the community as good or bad. Although each community manages to arrive at a consensus for a generation or two, history continues to frustrate the wish to settle on a definition of right actions and good people that all societies are willing to accept as reasonable. This fact keeps a number of philosophers and social scientists usefully employed debating the meanings of morality. Two issues remain stubbornly controversial. Should the adjective *moral* apply to behaviors or to individuals? Is it possible to defend any definition of moral that transcends the agent, his or her intentions, and the setting in which the agent acts? This essay tries to illuminate these questions.

Acts or People

Some philosophers, and a majority of the world's adults, want the term *moral* restricted to the actions that a majority in a community regard as right, appropriate, and good. Honesty, kindness, cooperation, responsibility, courage, and loyalty are the usual candidates. Arbitrary rituals, such as using a napkin when eating, are excluded because failure to honor them rarely evokes a harsh critical evaluation.

A smaller number of societies prefer that the adjective moral apply to individuals who are loyal to their personal definition of right, appropriate, and good, even if their actions occasionally violate the understanding of appropriate behavior held by members of the community. This is not a new idea. Zeno of Elea, a Greek who lived between 490 and 430 BCE, insisted that loyalty to one's private conscience was the primary criterion of a moral life. Contemporary Europeans and Americans celebrate Thomas More as a prototype of a moral person because he refused to carry out an order from his king requiring him to violate his religious convictions. Peter Abelard, the twelfth-century heretic Catholic cleric whose romantic affair with Heloise remains famous, wrote that the only human sin was to violate what one believed was morally right. Shakespeare favored this definition of moral when he had Polonius advise his son Laertes in *Hamlet*: "To thine own self be true."

Henry David Thoreau rephrased Abelard and Polonius in an 1849 entry in his journal: "The only obligation which I have a right to assume is to do at any time what I think right." Joachim Fest, a child during Hitler's reign, remembers his father telling him to memorize a Latin motto from the Gospel according to Saint Matthew: "Etiam si omnes—ego non!" which means "Even if all others . . . not I!" One of the dying father's last utterances to his son was, "I have made many mistakes, but I did nothing wrong."

America's ethnic and religious diversity invites respect for those who are loyal to the demands of their conscience. Hollywood promotes this view. The 1952 film *High Noon* stars Gary Cooper as the recently retired marshal of a small town whose conscience prevents him from leaving town to escape from a gang of four outlaws intent on killing him, despite urging from his new wife, the mayor, and friends who tell him that he is no longer respon- sible for the town's safety. When no man in the town volunteers to help, Cooper is forced to face the four outlaws alone because his moral code demands this posture. Some film critics claim that the scriptwriter of *High Noon* wanted to embarrass members of Congress who were afraid to oppose Senator Joseph McCarthy in 1950–51 when he accused loyal American writers, professors, and scientists of being communists.

Societies that are ethnically more homogenous, such as Japan and China, enjoy greater agreement on core values and reserve their praise for those who conform to the community's understanding of right and wrong.

These societies place greater value on the harmony of the collective than the autonomous conscience of a particular individual. The high incidence of genital cutting of girls and young women in the rural areas of many African nations affirms the power of a community norm. Adolescent girls submit to the ritual, despite their wish to avoid the pain, risk of infection, and muted sexual pleasure, because of a fear of social rejection for failing to adhere to the local value.

Although conforming to the morality of the majority is easier, a person who honors a standard that violates a private value is vulnerable to a blend of frustration and guilt. Some employees of mortgage companies who felt that selling large mortgages to unemployed adults was ethically improper but did nothing to halt the practice may have experienced this emotion. Chris Walsh in *Cowardice* suggests that the imperative to openly challenge dishonesty or injustice is weaker today than it was a century earlier. Even the frequencies of the words *coward* and *cowardice* in books written in English have decreased since 1800.

Do Social Networks Erode Private Conscience?

The increasing influence of social networks, such as Facebook and Twitter, may be making it more difficult for youths to honor their private moral standards. More than 90 percent of America's adolescents exchange Internet messages with peers at least once a day; about 5 percent spend so much time sending messages experts worry about an addiction. These exchanges shape group consensus on appropriate sexual behavior, drinking, recreational drugs, loyalty to parents, costume, attitude toward teachers, importance of academic achievement, and career choices. Since most youths converse with peers who hold the same values, each network validates the belief system of all members of the group.

A teenager who violates one of the group's consensual values is liable to be the target of a barrage of cyberbullying, which can generate anxiety and social isolation. Close to one-third of American adolescents reported cyberbullying by one or more peers during 2012. In rare cases the victims of harsh attacks are driven to suicide. Rebecca Sedwick, a middle-school adolescent who was a victim of cyberbullying, climbed the tower of an abandoned cement plant in September 2013 and jumped to her death. George Orwell's dark 1949 novel *1984* predicted surveillance by the government, not by one's friends.

The dynamics within today's social networks resemble those that characterized much of the world a thousand years ago when most adults lived in small communities in which residents quickly learned about the improper action of any member of the community. Under these conditions, the wish to avoid embarrassment and a loss of reputation was effective in curbing undesirable behaviors. It is not a coincidence that formal legal systems were introduced when communities became so large a majority realized that few if any residents would learn of an ethical violation.

Some Honest Attempts

Some social scientists who detected the public's unhappiness over the different usages of *moral* announced their willingness to resolve the ambiguity. Joshua Greene, author of *Moral Tribes*, advocates an older utilitarian rationale. An act is moral, Greene suggests, if it results in an increase in happiness for the largest number of equally worthy individuals. Greene's proposal is silent on the quality of the happiness as well as the fact that no agent can know who will be made happy and who unhappy by an action. More seriously, a utilitarian criterion strips Thomas More of his moral badge because his decision reduced the happiness level of his family, his many Catholic supporters, and perhaps his king as well. Thomas Piketty's refusal in January 2015 to accept France's prestigious Legion of Honor Award made millions of patriotic French citizens sad, but Mr. Piketty believed he was honoring a personal moral standard.

Shalom Schwartz of Hebrew University lists ten behaviors he claims reflect the moral standards held by most contemporary citizens in economically developed democracies. This list includes actions intended to attain a higher status, an achievement, hedonic pleasure, greater tolerance, new experiences, and social harmony. Contemporary Buddhists, Muslims, and Hasidic Jews residing in democracies would nominate a different collection of behaviors.

Jonathan Haidt, a psychologist at the University of Virginia, defends the universality of five moral imperatives: caring for others, fairness, loyalty, respect for authority, and sanctity of select objects and places. It is easy to find exceptions to each of these ethical demands for a particular agent acting in a particular setting. I suspect that a majority of adults in most cultures would agree on the morality of the following actions. A mother harms a man who is threatening to injure her child; a professor gives a conscientious student from a minority group a grade that is higher than he deserves because this act will allow him to keep his scholarship; a woman betrays her father to the police because he is about to commit a serious crime; a German citizen in 1938 refuses to respect the authority of an officer of the Third Reich; and Jesus's smashing of property in the synagogue.

Philip Pettit, a professor of politics at Princeton University, begins *Just Freedom* with the startling declaration that freedom is the only moral value every society has an obligation to honor. To be free of domination by and interference from any person or institution is Pettit's definition of freedom. As I began to think of the many objections to this blanket proposal, Pettit stopped me cold by adding a critical caveat. No person is automatically entitled to freedom if he or she does not possess the requisite skills, resources, or cooperation from others. Pettit's bold announcement boils down to the mundane freedoms that I, along with most of my friends, always understood we possessed. I am free to eat what I have the money to buy, own property I can afford to purchase, find a better job if I have the necessary talent and the desired job is available, and spend my leisure hours as I wish. Many affluent German citizens and officers who believed in and cooperated with the Nazi mission during Hitler's reign possessed those freedoms.

The Agent, the Action, the Place, and the Beneficiary

Scholars who insist on the morality of particular actions ignore the actor's properties. Nalini Ambady of Stanford University and her colleagues discovered that observers judged the immorality of sex workers more harshly when they were obese because these women were violating two moral rules rather than one. Americans were more critical of Richard Nixon when he lied about

Watergate than of Ronald Reagan when he secretly sent arms to the Nicaraguan fighters trying to overthrow the regime because they had disapproved of Nixon's earlier deceits. They assumed Reagan's intentions were patriotic.

The setting is also relevant. Acts that are acceptable in the bedroom are immoral in a public park. On occasion, passive bystanders at the scene of a crime are vulnerable to a bout of guilt simply because they were present. About one in five young adults who were in the recreational park the day of the mass shooting in Oslo, Norway in the summer of 2011 reported feeling guilty over their decision to go to the park that day.

The actions that allow a person to enjoy a sense of virtue, the state Hindus call "dharma," also depend on the intended beneficiary of a behavior. The actor, the actor's family, an ethnic or religious group to which the actor belongs, the local community, the nation, or the earth are all possible candidates. Consider a lawyer faced with the choice of working during a weekend to increase her chances of promotion or visiting her sister who, recovering from surgery, would enjoy seeing her sibling. She must decide whether she or her sister ought to be the primary beneficiary in this conflict. If the visit to the sister required our fictional lawyer to drive 250 miles, she might decide to add the earth as a potential beneficiary, for the trip would add carbon dioxide to the atmosphere. It is difficult, if not impossible, to erect a logically persuasive argument that would make one of these beneficiaries—the self, the sister, or the earth—the morally proper choice.

The belief that kindness to someone in need is always a moral act ignores the recipient's interpretation of the caring behavior. On some occasions, a recipient interprets another's generosity as reflecting a condescending moral smugness. Luis Buñuel's 1961 film *Viridiana* portrays a charitable nun who invites beggars, lepers, and pimps living in squalor in the city to live in the small houses that border the mansion she inherited from her father. Upon returning from a holiday, she finds that the recipients of behaviors she thought were kind have invaded the main house, destroyed her crystal goblets, and stained her tablecloth with food and wine. In one of the last scenes the nun is being raped by one of the beggars. Buñuel's message is that recipients of kindness who are unable to reciprocate and interpret charity as a sign of their subordinate status often feel anger rather than gratitude.

The African Americans Shelby Steele, in *Shame,* and Jason Riley, in *Please Stop Helping Us,* argue that white liberals who insist that blacks need special laws to help them ascend in status and dignity are unintentionally harming an unknown number who interpret their advocacy for such laws as reflecting a private belief that African Americans need help because they possess serious deficiencies. The blacks who are angered by that demeaning assumption achieve a measure of revenge by refusing to adopt the study and work habits their benefactors value. Steele cites Clarence Thomas's anger upon realizing that he was admitted to Yale Law School because he was black and not because the admissions committee regarded him as a brilliant student with great promise. Riley's claim that a criminal frame of mind is a more important cause of the large number of incarcerated black males than a racist criminal justice system is likely to frustrate black leaders.

The stigma attached to women who sell sex for money affirms the necessity of specifying an agent's thoughts and the context when judging the morality of an action or a person. The young women who provide sexual pleasures for money in order to pay their college tuition deny being prostitutes because they are free to pick their clients. Some sex workers insist they are not violating any private moral imperative. One Swedish sex worker told the social scientist Jay Levy, "I am really a good girl. . . . I like to do this."

These observations reflect the difficulty in nominating any behavior as inherently moral or immoral. Rather, one must specify the agent, his or her intentions, the setting, and the historical moment. The French protected freedom of expression for all religions for more than two hundred years. Nonetheless, French lawmakers, with public support, made an exception when they banned the wearing of the burka in public. A burglar told Emmeline Taylor of Australian National University that he robbed only the wealthy because they did not need what he stole and could replace the items easily. He insisted that he would never rob a poor or elderly person and confessed, "I went in a house once and an old woman was in her bed. I felt like a tramp. I've never felt so bad in all my life."

There are even exceptions to the broadly held prohibition against intentionally inflicting harm on an innocent victim. Members of the former Ottoman society forgave a new sultan who killed his brothers and the pregnant women in his dead father's harem when he assumed power. Seventh-century Mayan communities in Central America allowed a priest to sacrifice an innocent young woman in order to propitiate the god that brought rain.

The many Americans who argue that any behavior that harms another is always immoral may not appreciate that their grandparents held a more permissive view of justified killing during the nineteenth century. A policeman in the 2012 film *The Place Beyond the Pines* feels guilty after killing an armed criminal when he learns that the victim had a young son. I cannot think of any Hollywood film made before 1950 in which a cop who killed a dangerous criminal felt guilty over his action. I have difficulty imagining James Cagney, Edward G. Robinson, or George Raft, playing the role of an officer of the law, brooding over killing a bad man no matter how many children he had. A growing proportion of the world's population has become less tolerant than earlier generations of any behaviors that cause distress to an innocent. Even American youths who tease a classmate's clothing, physical appearance, or accent are likely to be punished or expelled from school.

Many Americans were outraged in the 1960s when the media described clinical settings where autistic children were given electric shocks as a strategy to help them establish adaptive behaviors. Although this practice helped some children learn more mature habits, usually cleanliness, sustained attention, and loss of stereotyped actions such as head banging or pulling at one's hair, this therapy never became popular because the public's repugnance over shocking children trumped any desirable outcome. The means have precedence over the ends when moral issues are involved. That is why a utilitarian criterion for all moral acts never enjoyed a prolonged period of popularity.

These examples—and many more could be cited—reveal the impossibility of nominating a particular behavior that adults from different cultures and historical eras would agree was a moral imperative to be honored under all circumstances. As I noted in the essay on words, full sentences are required before a community can arrive at a consensus on the definition of moral. Alasdair MacIntyre phrases this conclusion more gracefully in *After*

Virtue: "I can only answer the question 'What am I to do?' if I can answer the prior question 'Of what story or stories do I find myself a part?'"

History Again

Historical events continually tweak an existing moral belief, eliminate one that is no longer useful, or invent a new value. The ethical ideal in the Declaration of Independence stating that all humans are entitled to life, liberty, and the pursuit of happiness marks a watershed in a historical sequence that began in the city-states of Greece. Few scholars writing before 1500 claimed that large inequalities in wealth violated a moral standard. The ratio of poor to affluent families in most societies was large enough to persuade most citizens of the impossibility of economic equality. A tipping point seems to be passed when less than one-third of a community is qualitatively more destitute than everyone else. Under these conditions, a society is more likely to decide that a concern for the disadvantaged is an ethical demand.

The philosopher John Rawls recognized the widespread anger over the rising level of economic and social inequality in the United States during the 1960s and satisfied the public's need for a voice in his widely acclaimed 1971 book *A Theory of Justice*. This text, like Thomas More's sixteenth-century fantasy *Utopia*, argued that an equal distribution of resources to all members of a society was a moral imperative.

Thomas Piketty, the celebrated author of *Capital in the Twenty-First Century*, relied on his moral beliefs, not deductions from economic facts, when he wrote that the unfairness of serious income inequality required governments to impose a heavy tax on the wealthy. If citizens in democracies with high levels of inequality thought that the current level was a violation of a moral imperative, they would elect representatives who promised to correct this condition. The election results of 2014 in the United States and several European nations imply that most voters do not share Piketty's opinion.

Forty years after Rawls, the economist Amartya Sen, in *The Idea of Justice*, tweaked Rawls's message by arguing that every society ought to establish conditions that allow all citizens to be successful in any activity they choose to pursue. Sen's choice of the word *successful* ignores the brute fact that no society can function if everyone is an executive giving orders or a celebrity performing and no one is receiving orders or sitting in an audience. A corporation needs only one CEO, communities need a limited number of physicians, the Supreme Court cannot have five hundred associate justices, and the world is unable to award celebrity to every adult who wants to be an opera star, Olympic medalist, or news anchor.

Neither Plato nor Hobbes would have agreed with Rawls, Piketty, or Sen because they lived in a different time and place. The current ascendance of reduced economic inequality to a prominent position in the hierarchy of moral standards is understandable because this ethical ideal is needed to maintain harmony in ethnically diverse, democratic societies marked by a technological economy that has created a large divide between those whose education furnishes the needed skills and those who stop their education before acquiring these abilities.

Jeffrey Abramson's elegant review of the varied rationales for the optimal form of government in *Minerva's Owl* helps readers appreciate that the particular crises a community faces shape the solution that its scholars fashion. The civil unrest in anarchic seventeenth-century Europe made it likely that Thomas Hobbes would argue for a strong monarch. A century later, gentler conditions in England allowed John Locke to limit government power to protection of each citizen's life and property. Only after a crisis has passed do the members of a community understand why a particular ethical argument was appealing. Georg Hegel's phrase "The owl of Minerva flies only at dusk" captures this truth.

The Persistent Hope

Although humans hunger for at least one moral standard that transcends circumstances, nothing in nature transcends settings, neither the temperature of the oceans, the size of a finch's beak, a mother's decision to protect her child from harm, nor an economic principle. Jean Tirole, the recipient of the 2014 Nobel Prize in economics, punctuated his acceptance speech with frequent references to the fairness of a government regulator's decision regarding an industry and acknowledged that local circumstances determine what is fair or unfair. More than once Tirole told his audience, "One size does not fit all."

A demand for fairness emerges as early as the third birthday, when children begin to act as if they believe that the amount of praise or material reward a person receives ought to match the amount of effort expended. The widespread public anger at the currently high level of income inequality in America is fueled by the belief that too many adults did not gain their wealth fairly. It is the unfairness that is maddening. Few adults insist that everyone ought to enjoy the same level of material advantages. They accept the variation in wealth due to genes, luck, and hard work. Americans do not complain about the multimillion-dollar salaries and glamorous lifestyles of famous film stars, accomplished athletes, television celebrities, writers of blockbuster novels, or inventors of useful things. Oprah Winfrey, Tom Brady, and Bill Gates worked hard to perfect and maintain the talents that have given pleasure or a useful resource to millions of citizens.

Those who make multimillion-dollar incomes by trading currencies or selling equities, depositing their profits in offshore tax havens, however, did not work years to perfect a special talent, do not give pleasure to a majority, and often have to lie or exploit others in order to obtain their advantage. Hence, their wealth violates the public's understanding of fairness.

The absence of shame among those whose wealth was gained unfairly adds salt to the wound. Adam Smith was certain that eighteenth-century merchants would curb their excessive greed in order to avoid being criticized by neighbors. He was wrong. The current grumbling over inequality would be quieter if 90 percent of those with annual incomes greater than $1 million had risen from humble circumstances and worked twelve-hour days seven days a week to attain their wealth.

Those who believe in the absolute truth of their moral beliefs are driven in one of two directions when one of their ethical standards is challenged. They can become more rigid in defending their ideas or more tolerant of others' standards. The Sunnis in Iraq and Orthodox Jews in Israel chose the first strategy. Those who choose tolerance are at risk for a diluted feeling of vitality when they honor beliefs that are different from those they are willing to legitimize. A tolerance as permissive as "anything goes" can create a moral landscape that is so flat, the special pleasure that follows loyalty to a moral code disappears.

When too many members of a community are unsure of the actions that are forbidden, each is driven to invent some restraints. If those who fail this assignment also lack an admired talent and believe they are unacceptable to a majority in their community, the tapestry that is a metaphor for a coherent community frays. A pair of impoverished youths without any desire for material gain or revenge killed a homeless man in Albuquerque in 2014 on a whim. Although these events are rare, the fact that they occur at all is a sign of a torn tapestry.

Humans are unwilling to tolerate this state of affairs indefinitely because moral standards provide guides to decisions, rituals that affirm one's goodness, and assurance that social encounters with strangers will, most of the time, be marked by civility and honesty. The yearning for a clear statement of the moral obligations everyone in a community ought to honor explains why *The Wizard of Oz* and *Casablanca* continue to be rerun on cable networks. Courage, empathy, and a willingness to give up a desired pleasure if that sacrifice serves a higher purpose remain American ideals. Many have watched these films, made more than seventy years ago, a dozen times because the scripts satisfy the need to believe that these values are still alive, if only on a screen.

Intentions

Both uses of moral, whether describing actions or individuals, presume benevolent intentions. The thirteenth-century cleric Duns Scotus and the trial judge Morris Hoffman agree that a person's intention, not the outcome of an act, ought to be the basis for judging the morality of a behavior. Most regard a lie told to help another as more moral than one that benefits the agent. Americans who believed that J. Robert Oppenheimer's opposition to building the hydrogen bomb reflected his moral beliefs assumed he wished to avoid the deaths of millions of humans rather than help the Soviet Union. The man who jumps into a lake to save a drowning child but, because of his incompetence, drowns both himself and the child provides the classic defense of the role of intention in judging the morality of an action or a person.

I was surprised by David Sloan Wilson's argument in *Does Altruism Exist?* that because human intentions are too difficult to measure, it is acceptable to treat the consequences of an action as the definition of altruism in humans as well as animals. Physicists, however, would never ignore the significance of a hypothetical concept that explained the evidence simply because its measurement was difficult. That is why they went to considerable trouble building the Hadron Collider in order to detect the Higgs boson. The wish to regard the self as good explains why adults help strangers in need, even when they understand that a later reciprocal kindness is unlikely and no one will learn of the kindness. During a four-week interval in January 1998, an ice storm deprived millions of Quebec residents of electricity. Adults from regions unaffected by the storm sent money to the victims, knowing that the recipients of their kindness would not know the identity of their benefactors. Many Europeans are adopting a practice, initiated in Naples, of paying for two cups of coffee but drinking only one and telling the waiter to give the second cup to any stranger who appears to be needy. Despite these and other facts, some biologists and psychologists insist that altruism could not have evolved in our species unless it contributed to a person's fitness because the charitable agent expected a reciprocal generosity or his or her reputation in the community was enhanced.

When Adam Smith's declaration that eighteenth-century owners of small businesses would benefit their society by behaving selfishly was wedded a century later to Darwin's inferences regarding the mechanisms that contributed to the survival of a species, it became almost impossible for a natural scientist to propose any explanation of altruism that did not include the generous agent receiving some tangible prize. When I was a graduate student at Yale in the 1950s, the behaviorists, who honored a similar principle, insisted that no animal or human should do anything unless there was a reward (a tangible prize) for the action. I still remember an afternoon in 1951 when Neal Miller, a respected behaviorist who accepted the dogma that no human does anything unless he or she anticipates a tangible reward, told the twelve of us sitting at a table that he had been puzzled all morning because he could not figure out why his three-year-old son had turned on the garden hose.

The tortuous attempts to explain why many adults donate blood to a stranger, give money anonymously to a charity, offer a seat on a bus to an older adult, or stop to help a motorist change a tire with arguments that are loyal to Darwinian premises are analogous to Ptolemy's attempts to explain the orbits of the earth and near planets without violating the dogmatic premise that the sun revolved around the earth. Humans are kind to others because such behaviors allow them, for a moment, to enjoy the thought that they are good persons. There is no need to encumber explanations with tangible rewards. All that is required is to acknowledge two obvious properties that are probably unique to our species: humans think and some of those thoughts are evaluations of themselves and their actions as good or bad.

Can Science Help?

Many educated citizens believe that the results of scientific research might resolve some of the ambiguities surrounding the meaning of morality. My skepticism, shared with the philosopher Stuart Hampshire, rests on the fact that no natural phenomena invite a judgment of right or wrong. Neither the extinction of the dinosaurs nor the proliferation of rats that followed was moral or immoral. The concept of inclusive fitness, defined as the reproductive success of the individual and all his or her relatives, allows biologists to evaluate a mutation, behavior, or change in ecology as aiding or reducing fitness. But no biologist would claim that an animal that enjoys greater fitness is more moral.

Social scientists continue to squabble over the criteria that would permit the evaluation of a behavior, social condition, or law as good or bad. If 30 million Americans were at a higher risk for diabetes, stroke, heart attack, and a shortened life span because of a polluted water supply, a majority of Americans would regard this situation as immoral and demand that the Congress alleviate it as soon as possible. About 30 million Americans in poverty are at risk for these same disabling medical conditions in 2015. But at least one-third of Americans do not regard this state of affairs as a serious violation of their moral standards because they believe that a majority of the poor contributed to their unhappy situation. Hence, the government is under no moral obligation to ameliorate this condition.

Facts, independent of local circumstances, are rarely a sufficient foundation for deciding on the morality of an action. When the facts demanded the conclusion that black children were receiving a less adequate education in segregated schools, the Supreme Court in 1954 declared this practice unconstitutional. The Court in 1896 was aware of the same facts, but declared segregated schools constitutional. The public's beliefs must be added to the evidence. Facts can disconfirm the basis for a moral belief but cannot furnish the seedbed for a moral position because the community's sentiment, which changes with time, is always relevant.

A sole reliance on science to support or refute an ethical belief is a serious misuse of this important source of knowledge. The community's attitudes toward the proper roles for males and females are an example of this error. The prior essay summarized some of the biological differences between males and females. The current commitment to the moral ideal of equality between the sexes motivated Europeans and North Americans to declare that males and females ought to have equal representations in all careers and social positions, independent of any sex differences in biology.

Although sex differences in the frequency of rape and homicide seem partly due to biology, a society is not to be branded as foolish if it chooses to ignore the scientific evidence in order to honor a favored ethical belief. Americans demand that teachers treat aggressive behavior by either sex in the same way and courts impose similar punishments on men and women for the same violent acts. An ethical preference may have trumped scientific facts when the Pentagon allowed women to engage in combat. The Americans who advocate sex equality but want science to be an arbiter of laws should acknowledge the power of the moral argument rather than question the validity of the scientific evidence pointing to subtle biological differences between males and females. What is true in nature need not determine what members of a society adopt as their ethical code. Democracy, tolerance of diverse value systems, and freedom to make as much money as one chooses as long as it does not harm another are ethical values most

Americans celebrate. None is demanded by human biology. Viva human moral ideals!

The dominant role of science in modern societies has been accompanied by reluctance to base government decisions on ethical preferences. Politicians ask economists to compute the cost-benefit ratios for extending the life of eighty-year-olds by six months by having Medicare pay for heart surgery. Medicare paid close to $90 billion in 2012 to prolong the life of elderly patients by six months or less. Economists determined that each extra year of life for all Americans older than sixty-eight costs about $100 billion. No objective facts can establish the correctness of these expenditures. Nor can reason from evidence explain why the Karzai regime in Afghanistan paid $200 to each of the sixty families with a relative who was killed by an American gunship in 2003 but the American Congress awarded $2 million to the families of each Italian killed when an American Marine jet struck an aerial tramway in 1998.

Governments and private philanthropies have given many billions of dollars to scientists hoping they would discover what is true in nature so that citizens could free themselves of illusions and superstitions. The grateful scientists did what they were asked and concluded that all living things are accidental events devoid of any special purpose or meaning, all life will disappear in about 4 billion years when the increase in the sun's size and temperature evaporate the earth's water, no one should expect acts of kindness from a person who is not a biological relative nor anticipate help from a stranger who does not expect a reciprocal kindness, and any individual who does not serve his or her interests first is irrational. These were not the answers the public expected. The scientists' discoveries challenged the wisdom in the epigram "The truth shall set you free" and made it difficult for those planning a life to defend any ethical guide other than "Go for it now." This rule appeared to be the imperative the executives at the largest bank in France, BNP Paribas, followed when they ignored the many warnings from the United States that their practices were violating American law. When they admitted their guilt in June 2014 and agreed to pay a multibillion-dollar fine, they told shareholders there was no reason to worry because the bank had the necessary funds.

Proving One's Goodness

The human moral sense is an evolutionary novelty that emerges in most children during the second year when they become concerned with good and bad behaviors and people. Obviously, they wish to be among the good humans and therefore try to act in ways that allow them to apply this adjective to themselves. Their family and culture inform them of the behaviors and personal properties that define a good person. I noted that honesty, kindness, loyalty, and courage are usual members of this category. Many youths living in competitive, highly individualistic societies seem to have detected some of the disadvantages of these qualities and are searching for other signs of a good person. Many contemporary adolescents appear to believe that the ability to form and maintain many close friendships is one of the precious signs.

The selection of friendships as a feature of a good person was made easier by the feeling of anonymity in large bureaucratic organizations—businesses, high schools, and colleges—and densely populated cities. It is also relevant that smaller families and greater participation by women in the workforce meant fewer family gatherings during the year. These factors facilitated the selection of close friendships as a sign of the self's worthiness and friendlessness as a violation of a moral standard.

I have a vivid memory of a twenty-minute silent film that begins with a man walking on an isolated country road. When he trips, one of his legs becomes stuck in a sinkhole. The man waves for help whenever a car passes, but no one stops. After legs, arms, and trunk have sunk into the hole, a passerby steals some of his clothes lying outside the hole. In the final scene, when only his head is visible, another passerby stamps on it and the man disappears. The haunting 2007 Chinese film *Little Moth* portrays individuals as commodities to be bought and sold. In the final scene a crippled eleven-year-old girl, sold by her father to a stranger who used her to beg for money on street corners, sits alone on a deserted pavement by a highway as dusk approaches.

The authors of these two chilling scripts did not intend to tell viewers that the man in the sinkhole and the crippled girl lacked friendships. Rather, the message was that the muse of history, in a foul mood, wrote a chapter in the human narrative that deprived many individuals of the reassuring belief that most people are loyal, kind, and honest and at least one person cares deeply about them.

The Need for Reassurance

Unfortunately, it is impossible to avoid occasions of criticism, reprimand, failure, or committing actions that hurt another through betrayal, dishonesty, or aggression. These events generate a feeling usually interpreted as shame or guilt. Because the events that evoke these emotions are unavoidable, cultures that provide easy ways to reduce them have the most satisfied populations.

Many societies have invented religious and social rituals as well as life assignments requiring only modest effort to help the ashamed and guilty ease their pain. Eighteenth-century Europeans could find evidence of their moral integrity by suppressing urges to engage in actions fueled by lust, greed, anger, and jealousy. This assignment did not require anyone's help. It is more diffi-cult today to obtain assurance of one's moral integrity through suppressing the same acts because experts and the media remind everyone that sexual pleas-ures, wealth, personal freedom, and the expression of hostility contribute to good health. A pair of Danish investigators asked young adults who spent their evenings socializing in bars whether they drank beer, wine, or whisky at home before they went out drinking with friends. Many women who replied affirm-atively explained that they wanted to be "out of control" soon after their first drink at a party or bar. These women were taking John Updike's advice, "When in doubt we should behave, if not like monkeys, like savages— . . . our instincts and appetites are better guides for a healthy life than the advice of other human beings."

The belief that one is necessary for the welfare of another is an important source of a feeling of virtue. Historical events have made this belief harder to maintain because many can survive without the continual help of a spouse or companion. Day care centers care for young children, frozen foods and takeout meals make the talents of the assigned cook in a family unnecessary, several lovers of either sex are available to satisfy sexual needs that a familiar partner might not be providing, and in most places there is at least one lawyer, doctor, dentist, accountant, banker, butcher, baker, plumber, carpenter, and mechanic available when a problem arises.

The extraordinary material advances that brought longer lives, fewer infectious illnesses, electricity, potable water, computers, apps, and the opportunity to travel anywhere exacted the cost of rendering most individuals expendable and, in so doing, deprived them of the warm feeling that accompanies knowing that they, and they alone, are the only ones able to satisfy the wants of a particular other.

The attainment of a goal after considerable effort is another path leading to a moment of virtue. The machines and digital devices that penetrate most places have made it easy to obtain goals that used to require many hours or days of hard work. Many commentators recognize that the joy accompanying the pursuit of a goal lasts longer and is usually more intense than the feeling that bubbles up the moment the goal is attained. The smiles on the faces of students on graduation day could not have occurred without the effort that preceded the receipt of the diploma. The probability that any of the many thousands of scientists who are actively involved in research will make a significant discovery that will remain valid for ten years is extremely small. But they continue to expend energy and time in pursuit of this improbable prize because of the pleasure that accompanies the effort. A Dutch proverb reflects this truth: It's not the marbles that matter, it's the game.

The new social conditions frustrate many who are searching for a way to reaffirm their goodness when it is challenged. A century earlier Freud was certain that the superego's harsh demands were the primary source of anxiety. Contemporary adults are troubled because they cannot hear what their superegos are whispering. A cartoon in the New Yorker illustrates one man saying to another, "I did my job and grabbed my pile but no voice at eventide has cried, 'Well done.'"

This disappointment has become more common among members of modern Western democracies that are stripping themselves of sacred objects, actions, rituals, or obligations that can generate a feeling of agape because they transcend daily activities. The philosopher Roger Scruton argues in The Soul of the World that humans need to believe that a few ideas, behaviors, places, or objects are infused with a measure of sacredness.

The roles that used to enjoy a small measure of this mysterious property—clergy, scientists, artists, writers, physicians—have lost it because a few in these roles betrayed the ideals of selflessness, honesty, and humility that the public expected. The recent questioning of the ethics of some scientists prompted *Science* magazine to devote a section of its July 4, 2014, issue to the opinions of young natural scientists regarding the ethical issues they face as they begin their career. The practice in China of young scientists ambitious for promotion purchasing authorship of a research paper taints the sacred mission of science.

The instances of abuse of children and marital infidelity robbed motherhood and marriage of the sacredness they possessed centuries earlier. Humans traveling to places that had not been explored—the moon or the peak of Mount Everest—have tainted their symbolic purity. Artists can create objects of beauty and engineers can make objects with pragmatic utility, but neither can create sacred objects because that quality requires a person to invest an ordinary object with an imagined property.

Many contemporary youths are searching for at least one imperative that demands the unquestioned obedience Abraham displayed when God ordered him to kill his beloved son. The heroine in the Polish film *Ida*, which won an Oscar in 2015 for best foreign-language film, found such an imperative. By contrast, Mason Evans, the central character in the acclaimed 2014 film *Boyhood*, battles a confusion, shared with many youths, over what acts and ideas have intrinsic value. Mason is not satisfied with his estranged father's conclusion, "We're just winging it." The film ends with Mason's question unanswered and his passivity reflected in a comment to the girl at his side, "The moment seizes us." Jan Gerster's 2012 film *A Coffee in Berlin* contains the same message for German audiences. Both scripts capture the apathy of young adults in modern egalitarian societies in which every past ideology has revealed its flaws; concrete is replacing grass, harshness replacing gentleness, pragmatism replacing beauty, fucking replacing love, and hierarchy becoming a dirty word. This mood began in the 1950s with J. D. Salinger's novel *The Catcher in the Rye* and William Whyte's analysis of modern society in *The Organization Man*.

If nothing is sacred, nothing can be profane. Because acts that give or maintain life retain a tattered halo of sacredness, harming another without provocation remains the one act that all regard as a serious moral transgression. Even orphaned seven-year-old children living in the poorest slum of Bogotá, who witness crime on a regular schedule, told an interviewer that it is wrong to steal from or hurt others. The hunger for at least one sacred idea maintains some Americans' opposition to laws permitting abortion or preventing ninety-year-olds with only a few months to live from receiving expensive medical care.

The current historical setting renders large numbers of adults who were socialized to "be all they can be" vulnerable to a melancholic mood because they lack a healing ritual or action when they fail a task, encounter a rejection, lose a relationship, betray a friend, or harm another. Historical events have generated conditions that some commentators call "an age of narcissism." Others feel that "spiritually hollow" is a more accurate descriptor. How else can we explain the fact that, although books, articles, and films describe the insecurity, competitiveness, greed, and hundred-hour workweeks of those who choose to work for large banks or corporations, business is the most popular major among America's undergraduates? Men and women graduating from our best colleges are seeking a job with a Wall Street firm rather than choosing a career in medicine, nursing, biology, teaching, or social work where one's efforts might benefit others.

Apparently, a large number of talented American youths decided that making money was the only rational pursuit in contemporary society. This might be the first time in recorded history when a large proportion of advantaged youths chose a vocation that a majority in their society regarded as lacking in virtue. Shakespeare could not have predicted that in 2015 Shylock would be a role model for a sizeable number of Christians.

The failure of religion, science, capitalism, socialism, communism, or fascism to provide the community with the harmony it seeks leaves an unknown number of young adults with no ideology they can defend against all attacks. The writer Alfred Kazin wrote in 1955, "What I suffer from is the lack of a working philosophy, of a strong central belief in something outside myself, which my self can hold and for once forget the self." This lacuna leaves the seeking of material pleasures the only reasonable goal to pursue. The current zeitgeist bothers the *New York Times* op-ed columnist David

Brooks who, in the April 12, 2015 issue, asked readers to rein in their narcissism and commit to an ideal that pushed them toward the good.

If twenty-year-olds cannot assure themselves of their moral integrity by citing their gender, religion, ethnicity, education, talent, or an accomplished member of their family, because these properties place an unfair burden on the poor and minorities, the size of one's bank account becomes a default symbol of one's worthiness. No one is disqualified from this mission. Nonetheless, a majority are prepared to celebrate those who, with effort, did what they were supposed to do and perfected a praiseworthy trait or ability.

Who Is Number One?

An ethic that celebrates "winning" at all costs has created confusion over the ethical imperatives that ought to be honored. Many Americans are troubled by the fact that a large number who violated the traditional standards on honesty, fairness, or loyalty are rich, in positions of power, or celebrated by the media. Electronic traders on Wall Street able to detect an order from an investor in Chicago to purchase a large number of shares in a company block the trade before it can be completed, buy the requested equity, and milliseconds later sell it to the original buyer at a higher price, pocketing the profit. Although this practice seems immoral to many Americans, younger staff members at the Securities and Exchange Commission and the men and women engaged in this practice see nothing wrong in this activity. It simply reflects cleverness.

Students compete for the honor of being valedictorian; adults compete for size of salary, prizes, or celebrity; corporations compete for the largest profits and highest share price; nations compete to have the largest GDP, most Nobel Prizes, best universities, or most Olympic gold medals. The media devote more space to warning Americans about the possibility that China will soon replace the United States as number one in GDP than in describing the pollution of China's rivers, air, and land, its corrupt local governments, and the restrictions the central government in Beijing imposes on each person's freedom.

The obsession with being "number one" required three historical events to come together: an erosion of faith in any value other than an achievement that could be measured in terms of money, power, or fame; the growth of large institutions and corporations for which profit was the primary sign of success; and technologies that maximized institutional efficiency at the cost of the psychological state of the workers who made the success possible. The past few years have witnessed new businesses, depending on apps and iPhones, that allow consumers to rent a lawyer, doctor, driver, or even subjects for an experiment. Workers have neither job security nor any loyalty to their employer or client. They share many features with laborers who move from farm to farm picking whatever crop is ready for harvesting.

Simon Head notes in his book *Mindless* that managers at Amazon Corporation track each worker's activities over closed cameras; supervisors at Walmart outlets ensure that each store has fewer staff than needed. British government officials evaluate the annual scholarly output of each university faculty member in order to decide on salaries and job security; and federal bureaucrats in Washington punish hospitals serving poor populations for allowing too many revisits by the same patients. William Jennings Bryan pleaded with Congress as the nineteenth century ended to resist sacrificing America on a cross of gold. Today he would have replaced the burden of the gold standard with the heavier burden of maintaining maximal output in maximally efficient ways. Perhaps everyone should reread the Greek myth of King Midas, who was given the gift of being able to turn everything he touched, including his daughter, into gold.

A Less Than Conscious Sense of Responsibility

I have the intuition that a fair number of educated adults in wealthy, industrialized democracies live with a weakly articulated sense of responsibility for the members of past generations who polluted the land, seas, rivers, and atmosphere, destroyed forests, and exploited the weak and impotent. Margaret MacMillan, in *The War That Ended Peace*, described a somewhat similar mood among Europeans during the two decades before the onset of the First World War. Many influential commentators had claimed that industrialization and the competitive capitalism it birthed had corrupted a virtuous society by replacing the spirit of cooperation and religiosity found in small agricultural communities with a combination of fierce competition, a secular frame of mind, and dense urban centers with lonely residents. The feeling that accompanied the recognition of these sins had to be cleansed and war, it was argued, was one way to restore the society's purity.

Geoffrey Parker, in *Global Crisis*, tells us that a fair proportion of Europeans attributed the crop failures, mass hunger, and early mortality brought on by the unusually cold years that marked the middle third of the seventeenth century to God's decision to punish humans for their sinfulness. The British Parliament during the 1640s prohibited the celebration of Christmas, demolished all theaters, and publicly whipped actors as a way to eliminate sources of pleasure and thereby, hopefully, assuage God's wrath.

A similar dynamic can be seen in young children who committed a misdemeanor that was not discovered. Often these children commit a second violation in front of a parent in order to receive the punishment that will absolve them of the guilt attached to the first moral error. The student Rodion Raskolnikov in Fyodor Dostoyevsky's great novel *Crime and Punishment* seeks punishment for his murder of a pawnbroker. Although he kills her for her money, he leaves her house without taking most of the cash. As his guilt mounts in subsequent weeks, partly because no one suspects him of the crime, Raskolnikov begins to leave revealing clues. At the end of the novel he confesses to Sonya, the woman he loves, and is eventually arrested and imprisoned.

The boy Amir in *The Kite Runner* tries to cope with a corrosive guilt provoked by his failure to save his friend Hassan from being bullied. Amir throws fruit at Hassan, hoping to incite him to a retaliatory act that will punish him for his earlier moral error. The Old Testament allowed a warrior returning from battle to do penance for his acts of killing by prohibiting him from entering the camp for seven days. Medieval Christian communities also required returning soldiers to do some form of penance to absolve them from the guilt of their actions.

A number of women become prostitutes in order to be debased. They interpret their sexual experiences as deserved punishment for being a member of a dysfunctional family or allowing themselves to be passive victims of physical or sexual abuse. Self-blame and guilt occur among some widows or widowers who believe they should have done more to help their ailing spouse, rape victims who wonder whether they did something to invite the attack, youths who assume they were responsible for a parental divorce, and adolescents who suspect that their actions made a contribution to their poor grades, unpopularity, or unattractiveness.

Kelly Berg of the University of Minnesota and colleagues found that overweight women were especially susceptible to an episode of binge eating after a moral violation; it is possible to interpret the binging as a way to punish the self for the improper behavior. Spouses who recognize they were a bit too selfish or uncaring with their partner try to reduce their guilt by suggesting a night out or buying the partner a gift.

An ingenious experiment by Yoel Inbar and colleagues brought this process into the laboratory. College students who were first asked to write about a past event in their lives that made them feel guilty subsequently administered more intense electric shocks to their wrists than students who had written about a sad or neutral event.

These facts and others imply that humans are susceptible to accepting partial responsibility for undesirable conditions in their lives for which others bear the major responsibility. Readers who find this suggestion reasonable should be receptive to the speculation that thoughtful adults who reflected on the events of the past century might feel a bit responsible, and perhaps a trifle guilty, for their passive compliance to the rape of the earth, the murder of millions of innocents, the accumulating piles of nuclear waste and nonbiodegradable garbage, and the growing economic inequality between a struggling majority and a privileged minority. These adults might entertain the incompletely conscious notion that, perhaps, they and the members of their generation deserve to be punished with floods, droughts, and destructive storms for allowing these sins to be committed.

Some Hollywood studios, sensing that a fair proportion of comfortable white Americans are living with an unspoken guilt over being accomplices to the profanities of the past two centuries, converted the movie screen into a confession box by making award-winning films portraying the terrible cruelties and betrayals that one person or group inflicted on another. Why would anyone pay money to watch repeated scenes of white slave owners whipping helpless black victims in the film 12 *Years a Slave?* One possibility is that the white Americans who identified with these immoral antiheroes regarded the obvious damning of these men and women as a symbolic punishment that momentarily cleansed their conscience, as self-flagellations did for medieval Europeans.

Germans born long after the end of the Second World War watch films depicting the barbarous actions of the Nazi troops and officials who were their grandfathers, Israelis pay to see films portraying the unjust actions of their government against Palestinians, and Australians view films depicting the government's cruel treatment of Aboriginal families during the early decades of the last century. I suspect that the unpleasant feelings evoked by these scenes of cruelty provide audiences with an opportunity to acknowledge the crimes that past members of their society committed and, in that moment, accept a self-blame that they treat as a deserved punishment.

The political scientist Shelby Steele, author of *Shame,* argues that some white American liberals who insist on affirmative action and a generous transfer of public resources to poor members of ethnic minorities are moti-vated, in part, by a need to absolve a shame brought on by wars that should not have been waged, the persistence of racist attitudes, corporate greed, and increasing income inequality. Steele's book will anger these liberals for he violates political correctness by suggesting that their shame is not only unnecessary, it is also harming many blacks who are the targets of their char-itable views.

The Demand for Greater Equality

I sense the introduction of a new ethical value that appears to condemn any inequality, independent of its origin. The conservative magazine the *Economist* published a long essay in January 2015 bemoaning the fact that the children of college-educated American parents are attending the best colleges and landing the best jobs. The author of the essay failed to note that college-educated parents spend more time reading and talking to their children, taking them to museums, and encouraging conscientiousness in academic settings. Their children, in turn, adopt these values. Unfortunately, too many parents who did not attend college fail to do the same.

Americans have always celebrated individuals who do exactly what these college-educated parents are doing. It seems unfair to criticize the inevitable outcome of actions that a majority has always regarded as moral. A moral standard is persuasive when it is accompanied by a good reason for honoring its demands. There are good reasons why the multimillion-dollar incomes of many who work in the financial sector violate an ethic of fairness. However, declaring that inequalities in educational attainment, independent of their origin, are moral violations fails to provide an equally persuasive rationale. Moreover, it implies, albeit subtly, that the conscientious parents, rather than the mothers and fathers who failed to inculcate a value on academic achievement, are the moral transgressors. This logic would blame the scientists who invented painkillers for the deaths of youths who overdosed on opioids.

This essay returns to where it began by acknowledging the ambiguities that penetrate the concept of morality. Hopefully, readers have a richer understanding of why this is the case. The difficulty in naming a behavior that retains its moral status indefinitely has one advantage. Because social conditions change with time, the ethical code of a society must also change to adapt to the new circumstances. There are many who are moral paragons during their season, but few who are paragons across all seasons.

Epilogue

The importance of thoughts, feelings, and settings is woven into many of these essays as a corrective to the practice by both biologists and the media to award them marginal significance. The media tell the public regularly that climate change, new viruses, terrorist groups, and accumulating nuclear waste are worldwide problems whose solutions require new machines, chemicals, genes, and weapons, rather than a deeper understanding of the thoughts of individuals acting within their historical context. Thoughts were the origins of these worrisome conditions; new thoughts can contribute to solutions. It is even possible that the crises in Iraq, Syria, and Afghanistan might have been avoided if Osama bin Laden had not needed to mute the childhood shame he felt over his father's rejection of his mother by masterminding the attack on the World Trade Center.

The remarkable discoveries in genetics and neuroscience attribute more power to genes and brains than to the interpretations children and adults impose on the conscious psychological states their brains generate. This excessive emphasis on the material persuaded many members of the public unable to evaluate the validity of most scientific facts that they were helpless victims of their biology. Economists added to the misinformation by announcing that self-interest, which usually means a gain in tangible resources, was the only rational life strategy These essays have questioned these assumptions and hopefully strengthened the universal robust intuition that each of us is free to decide whether to be kind or cruel, conscientious or careless, loyal or deceitful, or to purchase an electric car that pollutes less even though it costs more than one that uses gasoline. If thoughts were returned to the privileged position they occupied in Pericles' Athens, individuals might appreciate they have more control of their future than experts have led them to believe.

Thoughts cannot be equated with sentences. The psychologist's practice of treating words as if they carved nature at its joints contrasts with the biologist's habit of first looking for puzzling phenomena and inventing a word only after an initial understanding is achieved. The scientists who invented the term *prion* wished to understand the cause of the symptoms of mad cow disease. Only after years of work pointed to a misshaped protein did they make up this word to name the presumed cause.

The psychologists who assumed that self-esteem and dysregulation named properties as real as eye color turned the penny on its head by declaring, with insufficient evidence, that these contextually naked terms explained why some youths failed in school or broke the law. If they had first studied the patterns of experiences and biological properties of those who displayed these actions, they might have discovered that combinations of temperamental biases, social class, cultural setting, and the profile of identifications were far better predictors of these behaviors.

Explanations that included these conditions would require longer sentences. Instead of writing, "Asocial youth drop out of school because they have impaired self-esteem and cannot regulate their impulses," they might write, "Youth with a temperament favoring a muted brain response to violations of community values growing up in a society in which they identify with the role of victim are at the highest risk for rejecting that society's ethical values." All outcomes occur in particular settings. The words that name a psychological property stripped of a subject, setting, and target have ambiguous meanings.

Nature is obsessed with particularities. An epigenetic mark might silence only one gene in white blood cells. The order in which questions are asked can affect the answers. Bilingual Chinese Americans describe themselves as possessing different traits when they answer in each of their languages. Social scientists have been more reluctant than biologists to acknowledge the relevance of the source of evidence for every conclusion. They prefer to be high-flying hawks taking in the big picture rather than frogs mucking around in the messy details of a pond.

Investigators who illuminate a puzzling phenomenon understand the importance of selecting the most fruitful level of analysis. The gene, not the chemical properties of carbon, is the optimal level for understanding the structure of a protein. The brain's microanatomy, not a single neuron, is the best level for those wanting to understand Alzheimer's disease. Thoughts are the most fruitful level for investigators seeking to explain the variation in the strategies people choose to deal with challenges.

The egalitarian ethos that has become a dominant value in many societies insists on a tolerant posture toward all groups and their beliefs. Not surprisingly, the host of benevolent changes that this idea made possible exacted a price. Youths socialized to respect those who honor values they had been taught were immoral find it hard to avoid the conclusion that all ethical ideas, with the possible exception of unprovoked harmful acts, are arbitrary. The recognition that one's moral beliefs are human inventions, rather than imperatives created by an omniscient oracle, prevents some youths from committing to any ethical demand. The current generation, taught to celebrate objective facts, finds it hard to adopt the advice of the Marquise du Châtelet to remain "susceptible to illusions for it is to illusions that we owe the majority of our pleasures."

Despite the material richness of daily life in industrialized societies, many live with a persistent unease. The brooding of heroes and heroines in popular novels, supported by the writings of social scientists, implies that the cause is a frustrated yearning for deeper, more trusting relationships and the acceptance of one or more moral imperatives that would free people from reliance on circumstances when deciding how to behave.

Czesław Miłosz asks his readers to resist the urge to surrender to the dispiriting meaninglessness of modern life because such a posture erodes the dignity that keeps melancholy at bay. Committing to some imperative, preferably one that accepts the welfare of others as a legitimate competitor to self, is an effective way to defeat the malaise.

Miłosz was surprised one afternoon by the sight of ducks splashing in a dirty puddle when only yards away a clean stream was flowing. He asked an old peasant sitting on a bench why the ducks ignored the stream. The man's reply, "If only they knew," might be a vitalizing mantra for those who are about to assume responsibility for their generation and that of their children. Montaigne would have smiled on reading Miłosz for he also believed "The profit from our studies is to become better and wiser."

Essay 1

Barger, B., R. Nabi, and L. Y. Hong. "Standard Back-Translation May Not Capture Proper Emotion Concepts." *Emotion* 10 (2010): 703–11.

Bergen, B. K. *Louder Than Words.* New York: Basic Books, 2012.

Caramazza, A., S. Anzellotti, L. Strnad, and A. Lingnau. "Embodied Cognition and Mirror Neurons." *Annual Review of Psychology* 37 (2014): 1–15.

Donoghue, D. *Metaphor.* Cambridge, MA: Harvard University Press, 2014.

Fodor, J. A., and Z. W. Pylyshyn. *Minds without Meaning.* Cambridge, MA: MIT Press, 2015.

Friederici, A. D. "The Brain Basis of Language Processing." *Physiological Reviews* 91 (2011): 1357–92.

Gallace, A., E. Boschin, and C. Spence. "On the Taste of 'Bouba' and 'Kiki.'" *Cognitive Neuroscience* 2 (2011): 34–46.

Lakoff, G., and M. Turner. *More Than Cool Reason.* Chicago: University of Chicago Press, 1989.

Mahon, B. Z., and A. Caramazza. "Concepts and Categories." *Annual Review of Psychology* 60 (2009): 27–51.

Miller, G. A., and P. N. Johnson-Laird. *Language and Perception.* Cambridge, MA: Harvard University Press, 1976.

Ogden, C. K. *Opposition.* Bloomington: Indiana University Press, 1967.

Pinker, S. *The Language Instinct.* New York: Harper Perennial, 2007.

Quine, W. V. *Word and Object.* Cambridge, MA: MIT Press, 2013.

Samsonovich, A. V., and G. A. Ascoli. "Principal Semantic Components of Language and the Measurement of Meaning." *PLoS One* 11 (2010): e10921.

Searle, J. *Mind, Language and Society.* London: Weidenfeld-Nicolson, 1999.

Wierzbicka, A. *Semantics.* New York: Oxford University Press, 1996.

Essay 2

Bartoshuk, L. M. "Comparing Sensory Experiences Across Individuals." *Chemical Senses* 25 (2000): 447–60.

Brendgen, M., and W. Troop-Gordon. "School-Related Factors in the Development of Bullying Perpetration and Victimization." *Journal of Abnormal Child Psychology* 43 (2015): 1–4.

Frances, A. *Saving Normal.* New York: William Morrow, 2013.

Kagan, J. *The Human Spark.* New York: Basic Books, 2014.

———. *The Second Year.* Cambridge, MA: Harvard University Press, 1981.

Kagan, J., and H. A. Moss. *Birth to Maturity.* New York: John Wiley, 1962.

Monod, J. *Chance and Necessity.* New York: Knopf, 1971.

Rottman, B. M., D. Gentner, and M. B. Goldwater. "Causal Systems Categories." *Cognitive Science* 36 (2012): 919–32.

Schacter, D. *The Seven Sins of Memory.* Boston: Houghton Mifflin, 2001.

Shallice, T., and R. P. Cooper. *The Organisation of Mind.* New York: Oxford University Press, 2011.

Widom, C. S., and C. Massey. "A Prospective Examination of Whether Childhood Sexual Abuse Predicts Subsequent Sexual Offending." *JAMA Pediatrics* 169 (2015): e143357.

Woodwell, D. *Research Foundations: How Do We Know What We Know?* Thousand Oaks, CA: Sage, 2014.

Essay 3

Colander, D. C., and R. Kupers. *Complexity and the Art of Public Policy.* Princeton, NJ: Princeton University Press, 2014.

Danto, A. C. *Andy Warhol.* New Haven, CT: Yale University Press, 2009.

Dodge, K. A., K. L. Bierman, J. D. Coie, M. T. Greenberg, J. E. Lochman, R. J. McMahon, et al. "Impact of Early Intervention on Psychopathology, Crime, and Well-being at Age 25." *American Journal of Psychiatry* 172 (2015): 59–70.

Erikson, E. H. *Childhood and Society.* New York: Norton, 1993.

Herdt, G. H. *Guardians of the Flutes.* Chicago: University of Chicago Press, 1994.

Kagan, J. *Psychology's Ghosts.* New Haven, CT: Yale University Press, 2012.

———. *Three Seductive Ideas.* Cambridge, MA: Harvard University Press, 1998.

Levin, Y. *The Great Debate.* New York: Basic Books, 2014.

Matsubayashi, T., Y. Sawada, and M. Ueda. "Does the Installation of Blue Lights on Train Platforms Shift Suicide to Another Station?" *Journal of Affective Disorders* 169 (2014): 57–60.

Milgram, S. *Obedience to Authority.* London: Pinter & Martin, 1974.

Pleskac, T. J., and R. Hertwig. "Ecologically Rational Choice and the Structure of the Environment." *Journal of Experimental Psychology: General* 143 (2014): 2000–2019.

Venkatesh, S. A. *Floating City.* New York: Penguin, 2013.

Vyssoki, B., N. D. Kapusta, N. Praschak-Rieder, G. Dorffner, and M. Willeit. "Direct Effect of Sunshine on Suicide." *JAMA Psychiatry* 71 (2014): 1231–37.

Essay 4

Chin, G., and E. Culotta. "The Science of Inequality." *Science* 344 (2014): 819–67.

Fernald, A., V. A. Marchman, and A. Weisleder. "SES Differences in Language Processing Skill and Vocabulary Are Evident at 18 Months." *Developmental Science* 16 (2013): 234–48.

Fiske, S. T., and H. R. Markus, eds. *Facing Social Class.* New York: Russell Sage Foundation, 2012.

Goffman, A. *On the Run.* Chicago: University of Chicago Press, 2014.

Hotez, P. J. "Neglected Infections of Poverty in the United States and Their Effects on the Brain." *JAMA Psychiatry* 71 (2014): 1099–1100.

Kraus, M. W., P. K. Piff, and D. Keltner. "Social Class as Culture." *Current Directions in Psychological Science* 20 (2011): 246–50.

Leonhardt, D. "In Climbing Income Ladder, Location Matters." *New York Times*, July 22, 2013.

Miller, G., E. Chen, and S. W. Cole. "Health Psychology." *Annual Review of Psychology* 60 (2009): 5–24.

Rosenvallon, P. *The Society of Equals.* Cambridge, MA: Harvard University Press, 2013.

Rumberger, R. W. *Dropping Out.* Cambridge, MA: Harvard University Press, 2011.

Schiff, M., M. Duyme, A. Dumaret, J. Stewart, S. Tomkiewicz, and J. Feingold. "Intellectual Status of Working-Class Children Adopted Early into Upper-Middle-Class Families." *Science* 200 (1978): 1503–4.

Wildavsky, A. *The Rise of Radical Egalitarianism.* Washington, DC: American University Press, 1991.

Essay 5

Bonner, J. T. *Randomness in Evolution.* Princeton, NJ: Princeton University Press, 2013.

Champagne, F. A., and M. J. Meaney. "Transgenerational Effects of Social Environment on Variations in Maternal Care and Behavioral Response to Novelty." *Behavioral Neuroscience* 121 (2007): 1353–63.

Comfort, N. *The Science of Human Perfection.* New Haven, CT: Yale University Press, 2012.

Dick, D. M., A. Agrawal, M. C. Keller, A. Adkins, F. Aliev, S. Monroe, et al. "Candidate Gene-Environment Interaction Research." *Perspectives on Psychological Science* 10 (2015): 37–59.

Grant, P. R., and B. R. Grant. "Unpredictable Evolution in a 30-Year Study of Darwin's Finches." *Science* 296 (2002): 707–71.

Kagan, J. *The Long Shadow of Temperament.* Cambridge, MA: Harvard University Press, 2004.

Kendler, K. S. "What Psychiatric Genetics Has Taught Us about the Nature of Psychiatric Illness and What Is Left to Learn." *Molecular Psychiatry* 18 (2013): 1058–66.

Lewis, R. *Human Genetics.* New York: Routledge, 2011.

Moore, D. S. *The Developing Genome.* New York: Oxford University Press, 2015.

Prinz, J. J. *Beyond Human Nature.* New York: Norton, 2012.

Richards, J. E., and R. S. Hawley. *The Human Genome.* 3rd ed. New York: Academic Press, 2011.

Wagner, G. P. *Homology, Genes, and Evolutionary Innovation.* Princeton, NJ: Princeton University Press, 2014.

Essay 6

Aspinwall, L. G., T. R. Brown, and J. Tabery. "The Double-Edged Sword." *Science* 337 (2012): 846–49.

Benedetti, F. "Placebo Effects." *Neuron* 84 (2014): 623–27.

Dunbar, R. I. M., and S. Shultz. "Evolution in the Social Brain." *Science* 317 (2007): 1344–47.

Floresco, S. B. "The Nucleus Accumbens." *Annual Review of Psychology* 66 (2015): 24–52.

Gazzinaga, M. S. "Shifting Gears." *Annual Review of Psychology* 64 (2013): 1–20.

Glickstein, M. *Neuroscience.* Cambridge, MA: MIT Press, 2014.

Groh, J. M. *Making Space.* Cambridge, MA: Harvard University Press, 2014.

LeDoux, J. "Coming to Terms with Fear." *Proceedings of the National Academy of Sciences* 111 (2014): 2871–78.

Pessoa, L. "Understanding Brain Networks and Brain Organization." *Physics of Life Reviews* 11 (2014): 462–84.

Satel, S., and S. O. Lilienfeld. *Brainwashed.* New York: Basic Books, 2013.

Essay 7

Baldwin, J. W. *The Language of Sex.* Chicago: University of Chicago Press, 1994.

Bruckner, P. *Has Marriage for Love Failed?* Translated by S. Rendall and L. Neal. Cambridge: Polity, 2013.

Cash, W. J. *The Mind of the South*. New York: Vintage Books, 1991.

Clark, G. *The Son Also Rises*. Princeton, NJ: Princeton University Press, 2014.

Collins, W. A., E. E. Maccoby, L. Steinberg, E. M. Hetherington, and M. H. Bornstein. "Contemporary Research on Parenting." *American Psychologist* 55 (2000): 218–32.

Dabashi, H. *Being a Muslim in the World*. Basingstoke, UK: Palgrave Macmillan, 2013.

El Feki, S. *Sex and the Citadel*. New York: Pantheon, 2013.

Kagan, J. *The Human Spark*. New York: Basic Books, 2014.

LeVine, R. A., S. Dixon, S. LeVine, A. Richman, P. H. Leiderman, C. H. Keefer, and T. B. Brazelton. *Child Care and Culture*. New York: Cambridge University Press, 1994.

McDonald, M. P. *All Souls*. Boston: Beacon, 1999.

Nuland, S. B. *Lost in America*. New York: Knopf, 2003.

Essay 8

Amici, F., F. Aureli, R. Mundry, A. S. Amaro, A. M. Barroso, J. Ferretti, and J. Call. "Calculated Reciprocity? A Comparative Test with Six Primate Species." *Primates* 55 (2014): 447–57.

Bickerton, D. *More Than Nature Needs*. Cambridge, MA: Harvard University Press, 2014.

Booth-LaForce, C., A. M. Groh, M. R. Burchinal, G. I. Roisman, M. T. Owen, and M. J. Cox. "Caregiving and Contextual Sources of Continuity and Change in Attachment Security from Infancy to Late Adolescence." *Monographs of the Society for Research in Child Development* 79 (2014): 67–84.

Bowlby, J. *Attachment and Loss*. 2nd ed. New York: Basic Books, 1999.

Darwin, C. *Origin of Species*. New York: Philosophical Library, 1951.

Kagan, J. *Three Seductive Ideas*. Cambridge, MA: Harvard University Press, 1998.

Meunier, E. "No Attitude, No Standing Around: The Organization of Social and Sexual Interaction at a Gay Male Private Sex Party in New York City." *Archives of Sexual Behavior* 43 (2014): 685–95.

Preuss, T. M. "Human Brain Evolution." *Proceedings of the National Academy of Sciences* 109, suppl. 1 (2012): 10709–16.

Tomasello, M. *Why We Cooperate*. Cambridge, MA: MIT Press, 2009.

Zeng, J., G. Konopka, B. G. Hunt, T. M. Preuss, D. Geschwind, and S. V. Yi. "Divergent Whole-Genome Methylation Maps of Human and Chimpanzee Brains Reveal Epigenetic Basis of Human Regulatory Evolution." *American Journal of Human Genetics* 91 (2012): 455–65.

Essay 9

Bok, D. C. *Higher Education in America*. Princeton, NJ: Princeton University Press, 2013.

Edmundson, M. *Why Teach?* New York: Bloomsbury, 2013.

Geiger, R. *The History of American Higher Education*. Princeton, NJ: Princeton University Press, 2015.

Kagan, J. *The Three Cultures*. New York: Cambridge University Press, 2009.

Mulcahy, C. M., D. E. Mulcahy, and D. G. Mulcahy. *Pedagogy, Praxis and Purpose in Education*. New York: Routledge, 2015.

Phillips, C. J. *The New Math*. Chicago: University of Chicago Press, 2015.

Essay 10

Buhr, K., and M. J. Dugas. "The Intolerance of Uncertainty Scale." *Behaviour Research and Therapy* 40 (2002): 931–45.

Goldstein, A., K. M. Spencer, and E. Donchin. "The Influence of Stimulus Deviance and Novelty on the P300 and Novelty P3." *Psychophysiology* 39 (2002): 781–90.

Kagan, J. "Categories of Novelty and States of Uncertainty." *Review of General Psychology* 13 (2009): 290–301.

——. *Surprise, Uncertainty, and Mental Structures*. Cambridge, MA: Harvard University Press, 2002.

Mendes, W. B., J. Blasovich, S. B. Hunter, B. Lickel, and J. T. Jost. "Threatened by the Unexpected." *Journal of Personality and Social Psychology* 92 (2007): 698–716.

Nelson, C. A., N. A. Fox, and C. H. Zeanah. *Romania's Abandoned Children*. Cambridge, MA: Harvard University Press, 2014.

Rhudy, J. L., A. E. Williams, K. M. McCabe, P. L. Rambo, and J. L. Russell. "Emotional Modulation of Spinal Nociception and Pain." *Pain* 126 (2006): 221–33.

Rolls, E. T., A. S. Browning, K. Inoue, and I. Hernadi. "Novel Visual Stimuli Activate a Population of Neurons in the Primate Orbitofrontal Cortex." *Neurobiology of Learning and Memory* 84 (2005): 111–23.

Ruby, P., A. Caclin, S. Boulet, C. Delpuech, and D. Morlet. "Odd Sound Processing in the Sleeping Brain." *Journal of Cognitive Neuroscience* 20 (2008): 296–311.

Whalen, P. J. "Fear, Vigilance, and Ambiguity." *Current Directions in Psychological Science* 7 (1998): 177–87.

Essay 11

Bedrosian, T. A., and R. J. Nelson. "Influence of the Modern Light Environment on Mood." *Molecular Psychiatry* 18 (2013): 751–57.

Brody, L. *Gender, Emotion and the Family*. Cambridge, MA: Harvard University Press, 1999.

Coates, J. M., and J. Herbert. "Endogenous Steroids and Financial Risk Taking on a London Trading Floor." *Proceedings of the National Academy of Sciences* 105 (2008): 6167–72.

Ekman, P., and R. J. Davidson, eds. *The Nature of Emotion*. New York: Oxford University Press, 1994.

Federman, D. D. "The Biology of Human Sex Differences." *New England Journal of Medicine* 354 (2006): 1507–14.

Gendron, M., and L. F. Barrett. "Reconstructing the Past: A Century of Ideas about Emotion in Psychology." *Emotion Review* 1 (2009): 316–39.

Gross, D. M. *The Secret History of Emotion*. Chicago: University of Chicago Press, 2006.

James, W. "What Is an Emotion?" *Mind* 9 (1884): 188–205.

Kagan, J. *What Is Emotion?* New Haven, CT: Yale University Press, 2007.

Leslie, S. J., A. Cimpian, M. Meyer, and E. Freeland. "Expectations of Brilliance Underlie Gender Distributions Across Academic Disciplines." *Science* 347 (2015): 262–65.

Scherer, K. R. "Profiles of Emotion-Antecedent Appraisal." *Cognition and Emotion* 11 (1997): 113–50.

Tsai, J. L., D. I. Simeonova, and J. T. Watanabe. "Somatic and Social." *Personality and Social Psychology Bulletin* 30 (2004): 1226–38.

Essay 12

Aksan, N., and G. Kochanska. "Conscience in Childhood." *Developmental Psychology* 41 (2005): 506–16.

Fu, G., F. Xu, C. A. Cameron, and G. Heyman. "Cross-Cultural Differences in Children's Choices, Categorizations, and Evaluations of Truths and Lies." *Developmental Psychology* 43 (2007): 278–93.

Greene, J. *Moral Tribes*. New York: Penguin, 2013.

Haidt, J., and C. Joseph. "The Moral Mind." In *The Innate Mind*, edited by P. Carruthers, S. Laurence, and S. Stich, 3:367–91. New York: Oxford University Press, 2007.

Hoffman, M. B. *The Punisher's Brain*. New York: Cambridge University Press, 2014.

Hofmann, W., D. C. Wisneski, M. J. Brandt, and L. J. Skitka. "Morality in Everyday Life." *Science* 345 (2014): 1340–43.

Kitcher, P. *The Ethical Project*. Cambridge, MA: Harvard University Press, 2011.

Levine, R. V. "The Kindness of Strangers." *American Scientist* 91 (2003): 226–33.

Parfit, D. *On What Matters*. New York: Oxford University Press, 2011.

Scanlon, T. M. *Being Realistic about Reasons*. New York: Oxford University Press, 2014.

Schmidt, M. F. H., and M. Tomasello. "Young Children Enforce Social Norms." *Current Directions in Psychological Science* 21 (2012): 232–36.

Scruton, R. *The Soul of the World*. Princeton, NJ: Princeton University Press, 2014.

Sen, A. *The Idea of Justice*. Cambridge, MA: Harvard University Press, 2009.

Wilson, D. S. *Does Altruism Exist?* New Haven, CT: Yale University Press, 2015.